'...like a tree planted...'

'...like a tree planted...'

'He is like a tree
  planted by streams of water,
that yields its fruit in its season
  and its leaf does not wither.'

Psalm I.

by

RICHARD O'DONOGHUE

GILL AND SON

DUBLIN AND SYDNEY

First published in 1967 by
M. H. Gill and Son Ltd.,
50 Upper O'Connell Street,
Dublin 1.
and
95 York Street
Sydney.

Printed and bound in the Republic of Ireland
by Cahill & Co. Limited, Dublin

FOREWORD

I wrote this book because Father John Forde, parish priest, Newcestown, Co. Cork, the literary executor for the late Father J. C. O'Flynn, insisted that I write it. To begin with, he gave me a suitcase filled with the notebooks and tape recordings of Father O'Flynn. These I supplemented by a series of interviews with members of the O'Flynn family, with past pupils of The Loft and with contemporaries of Father O'Flynn in the North Cathedral Parish and at Passage West. I was fortunate, of course, in that I had my own vivid impressions of Father O'Flynn to draw upon— impressions derived from a wonderful friendship of more than twenty years.

Because 'academic' is a word he hated I chose not to be academic in my portrayal of the man. Because life was what he loved I chose to present him 'live'. This I tried to do by selecting those episodes in which he seemed to me to have expressed himself most personally. The book, of course, is biased— marred, you may say, by my love for the man.

To Dr Michael P. O'Connor, to Desmond McAllister and to Dr Patrick Masterson, I wish to express my sincere thanks for their valuable criticism and suggestions. Double thanks to Dr O'Connor for undertaking to correct the proofs of this book.

Richard O'Donoghue

FOREWORD

CONTENTS

I

A special occasion

SUNDAY, 20 June, 1909, was ordination day at Maynooth. Archbishop Walsh of Dublin raised sixty-five young men to the priesthood. Among them was James Christopher O'Flynn, of the diocese of Cork.

When the long ceremony had ended the newly-ordained priests, robed in chasubles, gold, white and red, filed down the aisle two by two between rows of admiring parents and friends to the sacristy. The pealing of the great organ floated after them. The guests followed in some disorder. As they came through the double doorway into St. Mary's Square they broke up into family groups and waited around in shy confusion.

Presently the newly-ordained priests, having unvested, came out on to the Square. Father O'Flynn appeared in the doorway, looked about him, and seeing his group of four went over to welcome them. His proud mother embraced him; his sister, Cissie, kissed him; his brother Denny and stepbrother Con shook hands with him. He led them to a quiet place by the Infirmary. They knelt before him on the grass and bowed their heads. '*Benedictio Dei omnipotentis*. . . .' He gave them his first blessing. They kissed his anointed hands, and then stood up and chatted. Their happiness at seeing their Jimmy a priest—their warm congratulations—their smiles and tears of joy! His mother opened a little box; a silver pyx gleamed in white tissue paper. It was her present to her son. His father had sent him a book: *The Making of Ireland and its Undoing*, by Alice Stopford Green. Cissie gave her brother a beautiful hand-worked stole and Denny presented him with a purse of sovereigns—from his brothers. There were greetings and good wishes, too, from many friends in Cork. Then the O'Flynns were joined by Father Joe Devane and his family. Soon it was time for lunch. They walked along the cloister and into the students' refectory, a vast hall now gay with the chatter of more than three hundred guests.

After lunch they strolled through the park and the gardens. The O'Flynns were proud of their priest, walking between them in his new Roman soutane. Cissie thought he had got strong. She had not seen him since she had entered the convent in London five years before. All agreed that she looked lovely in her novice's habit of black and white. When was her final profession? Only eighteen months more. Reverend Mother was so good to let her over for the ordination, and a week at home.

Mrs. O'Flynn thought her son looked tired. She would see to it that he got plenty of rest and nourishing food when he came home. When would he arrive in Cork? On Wednesday. The cob and trap would be at the station to meet him. He would say his first Mass tomorrow in the convent at Lucan. Reverend Mother had everything ready. She was a sister of Cissie's Reverend Mother in London. They were both Barry girls from Cork.

They had arrived at the main gates of the college. They said farewell and parted.

The young priest walked slowly back from the gates. He passed through the deep archway that leads into St. Joseph's Square. Before him stood Pugin's Gothic façade: the twin towers in the centre; the archway beneath and the President's quarters above it; the line of dormer windows casting identical shadows along the roof; on the right, the apse of the college chapel, strong and cutting like the prow of a ship; behind it, and soaring above the roof tops, the spear-like spire. That grey granite pile, usually so austere and cold, had taken on a mellow and almost genial appearance in the warm sunshine of that June afternoon.

The clock in Stoyte House struck a metallic half-hour. Father O'Flynn quickened his step, crossed the square to the left, and entered the grounds of Junior House. . . .

Christy Slevin waited furtively in a doorway for him.

'Ah—there you are at last, sir!' said Christy. 'We thought you had forgotten all about us.'

Christy was the doyen of the college's fifty male servants, known as 'the Navs'. He was short and slight in build, his grey head was bald on top, and his slight limp had given him the nickname 'Hoppy'. He was dressed in his Sunday best, a stiff white collar and a black bow tie. His few remaining strands of hair were trained strategically across the bare dome of his head; for this was a special occasion.

'They're inside in the class-room waiting, sir. So if you're ready—'

'You're sure there's no one about?' asked the priest.

'The coast is clear, sir. The professors are in at dinner.'

'What's it all about, Christy?'

'A kind of presentation, sir'—he winked and held up a cylindrical cardboard roll—'but you'll see in a minute.'

Christy led Father O'Flynn into a large class-room, and up on to the rostrum. The room was filled with servants, who clapped when the young priest entered. There were about forty of them. Some wore their aprons over their grease-stained clothes; some were spruced up for the occasion. Most of them were aged between fifteen and twenty-five, but a few were in their thirties and one or two were grey-haired. They had been recruited from various places; industrial schools, orphanages, and from among the local labouring classes. They were the humblest element in the life of the college. They swept the corridors and dusted the rooms; filled buckets with coal, tended the fires, and polished the professors' boots; they washed and peeled potatoes, and rolled the great trolleys round the refectories, serving the students' meals. In their spare time some of them gambled, swore, stole and drank. It was the way in those days.

Father O'Flynn stood beside Christy Slevin while he extracted the scroll from its container and unrolled it. The servants' eyes were on the priest.

Of medium height, Father O'Flynn was very well proportioned. He was broad-shouldered, deep-chested and sturdy. His head was large and finely shaped, and crowned with a wealth of jet-black wavy hair. He held it high. His full expressive face with its Roman nose and deep blue eyes revealed a warm and sympathetic nature. He stood perfectly at ease, and his whole person radiated a masculine charm.

Hoppy Slevin adjusted his steel-rimmed spectacles, cleared his throat nervously, and in a rich West Clare accent started to read the address. 'The Navs' tittered as he stumbled a little through the opening lines and mispronounced a few words, but then he warmed to his subject and the words flowed easily. Obviously, he had rehearsed it.

'Dear Rev. Sir,

'We, the servants of St. Patrick's College, Maynooth, take the opportunity of your departure from amongst us to felicitate you on your recent ordination to the priesthood, and with a fullness of fervour, to pray every blessing on your future work.

'During the years of your college course that you came in contact with us, you have in an especial manner won your way to our hearts. We have learned to respect and to esteem you for your innate noble characteristics; to turn to you whenever in doubt or difficulty; to look to you whenever in need of encouragement or advice; to regard you at length as our guide and counsellor—yes, as our wise and sympathetic friend. We are deeply grateful for the magnanimous interests you have ever manifested in us, in a word for all you have done for us.

'You are called now to higher duties for which your great intellectual gifts, your ripe store of learning, and your deep religious zeal eminently qualify you. Our old connection then must be severed; but whilst we rejoice at the cause which takes you from amongst us, we feel at the same time the sorrow of parting.

'We trust in conclusion that you will often remember us in your prayers and in return we promise you an abiding place in our affections.'

The final brief paragraph, one of good wishes, was in Irish. The spirit of the Gaelic League, fostered by Dr. Hickey, Professor of Irish, was strong in the college among students and servants.

Then followed the signature: 'Christopher Slevin, on behalf of the Servants.'

Christy turned to the priest and handed him the scroll. He took it and was silent. Even to the toughest of 'the Navs', it was clear that the young priest was deeply moved. Several moments passed before he could reply.

'Yours is the most beautiful gift I have received for my ordination.'

It was obvious that the emotion of the priest had communicated itself to the servants.

This address of the servants of Maynooth College to a newly-ordained priest was without precedent. In those days there was no social contact between students and servants; there was, in fact, a rule against it. Here, had Father O'Flynn realised it, was evidence of an extraordinary response to his own extraordinary human qualities.

He spoke again. 'Thanks, thanks, and ever thanks.' He paused. 'Tomorrow, I will say my first Mass for you.'

Then, passing up and down between the desks, he gave each

of the servants his blessing, and they went back to their work. Father O'Flynn put the scroll into his deep soutane pocket and walked out to the glade to read his breviary and reflect on the events of the day.

It was a glorious afternoon. The park was deserted, for the visitors had departed. The path beneath the tall beech trees where he walked was mottled with numberless tiny pools of sunlight, the filterings of a summer's day. He looked up. The vast foliage, touched by a passing breeze, heaved a sigh, trembled in a myriad leaves, and settled again into a peaceful slumber.

He opened his new breviary and read Vespers for the day. Presently he put it carefully back in its leather case and, sitting down on a seat, he unrolled the scroll and read it. Hoppy could never have composed it, he thought. No! It was done by a firm in Dublin who specialised in these illuminated addresses. He winced at the hyperbole: '*Your great intellectual gifts, your ripe store of learning.*' He had always been content to jog along in the lower half of the class. He had never won a prize—except for elocution. He had made no impression on his professors for his brilliance at divinity; but this scroll would seem to suggest that he had impressed the servants with his humanity—a much rarer achievement.

'*You have in an especial manner won your way to our hearts.*' Had he? he asked himself, and read on:

'*We have learned to respect and to esteem you for your innate noble characteristics. . .*' What would his class-mates say if they read that? he mused.

'*We are deeply grateful for the magnanimous interests you have ever manifested in us. . .*'

What, in fact, had he done for them? He had, from time to time, been friendly towards them, had given what advice and help he could when asked for it. He smiled as he remembered one incident.

In his final year he had been appointed monitor and sacristan in Junior House. Within a week or so, he noticed that the altar wine was disappearing, half a bottle at a time. He mentioned the matter to some of his class-mates. They told him that this sort of thing had been going on for years. Some of the servants were stealing it, and drinking it on the sly. But nobody bothered, and apparently nothing could be done about it. But Mr. O'Flynn thought otherwise.

He kept a careful watch for the thief, and at last he caught him red-handed, opening the press where the wine was kept and taking out a bottle. The thief was a freckled red-headed boy of sixteen. He did not drink himself, but he sold it to others who did. He begged not to be reported.

'Here,' said Mr. O'Flynn to the youth. 'Take these keys! I am putting you in charge of the altar wine for the rest of the year. Its safety is now your responsibility. Don't let me down.'

It worked. There was no more wine missing.

But Father O'Flynn did not stop at that. He called together all the young 'Navs' he suspected of drinking. They met at the back of the handball alley. There he acted before them the horrors of drink, in his own inimitable way—a mixture of Lear in his madness and Falstaff in his cups. So realistic was the performance, so terrifying its effect on the goggling young servants, that he had little difficulty in getting them to take a pledge. It was the last of the under-world.

At the end of the term Dr. Mannix, the President, sent for Mr. O'Flynn. Could he explain why the bill for altar wine was so low compared with last year? The same number of priests were saying Mass in the Junior oratory. The young man said he preferred not to explain. Dr. Mannix insisted. Reluctantly he told him the whole story.

Dr. Mannix was not amused. 'Your methods, Mr. O'Flynn, though undoubtedly effective, are unorthodox and not to be recommended. You took a great risk in giving the keys to that servant.'

'Perhaps, Monsignor,' replied Mr. O'Flynn respectfully, 'Our Lord took a great risk too when he gave the keys to Simon Peter.'

And there the matter ended.

Now, under the beech trees, he smiled again as he remembered the effect of his acting on the Navs. It had been no lucky accident. Already, in the college dramatic society, he had given several excellent performances in Shakespearian roles: Laertes, Buckingham, Falstaff and King Lear. He was a born actor. His professor of elocution, Mr. McHardy-Flint, had himself been a pupil of the celebrated English actor, Sir Henry Irving, and it was McHardy-Flint who introduced the young Mr. O'Flynn to the world of William Shakespeare. Father O'Flynn described the event later:

'I came to Shakespeare from life. When first I met him I was, you may say, an adult. It was at Maynooth College, and I was twenty-two. The student who was to play Laertes fell ill. I was asked to take his place. I accepted, although up to that I was just an odd-jobs man around the stage.

'I remember McHardy-Flint, the producer, saying to me that most actors found it very difficult to act convincingly the rapid transition from towering anger to tears of sympathy for Ophelia in Act IV, Scene 5 of *Hamlet*. I tried it. I did not find it hard, for that sequence of emotions was known to me. I had observed this kind of thing among the people in my own district of Blackpool in Cork. Laertes was my first meeting with Shakespeare. I played the part as my heart dictated. They said I made a good job of it.'

But therein lay his problem. As a student possessed of such a talent, he had three possible courses of action. He could have decided that the exercise of his talent was incompatible with the priestly way of life and, like the man in the gospel, wrapped it up and buried it. That would have been the safe course. Or he could, while still a student, have decided to follow his natural bent and leave the seminary for the stage. That must have been a great temptation. In later years a well-known Irish producer was to say: 'If Father O'Flynn had not been a priest, he would have been one of the world's greatest actors.'

Or he could have decided to accept his natural gifts for what they were, develop them, and integrate them into his priestly life for the benefit of his fellow-men.

This last was his decision. He never regretted it.

Now he was an ordained priest. And like ripples from a stone dropped into a still pool, his thoughts spread out, beyond the day's events, beyond Maynooth College, back to his home in Cork; to his boyhood, and to the beginning of it all.

2

On Shandon hill

On Shandon hill stands Shandon Church, and above it Shandon steeple rises square in four telescopic stages of sandstone red and limestone grey, to a dome on which floats a great golden fish.

If ever a fish was out of water, if ever a fish was high and dry, it is the great golden fish on top of Shandon steeple. Gleaming high above the city, it is in a unique position to observe the comings and goings of the people of Cork, and of the Shandon area in particular. Playing the role of weathervane in a community ever curious to know which way the wind is blowing, that observing fish is itself the observed of all observers. The visitor, seeing it for the first time from St. Patrick's Bridge or the Opera House, usually remarks a little hesitantly:

'It is a salmon—isn't it?'

To which the citizen beside him usually replies:

'No, sir. It's a cod.'

Salmon or cod, it was a frozen fish that pointed towards Blackpool and the North Pole early on Monday morning, 12 December 1881. Below it, the higgledy-piggledy roof-tops, lanes, streets and cobbled spaces sparkled with frost. All the lakes and ponds of the city were frozen; the swans on the Lee paddled in the icy waters, and the pigeons in their lofts in Quarry Lane cooed querulously at the cold. On the steep hills of Shandon, what with slipping and sliding, plunging and falling, it was a hard day for horses. Up from the chimney stacks around Shandon, tall, squat, gapped and cowled, thin columns of smoke shimmered in the freezing air.

At number twelve Mallow Lane, as Shandon bells chimed eight o'clock, Jimmy O'Flynn was born. The blessed event caused no great stir, for this was the fourth son that Kate O'Flynn had borne.

Her husband, Con O'Flynn, had left the house earlier that morning for his day's work at the Butter Market. As he rounded the corner at the base of Shandon steeple he saw policemen tearing down notices from the walls and pillars of the Butter Exchange. He was just in time to read one of them. It was printed in heavy black capitals:

'NO RENT: PARNELL, DAVITT, DILLON, SEXTON, KETTLE, BRENNAN, EGAN.'

Then it continued in smaller print:

'Flay the Land Court—it is a sham and a fraud. Men of Ireland, it is a noble cause you are engaged in—it is a holy crusade against a hell-born class who has plundered you and yours; a class who has grown fat upon the blood of yourselves and your children.

'Hold the rent! Hold the harvest! Hold the land!

'LANDLORDS MUST GO! GOD SAVE IRELAND!'

It seemed that Con O'Flynn's fourth son had not been born into the best of all possible worlds. The times in fact were out of joint, and those who tried to set them right were clapped behind prison bars for their pains; Parnell and Dillon lay in Kilmainham Jail, and hundreds of other prominent Land Leaguers crammed Her Majesty's prisons during the holy season of Advent, 1881.

Two years earlier, in 1879, Michael Davitt, son of an evicted Mayo peasant, had begun this 'holy crusade against a hell-born class.' These Anglo-Irish landlords had, since the days of the Cromwellian and Williamite settlements, 'grown fat upon the blood' of the Irish peasants whom they tolerated as tenants at will upon their estates. But between 1850 and 1880, due to a change over from tillage to pasturage, a series of bad harvests and the consequent inability of their tenants to pay the exorbitant rack-rents, these same landlords evicted 373,000 families, amounting to about two million people. Sir Robert Peel, no great friend of the Irish peasant, commented: 'I do not think the records of any country, civilised or barbarian, ever presented such scenes of Horror.' Exasperated by this heartless treatment an outraged people cried:

'LANDLORDS MUST GO! GOD SAVE IRELAND!'

What with the Coercion Act in full force, her leading nationalists in jail, and the country convulsed with agrarian troubles, Ireland in 1881 was indeed 'a most distressful country.' But to Con O'Flynn there was one bright spot—the Cork Butter Market. He counted himself lucky to have got a job there. He had in fact two jobs. In the morning he tested butter in the great hall of the Butter Exchange, and in the afternoon he supervised the work in the cooperage which stood behind St. Mary's Hall.

He was happy at his work and took a pride in doing it well. Deftly he opened several dozen casks of butter that the inspectors allotted to him each morning, bored each one to its depths, extracted a sample, smelt it, tasted it and decided on its grading which he then chalked on the side of the cask before he passed it on to the chief inspector. At the cooperage it was his responsibility to see that all the new casks were up to standard, and he also had to examine the old ones that were sent in to be repaired. Each cask had to be of good quality, expertly made of sycamore or oak and of a specified weight. When a doubtful cask caught his eye he examined it thoroughly, and on discovering any flaw he rejected it as unfit.

The wages were small and he considered himself a poor man, but the work was permanent, and every Saturday without fail he handed his pay-packet unopened to his wife, who made every penny do the work of sixpence in running their modest home. He was a calm, even-tempered man, and deeply religious in an unobtrusive way. His health was not the best, for he suffered periodically from asthma. At home, he enjoyed peace and love with a wife whom he always described as 'the finest little woman in the world.'

'Pappy was the kindest, most lovable person in the world,' wrote his daughter, Cissie. 'In the house, he was a fountain of love. With him we all experienced fatherly affection in its most attractive form. Each of us had an equal share of his love — for he loved each of us with all his heart. We vied with one another in returning his love.'

On the following Thursday baby Jimmy, wrapped in a white christening shawl, was carried to the Baptistry in the North Chapel. Hannah Sweeney, his godmother, gave the name to Father O'Connell, who wrote it in the register:

'James Christopher O'Flynn, son of Cornelius O'Flynn and Catherine, née Uppington, born 12th December 1881, baptized 15th December 1881.'

Only in the family circle was he known as Jimmy; later on as Father Jimmy. Outside the home, at school, and among his friends, he was always called Christy; and after his ordination, Father Christy O'Flynn. But when he himself became aware of the tradition from which he came, he signed himself neither James nor Christy, but always, in his native Irish: 'Seamus O'Floinn, Sagart.'

It was Father O'Connell who performed the ceremony.

When it was ended, baby Jimmy was carried home again and handed back to his mother. She took him and placed him in the home-made cradle which her two-year-old, Johnny, had just vacated. There, in the little back kitchen at 12 Mallow Lane, Jimmy O'Flynn spent the first of the seven ages of man.

'Glory be to God—the weight of him!'

Hannah Sweeney had taken her godchild, Jimmy, in her arms. He was now a sturdy child of more than three years. His father was about to go down to the Glanmire Station to see Mr. Charles Stewart Parnell, M.P. for Cork city, pass by in his carriage; for he was due to arrive by train that afternoon. It was January, 1885, and Parnell was at the height of his brilliant political career.

'Can't you take the poor child with you?' said Mrs. O'Flynn to her husband. 'The breath of air will do him good.'

Father and son went out together. Jimmy toddled, rode piggy-back, and ended up on his father's shoulders on the steps of St. Patrick's Church. From there he saw Parnell pass by. It was his first memory.

As it was the half-day for the Cork business houses, the streets were thronged with thousands of enthusiastic admirers of the Chief. Four bands marched in the great procession; the Butter Exchange Band, the Blackpool Brass and Reed Band, Barrack Street Band and Fair Lane Fife and Drum Band.

The horses were unyoked from Parnell's carriage, and the stalwarts of Cork pulled it in triumph through the streets of the city.

That night, Con O'Flynn sat in the gallery of the Opera House, while Parnell addressed the citizens of Cork:

'I come back, and every Irish politician must be forcibly driven back, to the consideration of the great question of national self-government for Ireland. I do not know how this great question will eventually be settled. I do not know whether England will be wise in time and concede to constitutional arguments and methods the restitution of that which was stolen from us towards the close of the last century. It is given to none of us to forecast the future, and just as it is impossible for us to say in what way, or by what means, the national question may be settled, in what way full justice may be done to Ireland, so it is impossible for us to say to what extent that justice will be done. We cannot ask for less than the restitution of Grattan's Parliament with its important privileges and wide and far-reaching constitution. We cannot under the British Constitution ask for less than the restitution of Grattan's Parliament. But no man has a right to say to his country: "Thus far shalt thou go and no farther." We have never attempted to fix the *ne plus ultra* to the progress of Ireland's nationhood and we never shall.'

All Cork, all Ireland, was inflamed by those words. Their effect on the country was soon to be seen in the reception given to the Prince and Princess of Wales, who paid a state visit to Ireland three months later. Dublin quietly ignored the royal couple. The students of Maynooth College expressed their feelings by breaking all the windows in the front of the college and retiring in a sullen body to the far end of the grounds.

But Cork was more eloquent and emphatic in its disapproval. As the royal procession passed through the streets, a black flag flew from a pole which protruded from one of the top front windows of the City Hall, and on its end were two shackles, with chairs attached. An angry crowd lined both sides of the processional route. Hundreds of black flags appeared from under shawls and overcoats, and were waved derisively in the royal visitors' faces. There was a brisk trade in rotten eggs and over-ripe tomatoes, and these were pelted at the procession, leaving streaks of dripping yellow and red on the black polished sides of the passing carriages, and on the well-trimmed beards and bemedalled chests of the dignified Hussars who escorted them. The air was filled with booing and hissing. The horses wheeled around in disorder.

In the middle of this din the Riot Act was read, the cavalry charged, and many people were injured. But the people of Cork had expressed beyond all doubt their opinion of the distinguished visitors.

3

Unwillingly to school

ONE September morning in the wet and sunless year of 1886, Mrs. O'Flynn took her little son Jimmy by the hand and marched him off to school. Up to 'the Height'—as the top of Mallow Lane was called—past the Cathedral and down through Clarence Street, unwillingly he toddled. His unwillingless was partly overcome by a visit to the sweet shop en route. Jimmy placed a halfpenny on the counter, and old Muddie Sweeney, the proprietress, handed him a lump of home-made brown rock, a glutinous sweetmeat that gave hours of satisfactory chewing.

Out again in the street, he clasped his mother's hand and journeyed on to the unknown world of school. Children were flocking from all directions: in the Commons Road from Killeens, down from Dublin Hill, up along the Watercourse Road, and out from the many lanes that joined the main street; boys and girls, tall and small, many of them poorly dressed and bare-footed, skipping or running or dawdling by the way, and filling the streets with their laughter and shouting. It seemed to young Jimmy that the whole world was going to school that morning.

At the school gate Mr. Moynihan, the headmaster, greeted Mrs. O'Flynn. She handed over her son to him and quickly disappeared to avoid a scene. The master led his new pupil across the noisy playground and into the class known as Low Babies.

Years later Father O'Flynn stopped his car opposite the church in Blackpool.

'That's where the old national school used to stand,' he told his young nephew. 'It was demolished and the church was extended over the site. I spent nine years in that school and when I was ordained a priest I came back and said Mass and preached my first sermon on the very spot where I learned to spell O—X, ox.'

'Did you like school?' his nephew asked.

'Not a bit of it. I mourned every morning at the thought of spending the day in a desk looking up at a blackboard. Of course, there is no royal road to learning, and to pursue the truth means hard work, and hard work means mourning. But blessed are they that mourn in the pursuit of truth for they shall have great joy when they enter into possession of it. However, if the child is put on the wrong road by a false system of education then indeed he may mourn, for he has no hope of ever arriving at truth. There is no progress except along the way of truth; and our system of education has put the country on the wrong road for over a century now. From Low Babies to Leaving Certificate, verbalism prevails. The children are cut off from reality and the desire for truth instead of being fostered is stifled.'

'Will you look at that,' he said, pointing to a large hoarding that caught his eye.

'Farmers of Ireland—Grow more wheat,' his nephew read aloud.

'That's what I'd call a choice piece of verbalism,' continued Father O'Flynn sarcastically. 'Could you blame the farmers of the country for laughing at the Department of Agriculture for displaying such ignorance of nature's ways? If those three words are to make sense they must be taken as addressed to God—for he alone can give the increase. Even then 'tis the height of arrogance for the creature to speak to the Creator in the imperative. Ah—but what else can you expect but mental myopia from officials who have got where they are by distinguishing themselves under a system of education that is out of contact with reality.'

They got into the car; and Father O'Flynn, turning to his nephew, quoted one of his favourite passages from Newman:

' "How much better, I say, is it for the active and thoughtful intellect, where such is to be found, to eschew (the national school) altogether, than to submit to a drudgery so ignoble, a mockery so contumelious. . . . How much healthier to wander into the fields and there, with the exiled Prince, to find 'tongues in trees, books in the running brooks'! How much more generous an education is that of the poor boy who . . . contrived from the beach and the quay and the fisher's boat, and the inn's fireside, and the tradesman's shop, and the shepherd's walk, and the smuggler's hut, and the mossy moor, and the screaming gulls and the restless waves, to fashion for himself a philosophy and a poetry of his own!" '

Then he turned the key in the ignition and drove off.

Without going so far as 'to eschew altogether' the national school at Blackpool, young Jimmy O'Flynn began to fashion a philosophy and a poetry for himself. He observed life in the streets and lanes of the Shandon area; he observed it from his own peculiar point of view—a point of view that was intimately linked with his emerging artistic talents. And the first object of his observations was Dr. O'Callaghan, Bishop of Cork.

On Sundays, Jimmy accompanied his father to Mass at the North Cathedral. There he heard the Bishop preach. He was fascinated.

Having listened to a sermon on the Good Samaritan—one of the Bishop's favourite themes—Jimmy came home, stood up on a chair and impersonated the Bishop:

'A certain man went down from Jerusalem to Jericho. . . .'

It was clear that the boy was a born mimic. But his parents

were perplexed. Should they reprimand their son for irreverence or praise him for the excellence of his impersonation? His devout father was inclined to reprimand him. 'After all, the Bishop is the Bishop,' he declared. His perceptive mother was inclined to praise him. 'Such talent is God's gift,' she replied. So they suspended judgement and ignored him.

But Jimmy's brothers and sisters had enjoyed the performance immensely. They wanted more. 'Do the Bishop, Jimmy! Do the Bishop!' they urged him.

Jimmy obliged, stood up on the chair they had placed for him and began in a solemn voice:

'A certain man went down from Jerusalem to Jericho . . .' His appreciative audience repeated the phrase 'from Jerusalem to Jericho', for they were completely taken at Jimmy's exact reproduction of the Bishop's peculiar pronunciation and inflection of those words.

Mrs. O'Flynn, overhearing 'the sermon' for the third or fourth time, decided to intervene. 'Jimmy,' she said, 'that's wonderful. Now the street outside is full of funny people, far funnier than the Bishop. I promise to give you a penny every time you bring home a new funny act.' She was trying tactfully to direct her son's mimetic powers towards less venerable objects.

'I took my mother at her word,' said Father O'Flynn, 'and in no time I made a fortune in pennies.'

The streets and lanes became his studio and the people his models—and very varied and interesting models many of them happened to be. Father O'Flynn describes the scene as he knew it in the 1890s:

'Mallow Lane on a Friday was all buying and selling. Long lines of horses and carts, jennets and carts, and donkeys and carts, jogged in from Blackpool and down Blarney Lane from the west. You couldn't hear yourself talking with the bockety rolling of iron-banded wheels over the potholed streets, and the regular rasp of the chain-traces on the wooden shafts of the carts. Ruddy country women lined both sides of Mallow Lane from the Height right down to Goulnasporra at the foot of the hill. They stood on the edge of the street, their large wicker baskets on the footpath before them laden with chickens and ducks and geese, with fresh eggs at sixpence a dozen, and home-made butter at eightpence a pound which they handed you wrapped in a green cabbage leaf. In spring there were kids with silky white beards and tiny black horns peeping up between their hairy ears, and snow-white lambs bleating for the fresh green fields.

'In autumn, I often saw, stalking up the hill, a tall, lean, unshaven fellow leading a jennet piled high with bulging sacks, and shouting in a raucous voice: "Ballyhooly hurts! Fine black hurts!" He tethered his jennet outside Callaghan's pub and threw a fist of oats on the ground. Flights of pigeons swooped down from the steeples of Shandon and the North Cathedral, and jostled one another out of the way while they pecked the oats within inches of the jennet's nose.

'Halfway down Mallow Lane, where it is joined by Church Street on one side and by Cattle Lane on the other, is Crosaire na Spailpín. There as a boy I watched them gather, forty or fifty stout-looking fellows. They stood at the corners in groups with their heavy hob-nailed boots, home-spuns, and wide-brimmed felt hats, a pitchfork or spade in their hands and a little parcel of food tied to the handle. They were the spailpíns, labourers who hired themselves to work for a season on the estates and tillage farms to the north of the city. They were herdsmen and ploughmen and harvesters—powerful men to work. They came from places as far away as Charleville and Tralee. Some of them represented the surplus population of the poor districts in West Cork and Kerry; many had been evicted from their holdings for non-payment of rent. These latter were proud men, and were often filled with bitter indignation at the cruel injustices that they and their families had had to suffer at the hands of heartless landlords and their agents. They had seen the battering ram and the crow-bar of the police demolish their cabins and they themselves with their families swept out on the roads with scant feeling for human suffering.

'The powerful emotions of those evicted peasants who gathered at Crosaire na Spailpín are accurately expressed in one of our Irish songs: *An Spailpín Fanach*. The passion of wounded pride and fierce indignation is as intense in that song as it is in Lear's speech: *O, reason not the need* . . .

'When the agents and farmers appeared, there was the loud talk of men bargaining and haggling over wages. In those days the spailpín usually agreed to work for five shillings a week and his keep, and many of those poor fellows had to rear a family on that. A living wage, God help us!

'In and out through all this crowd tall tinkers moved with strings of pots and pans. When they had a few drinks in, they strutted and shouted as if they owned the lane, and cursed with a fury that I've never seen equalled except in the deprecatory psalms. Their red-headed wives and numerous ragged children begged and whined their way around the street.'

'Who taught the beggar to whine?' That was the kind of question that interested Father O'Flynn. He would give you an excellent inpersonation of a beggar, and then go on to explain that in the whine of the beggar we had something fundamental. 'Not art, but nature taught the beggar to whine, and nature is above art in that respect,' he would say. 'The whine is one of nature's elemental, universal and unchanging modes. It is nature in the beggar that dictates the tone, the cadence and the rhythm of that whine—and all that accompanies that whine in stance, gesture and look. The arguments or the words of the beggar can leave us unmoved—but the whine goes straight to our hearts and opens our purse more effectively than any words. In nature the whine is compelling; in art, especially in Shakespeare, it can be overwhelming.'

Jimmy O'Flynn had an ear for street cries. He describes some of the cries of the Shandon area:

'A tall bony woman, bare-headed, her shawl wrapped tightly round her, laboured up the hill under the weight of fish in the great basket slung over her shoulders. Her large head and ruddy masculine features would have looked well on the shoulders of a Grenadier Guard. She cried as she strode along: "Fine fresh mackerel! Fine fresh mackerel!" She pronounced the word "make-er-el," and to my ears the tune of it was sweet and happy.

'A second fishmonger wheeled her fish before her in a child's perambulator. She cried: "Fine cruddy hake! Fine fresh hake!" Her voice was deep and full, and gave lovely expression to her rather melancholy tone. Orsino in *Twelfth Night* described it well when he said "*it hath a dying fall.*"

' Then there was Katie Barry up on the Height who sat behind a wooden tray placed across two orange boxes and sold fruit. "A penny each the wine-apples!" she cried, and added: "a glass of wine in every apple!" Then she'd laugh at her own wit, and her laugh was loud and musical. Near her stood a little girl beside a box of onions. She was a frail child with a pale, thin face and large, brown eyes. She stood in her bare feet, holding up a string of Spanish onions that reached to the ground. "All for a pinny! All for a pinny!" she chirped in a pathetic monotonous tone, like a tiny bird that had fallen out of its nest.

'Not far from her stood a haberdasher who held before her a tray full of pins and needles and reels of thread. She held up a sheet of pink paper and cried: "A pinny a sheet the pins! A pinny a sheet the pins! Made in Japan! Made in Japan!"

'But the street cry I loved most was the cry of the old woman who sat at her stall down in Goulnasporra. She sold goose-

berries and plums in the autumn: "Fine free ha'penny plums!
Fine free ha'penny!"

'As I grew older I noticed that all those street cries—and
there were many more in those days—were built on three
notes: just two tones and a half-tone. Great was my surprise
when I discovered, while listening to the priest sing high Mass
in the Cathedral, that those cries are at the heart of the Pater
Noster. In the Plain Chant setting of that prayer you have only
one note above those street cries taken three times, and one
tone below taken once, and all these notes are in the middle
register of the voice. Anyone with a note in his head should
be able to sing the Pater Noster—the Common Prayer set
to the tune of the common cries of men.'

It was on one of those market days, when he was about
twelve years old, that Jimmy had an experience that impressed
itself indelibly in his memory and gave a specific direction to
his keen musical talent.

He was upstairs in the bedroom looking out the window at
the people in the street. A little old man with a ragged coat, a
battered hat and a stick, shuffled along the footpath and stood
outside Jimmy's door. He sang a few ballads, and as he was
singing he held a cap in his hand to collect pennies from the
passers-by.

Jimmy took stock of the stranger. To him it seemed odd that
the man should have a hat on his head and a cap in his hand. He
came down to the hall-door to watch at close quarters. The old
man, it would appear, was a traditional Irish singer. Very
likely he had come to the city from the Irish-speaking district
of West Cork, for he sang an Irish song, *Madarín a Ruadh*, in
traditional manner. The song is in the form of a dialogue
between a farmer and a fox who stole his goose. The dramatic
quality of the song and in particular the old man's way of
singing it appealed at once to Jimmy. He asked the man to sing
it again, and gave him the penny he had got from his mother

for his impersonation of a tinker selling holy pictures. Each Friday for about six weeks the little old man walked down Mallow Lane, sang his songs and collected pennies in his cap. Jimmy was always waiting for him, and put his penny in the cap to hear him sing *Madarín a Ruadh*. Then the old man came no more. Jimmy never saw him again. But he had the song in his heart and could imitate perfectly the old man's way of singing it. It was his first taste of the old Gaelic world, and instinctively he loved it.

Among those who helped him in the fashioning of a poetry and a philosophy of his own, Father O'Flynn considered that Jimmy Murphy, the cobbler, played an important role.

Jimmy Murphy, the cobbler, had his little wooden shop down in Goulnasporra. On top of a table, facing the window, Jimmy sat with his legs crossed while he worked away intently at the job in hand. The place reeked of leather and wax. On weekends it was packed with fellows getting measured for a new pair of boots.

Jimmy O'Flynn liked to visit the cobbler's den, for he was very friendly, had a fund of songs and stories, and a wonderful way with children.

'I noticed,' said Father O'Flynn, 'that Jimmy did not use a tape or rule to measure his customer's feet; instead, he used very thin laths—kippers they used to call them in those days. These he cut to the length and breadth of the foot and then tied the two kippers in the form of a cross. It was from this that Jimmy built each pair of boots. The boots he made fitted perfectly and were expertly finished.

'Murphy's the cobblers was *the* place in the Shandon area for news. You could find out everything there, from who died that day in Skye's Lane to what Tim Healy said about Parnell in the House of Commons the day before. In those days all the talk was about Parnell and the bishops and Kitty O'Shea. The North Parish was strong for Parnell until the news leaked out from the cobbler's shop that he had married Kitty O'Shea in a registry office in London, in July, 1891. That put the tin hat on it. Most of the people in the North Parish now turned against Parnell. But even then there was plenty of for-and-against, and arguments that began in the cobbler's shop often flared up into a fight. In a few minutes Goulnasporra was like Flanders. The fight spilled out into the street; the men fought the men and the women clung to one another. The street was filled with their shouts and screams. The ducks, the chickens and the geese took up the cry, cackled and crowed and flapped their wings, and filled the street with feathers. Donkeys and jennets broke from their tethers and bolted down the street, throwing everything into confusion. Then the policemen from Shandon Barracks appeared at the bottom of Mallow Lane. The warning was given, the fighting stopped, and the men and women ran into the pubs for asylum. The men got out through the back doors and then took off up the lanes. The women huddled into the snugs, their shawls hanging loose about them, their hair streeling and dishevelled. They dragged their feet in a pair of their husband's boots, with no laces and the tongues hanging out. They sat down around the table, ordered a half-gallon of Murphy's stout, and passed the time blathering and caterwauling, their stomachs growing fat from porter'.

The cobbler was keen on music. He sang in the choir at St. Mary's and played a clarinet in the Butter Exchange band. He had a large collection of ballads, and it was from him that Jimmy O'Flynn learned *Fineen O'Driscoll the Rover* and *The West's Awake*. He also had a habit of tapping out little rhythmic patterns on the table. These fascinated young Jimmy.

'How many different ways could you tap like that?' Jimmy asked the cobbler.

'There's no end to the number,' he replied.

'But you can take it as gospel,' he continued, 'that all the music in the world is written in either one-two or in one-two-three.'

'What's one-two?' the boy asked.

'That's one-two,' the cobbler demonstrated, placing the boy's fingers on his wrist so that he could feel the pulse. 'And,' he continued, 'you can take it from me that the best music is written in one-two.'

'Why in one-two?' the boy asked.

'Because that is the beat of the human heart—and the best of music moves with that beat.'

Whenever Jimmy happened to be passing by the cobbler's shop and saw that the cobbler was alone, he would drop in to get a new song or ballad or to listen to the cobbler tapping out little tunes on the table.

'I learned something about the different beats and time signatures from the cobbler. He used to illustrate these by tunes on the clarinet or bits of songs. I think he was flattered by my questions and the interest I took in his music-making. It was due to him that I became very much aware of the different rhythms all around me, in the streets, at school and wherever things moved.'

As soon as Jimmy O'Flynn discovered a new rhythm, off with him down to the cobbler and they would tap it out on the table and make a little tune of it, and make it say something by putting words to it. The donkey and cart flying down Blarney Lane said:

'Clickety-clack, I'm off on a hack, flying down Blarney Lane,' while the horse pulling the load up Mallow Lane said:

'Plod, plod, keep on pulling. . . .'

Then one day Father O'Flynn remembered the little old man and his song *Madarín a Ruadh*. As a matter of interest, he tried to fit it to one of the cobbler's time signatures. Try as he may he could not. He brought his problem to the *maestro* himself.

'Listen to this song, Jimmy,' he said and sang *Madaírn a Ruadh* as he had learned it from the street singer.

'What time is that in, Jimmy?' he asked.

'Start it again,' the cobbler requested. And once again Jimmy sang it through, while the cobbler tried to tap out the beats on the table.

'What kind of an old song is that?' said he. 'You must be singing it wrong for it isn't one-two and it isn't one-two-three.'

'I'm not singing it wrong. That's how the old man sang it, and I paid him six pennies to teach it to me.' Jimmy was very sure of himself.

'Well, all music is writ in either one-two or one-two-three.' The cobbler reaffirmed his musical *credo*. 'But what you've been singing is neither—it can't be music.'

'It is music!' said Jimmy, flashing with anger. 'It's a different kind of music, and it is far more beautiful than any of your old "come-all-yes" in one-two or one-two-three.' And he walked out of the shop. It was the end of a musical friendship, for Jimmy did not darken the cobbler's door for many a long day.

4

The O'Flynns

'WHAT in God's name will we do with Jimmy? All this singing and play-acting—where is it going to lead him?'

Mrs. O'Flynn had a problem and was talking it over with her husband, whose health had been failing of late. His asthma had become chronic; shortly he would have to give up work. The time had come to put their heads together and plan for the children's future.

Kate O'Flynn (*née* Uppington) was petite, slim and vivacious. She had a keen eye to business—much more so than her quiet husband—and she was an excellent manager. She had peculiarly penetrating eyes. A friend of the family said of her: 'She could see vulgarity behind a stone wall or a double doctorate.' She had only to look at one of her children and he or she recognised at once the authority in her eyes. She was strict with them; insisted on prompt obedience and got it. She decided what they would do, where they would go and what company they could keep. She often remarked that as there were seven of them she could not see where they could get better company than with each other in their own home. She made that home attractive and encouraged her children to invite their friends.

A cousin who had returned from America after thirty years, seeing the efficient way Mrs. O'Flynn delegated the various chores to each of her children; saw them out the door to school each morning all as neat as new pins; had hot meals ready on the table when they returned in the afternoon, and saw to it that they did their home-work carefully, exclaimed: 'Gosh, Jimmy, your mother should be a quarter-master general in some great army!'

Kate Uppington was the child of a mixed marriage. Although she had seen her father and brothers go to Service in St. Ann's Protestant Church, while she with her mother and sisters attended Mass in the North Chapel, she suffered neither confusion nor doubt about her Catholic faith. On the contrary. All her married life it was her custom to attend seven o'clock Mass every morning, hail, rain or snow, in the Presentation Convent, Blackpool. Her daughter, Cissie, recalls one winter morning when a heavy fall of snow had blocked up the hall-door. Her mother opened the window and called a passer-by. She handed him a shovel. He cleared away the snow-drift. She got out to her usual morning Mass. She had time for everybody and everything except humbug and sham. She was without social pretensions, never employed a maid, and all her ambition was for her children.

Their future depended upon the decisions she would take now. She called a round-table conference to take stock of the situation.

They had three grown boys, Denny, Paulie and Johnny, who were of an age to work; Jimmy, their fourth child, was in Middle Grade at the North Monastery, and his younger brother Josie and his two sisters Cissie and Monica were still at the Primary school. She aimed at setting her sons up in a business of their own. 'No point in working for others like their poor father and have nothing in the heel of the hunt, if they can pull together and work for themselves,' reasoned Mrs. O'Flynn.

'Whatever ye do, keep out of butter,' the father warned his sons. The Danes had captured the market. Butter was on the way out. What then to do?

'Sheep were doing well,' Denny remarked—he was apprenticed to a butcher.

'There's money in cows,' Paulie said.

'What about a butcher's shop of our own?' Denny suggested.

'That's not a bad idea at all.' They all agreed.

'And to begin, we could rent a stall in the market,' Johnny, the quiet member, added.

Plans were made, the ground surveyed and a stall was duly rented in Mutton Lane that connects Patrick Street with the City Market. Denny, the eldest, was put in charge. Paulie went to the fairs to buy the sheep and cattle. Johnny looked after the slaughter-house up in Ballymacthomas. Business boomed. The O'Flynns moved from Mallow Lane to a large house in Blackpool.

Each night the three elder brothers came home from work together. Denny carried a Gladstone bag with the takings from the stall. Their mother had drilled them to take off their muddy boots in the yard and to change into slippers. Jimmy scraped and polished the boots and placed them near the range—to have them dry for the morning. The brothers sat round the kitchen table. Their mother served them a supper of bread and beef-tea, from a pot that simmered on the range. 'Beef-tea lies light on the stomach at night,' she held. The supper over, the *Cork Examiner* was read and the prices of hoggets and wethers, of bullocks and heifers noted and discussed.

Then the newspaper was spread out on the table, and Denny emptied the contents of the Gladstone bag. His brothers helped him to separate the copper, the silver and the notes. They counted the coins, stacked them in rows, checked them and scooped them into paper bags marked copper, silver and gold—for sovereigns and half-sovereigns were in circulation at the time. The notes were carefully counted, rolled in a bundle, and tied with an elastic band. Mrs. O'Flynn made the final check and noted the amount in an account book that she kept under lock and key in the sideboard drawer. The money was put back in the Gladstone bag and Denny banked it the next day.

Then they all knelt down before a picture of the Holy Family, and their father led them in night prayers. . . .

But what to do with Jimmy? That problem had remained unsolved.

''Tis only fair that he pull his weight like his brothers,' Con O'Flynn suggested.

'But how?' Mrs. O'Flynn asked. 'I can't for the life of me see Jimmy standing inside a counter with a butcher's block and chopper.' She made inquiries, and at last found an opening for him as a clerk at Ogilvie & Moore, a wholesale warehouse in Parnell Place.

Nothing could have been more uncongenial to him—cooped up in a counting-house, pushing a pen all day.

'I'd rather break stones on the side of the road,' Jimmy said to his father when they were out walking together on one of Jimmy's half-days. They had a mutual interest in local history, and as they walked along Blackpool they made a list of the names of the streets: York Street, Clarence Street, Great Britain Street, Berwick Lane, Gray's Lane, Peacock Lane, Hatton's Alley, Allinot's Lane, Hodder's Lane, and Blasby Street.

'For all those names mean, we could be walking through an English town,' his father said. 'But further out beyond the Commons Road you'll meet with names like Kill an Ab, that is, the Church of the Abbot, and upon the right Kilbarry, the Church of Finbar, and Kilcullaig, and out further Killeens— the little church. On the hill on the left are Farranree and Farranferris—the land of Pierce. The seminary up there is where the Bishop lives. . . .'

Walking through Blackpool, Jimmy and his father passed the flax factory, a weaving industry, a distillery, and over a dozen tanneries.

'Why are these industries all out here?' asked Jimmy.

'Blackpool and the Shandon area,' explained his father, 'became what they call the industrial centre of Cork during the eighteenth and early nineteenth centuries. The fact that the train from Dublin stopped at Kilbarry, until the tunnel was built in 1858, helped to do this.

'The Protestant element who ran the industries were loyal to the memory of William of Orange. They had their bands and their drums and their Twelfth of July celebrations there in Blackpool—just as they have in Belfast. They're the Ascendancy, from whom came the Lord Mayors of Cork and the Corporation, who ruled the city for nearly three hundred years. They cared nothing for our Irish traditions, and so they named the streets in their own way.'

They stopped opposite Daly's margarine factory. His father said: 'In the time of Queen Elizabeth of England there stood on that site Shandon Castle. Here the Council of Munster sat. As Dublin Castle ruled Leinster, Shandon Castle ruled Munster in the name of Queen Elizabeth. In those days Cork was a walled city, built on the marshy island between the two channels of the river Lee.'

It was in this way—not from the textbooks at school—Father O'Flynn maintained that he was first stimulated to take an interest in local history.

Jimmy was not very good at games; he was more a solo performer. It was at this time that he became very keen on bodybuilding. He attended regularly at the gymnasium run by the League of the Silver Cross in St. Mary's Hall. There he excelled as a weight-lifter, and at throwing the half-hundred over the bar. He could beat any youth of his own age and several others who were much older.

After two years at Ogilvie & Moore, he opened his mind to his mother.

'Mamma, I think I'd like to become a priest.'

'You'd like to become a—what?' She was astonished.

'A priest.'

'Put the idea out of your head, child of grace.'

'Why?'

'For the simple reason that one half of the family is Protestant—that's why. The Lord must be hard up for vocations when he has to call on one of the O'Flynns!'

'But we're all Catholics in this house.'

'Yes. In this house—but what do you suppose the Bishop would think when he poked around and discovered that the other half was Protestant?'

'What about it, if the Uppingtons are Protestants? They're decent people, and were always good neighbours too. There's nothing to be ashamed of—whatever the Bishop may say.' Jimmy was beginning to show some of the forthright spirit of his mother; a chip of the old block.

'Tell me, Jimmy,' she asked, 'what kind of a priest were you thinking of becoming?'

'A priest like Father O'Sullivan in the North Chapel.'

'A secular priest?'

'A secular priest.'

'In the diocese of Cork?'

'I hope so.'

'That's completely out of the question.'

'Why?'

'Because 'twould take a mint of money to put you through Maynooth—and it gives us all we can do to make ends meet. So stick to your job—'tis more in your line.'

And there the matter rested. Jimmy went back to the grind-stone.

'All work and no play makes Jack a dull boy.' No one could say the O'Flynns were dull. They were the friendliest, merriest family in Blackpool. They were a talented family and had similar tastes—music, poetry, drama, opera. Each of the children was gifted with a voice of good singing quality. The two girls learned to play the piano—Cissie, the organ as well; Denny learned the violin.

Their clear-sighted mother put first things first and saw to it that her children gave generously of their time and their talents to the Lord. ''Tis loving and giving that makes life worth living,' she told them. She herself when a girl had sung in the choir in the North Cathedral. Each of her children sang in one or other of the city church choirs. On Sunday mornings there was a general exodus from the O'Flynn home. Paulie and Jimmy sang in the North Cathedral choir conducted by Herr Schwartz; Denny and Cissie sang in St. Augustine's; Josie and Monica in St. Mary's on Pope's Quay. The boys were members of the Sick Poor Society, and after Mass they collected from door to door and visited the sick poor in their homes. Jimmy developed an apostolate of his own. He rounded up the poor children in the lanes about the Cathedral and led them to the Children's Mass.

On Sunday, they usually had a musical evening in their home. Their repertoire was large, for besides singing in church choirs, Monica and Josie were members of the Cork Operatic Society, and Denny and Cissie sang in the Cork Choral Union. Solos, duets and trios from the operas *Maritana*, *The Bohemian Girl*, *Faust* and *La Bohème* were repeatedly sung. Denny played the intermezzo from *Cavalleria Rusticana* on his violin, accompanied by Cissie on the piano. Monica gave solos from the lighter operas, *The Geisha Girl*, *The Country Girl*, and from Gilbert and Sullivan. Her most popular party piece was *The Moon and I*. Cissie and Jimmy sang the duet *Hear me, Norma*.

On Christmas Eve in the O'Flynn home it was the custom to sing carols. The house was decorated with holly and ivy, and mistletoe hung over the door. A big fire blazed in the grate and there was lemonade and cake for all. The family was augmented by some of Jimmy's student friends. They gathered round the piano on which Cissie accompanied the singers. Mrs. O'Flynn led off with the first verse of *Silent Night*, then all joined in in harmony. They sang the favourite carols of the day and always ended with *In Dulci Jubilo*—an old German Christmas hymn—in four parts with Jimmy conducting, à la Herr Schwartz, and singing his line as well. Then all went out to Midnight Mass.

Jimmy had a large repertoire of impersonations, songs and dramatic pieces. Favourites with his audience were *The West's Awake; Finneen O'Driscoll the Rover;* the recitations *Kissing Cup, Top o' the Morning,* and especially the song *Drinking*. His rich voice gave full value to this latter song with its descending scale passage on the letters D-r-i-n-k-i-n-g. He never failed to thrill his listeners with the last note, which he seemed to drag up from his boots; it vibrated in his head like the 32-foot bass pipe in the organ at the North Cathedral.

This song ended, his audience invariably called for *My Boots are Tight,* an unpretentious monologue that depicted all the phases of the intoxicated mind. Jimmy could do the drunk to perfection. He had drawn his interpretation from live models all around him. He began by turning his back on his audience while he ruffled his black curly hair and splayed it down over his forehead. When he faced them again, he was the thing itself—just nicely under the weather, leaning against an imaginary lamp-post outside a public house. He began with a few bars of a song *In Cellar Cool I'm Drinking*. The dull glassy eyes, the slow opening and shutting of his eyelids, the relaxed mouth and loose lips, the mobile features, all his fumbling gestures and unsteady stance blended to form a perfect picture of the drunk. The progress in intoxication was excellently done as he slipped imperceptibly from mood to mood; singing, straightening up when the policeman passes; fumbling for a match and lighting his pipe; greeting an old friend with

mawkish sentiment; the quarrelsome attitude; the reconcilia-
tion; the stupid laugh—the stupor and oblivion. The truth and
sincerity of each phase of this rather long piece always evoked
wonder and rapt attention in his audience. Those who saw
him do it for the first time were often shocked; those who had
seen him do it many times over the years said it always
remained fresh and fascinating. *My Boots are Tight* remained
part of his repertoire till the end.

But his desire to become a priest persisted. He turned to his
father, who advised him to speak to Father O'Sullivan. He did.
Father O'Sullivan called to the house and had a talk with
Jimmy's parents. Mrs. O'Flynn confessed she had been testing
her son's vocation.

'After all, he's a bit of a dreamer,' she said, 'and dreamers
are easily deceived.'

'There's a place for dreamers too in the Church,' Father
O'Sullivan said.

And so it was arranged that Jimmy should go to the junior
seminary at Farranferris. He entered it in September, 1899.
Though three years older than the others in his class, he fitted
in quite well.

In his first term at college he became friendly with Mick
Twohig, a fine Irish speaker and a good singer, from Bally-
vourney. He taught Jimmy the beautiful Irish love song
Eibhlín a Rún, in the traditional manner.

'I went home at Christmas and was as proud as punch to sing
it at the family parties,' he said. But it gave rise to a problem.
His sister, Cissie, who could accompany almost any song on the
piano was unable to work out an accompaniment for *Eibhlín a
Rún*. 'There's something queer about the time of it,' she said.

Jimmy took his problem to Herr Schwartz, the organist at
the cathedral.

'Listen to this, sir,' he said to the professor, and sang a verse
of *A Nation Once Again*.

'Now listen to this,' he said, and sang *Eibhlín a Rún*. 'Can you explain the difference to me—my sister could not accompany this Irish song.'

Herr Schwartz explained to Jimmy that the Irish song was a much older kind of music than *A Nation Once Again*, that it was similar to the Church's Plain Chant.

Herr Schwartz demonstrated by singing a Plain Chant *Kyrie Eleison*.

'Your Irish song and the *Kyrie Eleison* are built on the ancient modes. *A Nation Once Again* is built on the modern scale and is played to a strict beat.' The professor hummed a tune and beat time with his hand.

Jimmy saw the light.

'This song moves like a man marching—left-right; like a man rowing—heave-ho,' he said.

'Exactly,' said the professor, 'the regular beat is there all the time!'

'But *Eibhlín a Rún* does not move like that' said Jimmy.

'No,' agreed the professor, 'it moves in what is called "free rhythm". It is a more natural kind of movement.'

'That would be more like the movement of the waves than the rowing of a boat?' suggested Jimmy.

'Or better still, like the flight of a seagull,' added the professor.

Jimmy thanked Herr Schwartz. His problem was solved.

On thinking the matter over he concluded:

'The cobbler held that music is a succession of notes written on paper and enclosed in bar-lines, with a regular beat—and that whatever cannot be measured in that way is not music. He has mistaken the means for the end: for in art the means can be measured but not the end. He did not realise—as many people better educated than he seem not to realise—that the sighing of the wind and the rolling of the waves and the song of the thrush are also music—but not note after note. These sounds move in liquescent lines and give us a rhythmic woof.

It is these natural rhythms that inspired the makers of our traditional Irish songs—an older and in my opinion a more beautiful form of music.'

Bishop O'Callaghan resided at Farranferris. Jimmy knew him of old. Now the Bishop got to know Jimmy. He was made prefect in his final year. Part of his duty was to ride in the carriage with the Bishop on Sundays to St. Nicholas' Church in Blackpool. There the Bishop celebrated Mass and preached. It was Jimmy's function to read the notices. Having done so, he sat down and listened to the sermon.

'A certain man went down from Jerusalem to Jericho. . . .'

His mother had warned him, but he couldn't resist the temptation. Back in the college, at a 'free study' at end of term, Jimmy was asked to sing. He did not sing that night. He 'did' the Bishop instead: 'A certain man went down from Jerusalem to Jericho. . . .'

The study was silent when he had finished. Nobody clapped. He looked around.

The Bishop stood at the door. . . .

'Thanks be to God, the poor Bishop had a fine sense of humour—or that was the end of my vocation,' said Father O'Flynn years after.

The Bishop selected seven men and sent them on to Maynooth. They were Denis Murphy, Ned Galvin, Jim Cashman, Jer Cullinane, Jimmy McGuckin, Edward Fitzgerald and Jimmy O'Flynn.

On the second Tuesday in September 1902, the seven assembled on the platform at Glanmire Station. They bought their single tickets and saw that the luggage was loaded on the train.

They alighted at Hazelhatch. They had never been so far from home. A line of jarveys was there to meet the train. The Corkmen were shy—but shrewd.

'How far is it to Maynooth?' they asked.

"Tis five long miles and a bit,' a jarvey replied.

'How much do you charge for a lift?'

'Seven-and-sixpence per head.'

'And what about the luggage?'

'The college will send a special wagon for that. The luggage is carted free.'

The Corkmen withdrew and huddled in consultation.

'There's a lot of spending in seven-and-six,' one of them said.

'What's five miles of walk?' said another. 'We often did more than that for recreation on our half-day at Farrna.'

'I've a mouth-organ,' Ned Galvin said, 'and I can play a tune on the way.'

'I've a tin whistle,' said Jimmy O'Flynn. 'I can take over when you're tired.'

Along the dusty road they marched, Ned Galvin at their head playing on his mouth-organ. Jimmy took over after a while on his whistle and played *Clare's Dragoons*. They arrived at the gate of Maynooth, their money in their pockets.

With so much saved they could now be flush, and at Jimmy's suggestion they made a last concession to the old Adam; they went into a shop and had lemonade and biscuits.

Then they brushed the dust from their new black suits, queued at the gate lodge to sign the register and disappeared through the great archway in Stoyle House.

For the next seven years, Jimmy O'Flynn, in common with some six hundred other clerical students, lived by the bell. It roused them each day at 6 a.m.; summoned them to prayer, to Mass, to class, to meals, to study, to recreation and then to bed again at 10 p.m.

'We are such stuff as priests are made on,' Jimmy remarked. 'And our little lives are rounded with a bell.'

5

'Dark Rosaleen'

> 'O my Dark Rosaleen,
> Do not sigh, do not weep!
> The priests are on the ocean green,
> They march along the deep.'

''Tis strange the way things turn out,' Father O'Flynn reflected. 'I had made all arrangements with Dr. Cottor of Portsmouth to minister in his diocese for five or six years after my ordination, but at the last minute my own bishop, Dr. O'Callaghan, decided to keep me at home.'

Had Father O'Flynn gone to Portsmouth in 1909 it is unlikely that he would have developed into the complete Irishman we have known him to be, for he would never have come in contact with the vital source of his inspiration—the Munster Gaeltacht.

Dr. O'Callaghan cancelled the arrangement with Portsmouth, and appointed him to the staff of the seminary at Farranferris to teach elocution.

With his talent for acting, his well-developed voice and his love of Shakespeare, the appointment pleased Father O'Flynn very much. He entered on his task with enthusiasm. Later he wrote:

'I began in Farranferris in 1909. We put planks on porter-barrels and covered them with an old carpet, and each year produced a full-length play of Shakespeare's. Encouragement

came from my Bishop, Dr. O'Callaghan—God be good to
him—and from his relative, Dr. Sexton, the President of the
College. By means of Shakespeare I aimed not only at helping
the students to speak correctly, but at a cultivation of the noble
emotions—education of the heart.'

That work he continued to do for over fifty years.

Early in 1910, Father O'Flynn was appointed to serve as
chaplain in the Cork Asylum, a very large mental hospital on
the Lee Road. As the quarters for the chaplain were not ready
Father O'Flynn lived at home with his parents for about ten
months, and every morning he set out at 7 a.m. in a cob and
trap for the Asylum. There he said Mass, administered the
sacraments, visited the patients each day and frequently
entertained them with his songs and dramatic pieces.

'He was a ray of sunshine whenever he visited us in the
wards,' was how Nurse Anna O'Dwyer described Father
O'Flynn. He remained there until October 1920.

'When I was ordained here in 1909, I was a Protestant.'
Father O'Flynn, a twinkle in his eye, shocked a student
audience at Maynooth in the course of a lecture on Irish
music in November 1916. It was his way of saying that he
had come to manhood—and to the priesthood—without any
intimate knowledge of 'the Irish thing', the language,
folklore, songs and dances which mirrored the Gaelic mind
and which he affectionately called 'Dark Rosaleen'.

The event that changed his outlook, and to a large extent his
life, was a visit he paid to the Irish-speaking district of Ballingeary in West Cork. He went there on the invitation of a
friend, Father James O'Callaghan, who was curate at Inchigeela.

'Come down for a few weeks in the summer, you are sure
to enjoy yourself. The scenery is magnificent and the people
couldn't be nicer,' his friend had written him.

Father O'Flynn accepted the invitation and he described his
reactions:

'In 1910 I visited the Irish-speaking districts of West Cork and for the first time came in contact with the old Gaelic world. There, rummaging among the ruins of the nation, I discovered the remnants of a supremely beautiful culture of emotion in language, story, song and dance still living in the hearts of these people, that completely captivated me.'

Captivated he must have been, for summer after summer he spent his holidays in one or other of the Irish-speaking districts of Munster: Ballingeary or Gougan Barra, or Ring in County Waterford. But his favourite haunts lay far to the west in Kerry: Dunquin, the Blasket Islands and Ballinskelligs. There he revelled in the beauty of mountainous promontories, sheer cliffs and wheeling seabirds. From Coomakishta and Bolus Head he looked on breath-taking seascapes and saw frail currachs dance dangerously in Dingle Bay.

In this old Gaelic world the people were his chief interest. His sincere and easy manner opened the door to the heart of these people. Frequently he would go out in the boats with the fishermen or help the farmers save the hay. At night he spoke with them and their families in their homes. He was charmed by their unsophisticated ways, their simple hospitality, their natural mode of expression, their kitchen homeliness and their strong Catholic mind.

'Whenever I get the smell of home-made bread,' he used to say, 'it recalls to my mind a cottage in Ballinskelligs with its hanging bastible and turf fire, its whitewashed walls, rough deal furniture and fuchsia in a jam jar on the window.'

Before his visit to Ballingeary, Father O'Flynn had learned Irish—'but only from books,' as he put it. Now, having heard the language spoken fluently by native speakers with the *blas*— the true accent and pronunciation—his desire to master it was whetted. He returned to Cork, joined a Gaelic League class and fell to with a heart and a half to learn his native language.

'We get ideas,' he used to say, 'but ideals get us.' The ideal of

a Gaelic Ireland soon possessed him and urged him to work
with tremendous enthusiasm to make that ideal a living reality:

> *I could scale the blue air,*
> *I could plough the high hills,*
> *Oh, I could kneel all night in prayer,*
> *To heal your many ills!*
> *My Dark Rosaleen!*

In 1911, the Christian Brothers at the North Monastery
Schools celebrated their centenary. They decided to put on
a pageant of Irish mythology and history and invited their
past pupil, Father O'Flynn, to act as producer. He was very
pleased to do so.

This put him searching the shelves of the libraries in Cork
for books on Irish mythology. He read avidly all he could lay
his hands on. The pageant was an outstanding success, thanks
to him.

On 10 May 1912, Father Peter O'Leary (An t-Athair Peadar
Ó Laoghaire) and Kuno Meyer were elected Hon. Burgesses
of the city of Cork, the former in recognition of the priceless
services rendered by him to the Irish language and the Irish
literary movement generally, the latter for his scholarly
researches and editing of Early Irish and Middle Irish manuscripts.

Father O'Flynn was in charge of the reception committee.
He had the boys from the North Monastery, dressed in the
costumes of the pageant of the previous year, lined up outside
Glanmire Station to greet the distinguished visitors. The
'Mon' boys gave them a rousing welcome.

Later that day, Father O'Flynn was walking along Patrick
Street with An t-Athair Peadar. They came to Guy's, a photo-
grapher's studio.

'Come in and we'll have your photo taken,' invited Father
O'Flynn.

'I've no mind for such vanity,' said An t-Athair Peadar.

'The times demand it,' argued Father O'Flynn.

'Well—if it will help the cause we'll go in.'

And in they went and had a photograph taken together. Father O'Flynn numbered this photo among his most cherished possessions.

The Irish Outlook, a weekly review of literary and social events, said of Father O'Flynn in July 1912: 'There is a strong magnetic quality in his personality; the magnetism that sways, that encourages, that inspires with hope and confidence. He is enthusiastic and has a multitude of interests, all national in character. His energetic mind is devoted to the re-establishing of the native language, and swayed by his enthusiasm many readily enrol themselves under his intrepid banner. As an orator, he possesses eloquence of a high order; his erudition is indisputable and his power to grip and hold an audience is unique. . . .'

In the summer of 1912 Father O'Flynn was accompanied on his visit to the Gaeltacht by Dr. Osborne Bergin. He recorded an experience he had:

'I recall a summer's evening in the Pass of Ceimaneigh. Dr. Bergin and myself were sitting on a rock, motionless and listening to a labourer speaking to us in Irish. He was a magnificent specimen of a man. He stood facing us, tall, powerful, erect and perfectly at ease. The handle of a spade lay lightly in his left hand; with his right hand he emphasised his conversation.

'I sat there, looking, listening, admiring the lovely picture. His conversation I could not fully understand, for he spoke fluently, and my humble knowledge of Irish was imperfect. But I know the Shakespearian drama, and the need the human spirit has, when deeply moved, to express itself in the iambic and in an adequate emotional form. I was an ardent student of natural expression. There before me was the thing itself. That labourer's voice was delightful to my ear. I recalled the saying of Pedersen of Copenhagen that Irish is the language of the sweetest sounds—a diamond on the lips of those who spoke it. I longed to know what the burden of that speech was that made that man's eyes scintillate, his face so expressive, his gestures so emphatic. What a study in expression for one searching in a hundred books, as I was, for light!'

No doubt, Father O'Flynn had the labourer of Ceimaneigh in mind when he wrote:

> And as I listened I often said are we
> That noble race? Are we so utterly
> Uprooted from our soil, as not to know
> That that man there and we are Irishmen?
> He is—but what am I? In language he
> Excels, and in a perfect utterance.
> In folklore and mythology, in ways
> Of thought, in poetry, music, stories, dress,
> Tradition, history, all that a nation wants
> Its man to be, he is. The scholar haunts
> His house, to hear the most melodious tongue. . . .

'Every day I was absorbing spiritual food from a tradition that no other nation in Europe can boast of—a thing that has come more from heaven than from earth. I got from the old songs the same stirrings of heart and soul that Shakespeare must have got from his observations of the human scene, and it was the enchantment of the music that set me on the track of the poets and bards.'

Among the many lasting friends he made during these promise-filled summers in the Gaeltacht, Father O'Flynn owed much to Daniel Corkery. He delighted in Corkery's vision of the Golden Age:

'Except for the portions of Eastern Europe which belonged to the Greek Empire, Ireland was the most important centre of sacred and profane learning from the sixth to the ninth century (*Irish in the early Middle Ages:* Rev. Father E. Cahill, S.J.). One reads such a tribute and sees again in vision the lonely neglected places where one has come upon all that is left of one or other of those great schools—places seldom visited, by a gentle river, or within a deep glen, or on a hillside over the sea, so withdrawn, so still, that it is almost impossible to raise the faintest vision of them as they once were—filled with ardent and serious students from far and near—from Gaul, England, Germany, Switzerland, Italy, Hungary, even from Christian Africa. Rosscarbery, above the southern sea, is as quiet a little place as any in the world, yet its old name, Ros Ailithir, tells us that it was pre-eminently the place to which the most distant foreigners came—the Promontory of the Pilgrims. And in thousands they came. It is the French Benedictine, Gougaud, who tells us that these students—"the élite of foreign nations", in his phrase—became "so fascinated by the life there as to find it impossible to tear themselves away." Gougaud is almost of our own time; to his words it may be well to add those of the Venerable Bede, one who was contemporaneous with those schools: "The Irish most readily received them, and provided them daily with their food without charge, and books also to read, and free instruction".'

What especially delighted Father O'Flynn in Corkery's description was the ideal of the liberal pursuit of knowledge; the zeal of the scholars, the humility of the teachers and the spirit of hospitality. The Irish revival meant far more to him than the language, games, music and dancing. What he aimed at was 'the restoration of the ancient purity of spirit, of neglected virtues and ideals, which would act as a defence against the demoralising tendencies of the age we live in.' He always saw Ireland in a European context and his love of Shakespeare and Dante played a most important part in his appreciation of things Irish.

In contrast to his ideal, what he saw all about him in Cork city saddened him. Apart from the enthusiasts he met in the Gaelic League, the vast majority of the people were apathetic or even opposed to the ideals of a Gaelic Ireland.

'What can we expect,' he said, 'of a people who have been truncated from their tradition? They know not whence they come! Cork city has been for centuries under the English spirit of conquest. Its people have never known the true Irish tradition or what it might have made of them. They were barred from their native culture, and their native culture was barred from them, and they were taught to believe that they were well rid of it.'

> Woe and pain, pain and woe,
> Are my lot night and noon,
> To see your bright face clouded so
> Like to the mournful moon,
> My Dark Rosaleen!
> My own Rosaleen.

That which delighted Father O'Flynn above all else in this world of the Gael was, as one might suspect, its music and its songs.

'I went about the Gaeltacht areas in Waterford, Cork and Kerry listening to the traditional singers and learning from them their songs. I was like the man in the gospel parable who went about seeking pearls.'

He was charmed by the way in which those traditional singers sang their songs.

'I never heard more perfect movement in sound than in the Gaeltacht singers. Even the raucous voice of the peasant in perfection of music motion sounded to my ears as far above the accurate note-singing of the professional singer as the delight of the spirit is above the tinkling of the tympanum.'

These traditional Irish songs differed considerably from the modern art song. They were structured on a word accent and a free rhythm. In the best of them one finds a perfect wedding between the poetry and the melodic line. The great accents give the dynamism to the melody and it is the task of the singer to fit in artistically all the lesser accents and grace-notes without doing violence to the verse and without breaking the flowing line of the main melody. Ideally this called for not only a good singing voice, but also for a fairly high degree of creative ability in the singer. These songs were not written down and rarely is the author known. They were handed down mouth to ear, and each singer sang the song as he felt it at the time of singing—for the true traditional singer is always an individualist. It was a *genre* of art that appealed immensely to Father O'Flynn. He loved the old songs he found in the Gaeltacht and likened them to the nectar preserved pure in the honeycombs that had been blackened with age in the Egyptian tombs—but which was as pure and luscious as the day it was distilled by the bees many centuries ago.

His own musical talents, his sense of drama and the ability to identify himself with the mood of each song and make it his own, all fitted him to be a fine exponent of the art of traditional Irish singing.

His interest in Irish music brought him in contact with Father Hennebry, lecturer in Irish music at University College, Cork. They became great friends. They met frequently in the chaplain's quarters at the Asylum. They discussed the structure and interpretation of the songs that Father O'Flynn had collected or was studying from manuscripts. He was never satisfied to take a song from a manuscript only. These folk-songs needed the living tradition to interpret them. He always sought someone with that living tradition to sing the song for him before he made up his mind on the interpretation.

On one of these visits, Father Hennebry had a recording of a native singer from Ballymacoda on his phonograph. He played it several times, and tried to sing it after the manner of the recorded voice. He found some of the intervals quite elusive, and could not sing them to his satisfaction.

'What do you think of it, Seamus?' he asked.

'I could do it as well as that singer myself,' Father O'Flynn replied.

'Come on, then—let me hear you do it!'

And Father O'Flynn sang the song so well that his listener was amazed and delighted.

'Seamus,' he said, 'you can do it as if to the manner born. Put on a tall hat and go teach the whole nation the tradition it is in danger of losing.'

'Why the tall hat?' asked Father O'Flynn.

'Because, without that bit of grandeur, no one will listen to you these days.'

Father O'Flynn was now a man with a message, a man with a mission. Such men need transport. He purchased a Red Indian motor-cycle with a combination side-car, and travelled Munster teaching the art of traditional Irish singing to all who had a mind for it.

His enthusiasm for things Gaelic caused him to clash with the Lord Mayor of Cork and the Corporation as the following incident shows.

On 8 January 1915, under the Lord Mayor's privilege, the following motion was passed at a meeting of the Cork Corporation:

'That the resolution passed by the Council conferring the Freedom of the City on Professor Kuno Meyer be rescinded, and that his name be erased from the Roll of Honorary Freemen of the Corporation of Cork, on account of his action and recent speech in New York, fomenting in the United States a movement amongst the Germans and an irresponsible section of the Irish population against the Empire.'

The Lord Mayor then proceeded to strike out the name of Kuno Meyer from the Roll of Honorary Freemen.

The people of Cork accepted in silence the decision of their public representatives; all except Father O'Flynn. Alone, he appeared before the Corporation, and protested passionately against this piece of 'fashionable humbug', as he called it. Because he had not waited to collect the signatures of twenty responsible citizens he could not, under the rules, be listened to. But his protest was justified by subsequent events.

On 14 May 1920, the name of Kuno Meyer was restored to the Roll of Honorary Freemen of the City of Cork when Terence McSwiney was Lord Mayor.

A sower by temperament, he was at his best when giving. Each week he visited the primary schools of the North Monastery and taught Irish songs to the boys. Here is how he appeared to some of his pupils in those days:

'Father O'Flynn was broad-shouldered, sturdy and very masculine. Although he was not tall, his forceful personality made him seem huge in our boyish eyes. Because of his strong national sentiments we admired him greatly. He was our hero. His forcefulness was balanced by his extraordinary sympathy. He was quick to see a boy's point of view, and his charming smile and hearty ringing laugh endeared him to us. Almost everything he said was given fuller meaning by his gestures. This fascinated us boys.

'He came once a week for half-an-hour and taught us songs in the Gaelic tongue. As soon as we became proficient he joined in singing them with us, and on these occasions he ceased to be our teacher and lived again as a boy among us. It seemed as though he transplanted something of himself into each of us. And so we left him, not just another pupil with a lesson learned, but rather as a disciple whom he, the master, had lifted up into another and a finer plane.'

Another of his pupils in those days wrote:

'My contacts with Father O'Flynn stand out in my memory as quite different from all other contacts I ever had with priests when I was a boy. There was some quality about him of bigness and warmth and—what is it?—cultural mastery and achievement, that used to give me a glow and uplift I never got from any other priest.

'I recall being in his chaplain's room in the Asylum with two other "Mon" boys sometime in 1915—a boy named Hawkins and a lad named Ernie Devlin. The three of us had been chosen to go to him for coaching in a song to be sung at a concert in the City Hall. I can still recall myself being freshly washed and combed for the visit, and how patiently he went through the song with us. The first line of the song came frightfully hard to me: "*Aréir ar mo leabadh go natuireach léanmhar.*" I couldn't get the interval between "*natuireach*" and "*lean*". Hawkins got it, and was chosen to sing at the concert.

'When the practice was over, he had tea brought in for us; very weak tea, I remember, and he told us that if we knew about the harm strong tea does to people's minds we would never drink strong tea again.

'Some time after that visit I met him again in Old George's Street, and he passed by me without recognising me. My heart fell. Then he turned and called me by name, and smiled and shook hands warmly; and the rest of the day—the rest of my life—was the brighter for it.'

Belfast city has a special place in the hearts of those who love Irish music, for it was there that Bunting took down from the last of the old Gaelic harpers their exquisite melodies. Bunting's collection showed Irishmen that they possessed a glorious heritage in music.

A century later Carl Hardebeck came to Belfast from England. He heard some traditional singers sing their unaccompanied songs in Irish. He was at once enamoured with their beauty, and resolved to devote his life to the study and cultivation of that musical form. He was particularly sensitive to the relation between each melody and the poetic sub-structure. He learned the Irish language and became familiar with the poetry. He travelled in the Gaeltacht of Donegal and sat by the firesides of the people, recording in braille—for he was blind—the words and tunes they sang for him. In the piano settings he made for these songs he aimed at preserving their rhythm at all costs, and he composed his accompaniments to point the melody and not smother it as others less sensitive than he had done.

'I look upon an Irish song,' he often said, 'as I look upon a beautiful lady. My accompaniments are merely gifts of pearls that serve to emphasise her beauty.'

Few of his contempories recognised the merits of Hardebeck, for they had been trained in a musical tradition very different from that of the Irish modal melodies. One of the few who did was Father O'Flynn.

Father O'Flynn met Carl Hardebeck for the first time in Belfast in 1915 and they became fast friends. He recalls the occasion:

'I remember being in St. Mary's Hall, Belfast, in 1915. Mr. Francis Biggar, to make the nation feel what it was fast losing, the noblest musical culture ever a nation had, called together all who loved our native music. He made a glorious night of it, welcoming us with princely hospitality. That night of enthusiasm in St. Mary's Hall for the crumbs of tradition that had fallen from the once rich table of our ancestors is in my memory locked. And if the crumbs could stimulate that insatiable desire Dr. Bergin had and Carl Hardebeck had and Mr. Biggar had, all who love our nation should gather those crumbs; for nothing remains to inspire us if the crumbs be lost. Nor will the painting of the crumbs inspire: museums, collections of folklore, books, letters, words, have no taste. The ear must hear, the eye in the soul must see, the whole man must experience the reality of our living tradition, if all the sacrifices of the past are not to be in vain.'

Father O'Flynn had little time for politics. He was surprised, therefore—pleasantly surprised—to discover that his arrival in Dublin on Easter Monday 1916, coincided with the Rising.

'Tommy O'Reilly and myself had set out from Cork that morning on my motor-cycle. We took turns at driving. I was booked to give a talk on Irish music to a group of Gaelic Leaguers in Parnell Square that evening.

'Driving along James' Street we were halted by a line of British bayonets. We were ordered off the motor-cycle and escorted into a hospital nearby where we were questioned. I explained that I was a priest on a peaceful mission.

"You don't look like a priest," the officer said, and I had to admit that he was right for I was dressed in an old leather coat, a leather cap and goggles and rubber boots—all of them covered in dust from the roads.

"What's in the Gladstone bag?" the officer asked me.

"My nightshirt and razor," I replied.

'He opened the bag and emptied the contents on to the table. He looked through my lecture notes and I was thanking my stars that the final remarks were written in Irish—for they were anything but complimentary to the British regime in Ireland.

'"You can forget about your lecture on music tonight," he said. "There's a rebellion on since this morning."

'My first instinct was to cheer. I rejoiced that there was still some savour left in the salt of Irish nationalism. But because of the company I was in, I kept silent.'

Father O'Flynn and his friend returned to Inchicore and found hospitality at the Oblate Fathers' House.

'It was a fine spring evening, and as all seemed quiet Tommy and I made our way into the centre of Dublin. There was no shooting, and hundreds of people had gathered to see what was happening. Volunteers were moving swiftly along the quays and side streets, erecting barricades.

'In O'Connell Street groups of people waved and cheered to the men in the windows and on the roof of the G.P.O. Now and then they returned the cheers. I gave the poor fellows my blessing.

'"At long last—at long last, thank God, I feel that Dublin belongs to the Dubliners," I heard a man in the crowd shouting.

'"And please God, Ireland will belong to the Irish before long," I said to Tommy.

'Down a lane off O'Connell Street we got a hurried look at the Proclamation posted on a wall. On seeing the name of Padraig Pearse among the signatories, I was amazed. I had thought him to be too gentle a person to take a gun in his hands. When first I had met him four years before all our talk was of poetry and Shakespeare. He was very interested in what I was trying to do by means of Shakespeare at Farranferris. He had so much of the truth about education, so much the nation needed, and now to drop all that and take to arms!

'I rejoiced that a blow was being struck for our freedom and I was proud to be present in Dublin the very day it was struck.

> Oh! there was lightning in my blood,
> Red lightning lightened through my blood,
> My Dark Rosaleen.

The apparent failure of the Easter Rising did not distract Father O'Flynn from his work for the revival of the Gaelic tradition. He became president of the Gaelic League in Cork city; acted as chairman of the Munster Feis; and was the inspiration and driving force of many other Gaelic League activities. In the autumn of 1917 he gave a series of six lectures to Gaelic Leaguers in Bolton Street Technical School, Dublin, on Irish music and the Shakespearean drama.

In 1918 Father O'Flynn became a member of the newly-appointed sub-committee of the Cork Municipal School of Music. At once he set out to realise one of his most cherished designs. He travelled to Belfast and begged Carl Hardebeck to accept the positions of Professor of Irish Music and the Head-mastership of the Cork Municipal School of Music; Hardebeck agreed. Back in Cork Father O'Flynn did not find it too difficult a task to persuade the committee to agree to his proposition. Among the members were such ardent nationalists as Terence MacSwiney, Daniel Corkery and Father Thomas, O.F.M.Cap. But as soon as the appointment was made public there was an immediate and violent reaction. All but one of the teaching staff resigned in protest at the appointment of a German as headmaster. They were replaced by a complete new staff.

The Federation of Discharged and Demobilised (British) Soldiers and Sailors by formal resolution 'objected to the appointment of a German to either the Headmastership or Professorship of traditional Irish music.'

Father O'Flynn, who was considered the chief instigator of this German plot, received a warning signed 'Tubs o' Blood'! It threatened that if he brought Hardebeck to Cork, he himself would be thrown into the river Lee. Father O'Flynn reacted by saying at the next committee meeting: 'Whoever attempts to throw me in the Lee will come in with me!'

When the time came for Carl Hardebeck to come to Cork, Father O'Flynn went to Dublin to meet him en route from Belfast. Things had now come to such a pass that two detec-tives accompanied the professor and the priest on their journey to Cork, and when they arrived at the Glanmire Station they were met by six armed policemen who accompanied the professor to his lodgings.

Father O'Flynn described the sequel:

'Shortly after Hardebeck arrived "Tubs o' Blood", in the person of two toughs, attacked me one night as I was coming home along the North Mall—but they fled when they saw my friend James O'Callaghan coming to the rescue. I remained on terra firma, and Hardebeck remained as Headmaster in the School of Music.'

The *Oireachtas*—the annual festival of language, song, poetry, music, dancing and games of the Gaelic League—was held in Cork city from 3 to 9 August 1919. Father O'Flynn had worked on several of the committees to ensure the success of this event.

It was a week of glorious summer weather. Early on Sunday morning the streets were gay with waggonettes and side-cars bringing large numbers of people into the city for the opening of the festival. Crowds were also arriving by special trains, and many from the city borders came on bicycles.

That afternoon, in the Gaelic Athletic Grounds, Blackrock, the Irish Volunteers Pipers Band played the Cork and Kilkenny hurling teams on to the field. Dr. Cohalan, the Bishop of Cork, was introduced to the captains by Father O'Flynn. His Lordship threw in the ball.

Irish was spoken by the vast majority of those present at the match. 'It seemed,' commented the *Cork Examiner,* 'that in a few years Irish will be again the language in this city.'

That evening a special meeting of *Coalacht Mhuire*—the Irish Confraternity—was held in the North Cathedral. Rosary, sermon and hymns were all in Irish. The Rosary was said by Father O'Flynn, and Father James O'Leary, P.P., SS. Peter's and Paul's, preached on faith and the Gaelic mind.

At the concert in the City Hall Mr. Liam de Roiste, M.P., in the absence of Mr. Eoin MacNeill, formally opened the Festival. He welcomed delegates from all parts of Ireland, England and Scotland, and assured them that a very warm welcome awaited them wherever they went in Cork city that week.

Satisfaction at the progress made in the Gaelicisation of the nation and great hope for the future success of that work was expressed by all the committees that week.

At the choral competition on Sunday night in the City Hall, Father O'Flynn won first place with his girls' choir from St. Marie's of the Isle. The two prescribed songs were *Seán Ó Duibhir a' Gleanna* and *Eibhlín a Rúin*. Mr. Carl Hardebeck, the adjudicator, paid a glowing tribute to the high standard of the choral singing. He said that he had heard some excellent rendering of these traditional Irish songs in different parts of the country, especially in Tyrone, but he had never heard anything to equal the singing of Father O'Flynn's choir from St. Marie's of the Isle. They were absolutely perfect, he said, and possessed the true Irish tradition of singing.

Marcella Ní Mhuirthille from Bantry, the recognised authority on traditional singing and one of the best traditional singers of the day, congratulated Father O'Flynn on the manner in which he had taught his choir, and said that only a choir of angels could equal them in sweetness.

Father O'Flynn was also assured of the orthodoxy of his tradition by the famous Gaelic story-teller and folklorist from Ring, Co. Waterford, An Fear Mór.

'To teach again what one has learned is the best assurance of the right understanding of the message of tradition. It makes assurance doubly sure that one has the tradition correct,' said Father O'Flynn that week. 'I asked An Fear Mór and his fellow-workers of Ring to hear my work' (choir singing traditional Irish melodies). 'They listened, and unhesitatingly put their seal on it. I felt twice the man.'

It was in fact a tremendous satisfaction to him, after nine years of loving labour at the language and music, to have been accepted by the leading figures in the Gaelic world as one of themselves.

He said on that occasion: 'Music for our ancestors was life sublimated. They had no idea of notation. They had a poetic vision of life, and in their music they expressed that vision and sublimated that life. Like David the psalmist in Psalm 18, our old Irish people found uplift in the glories of the universe; aye, and in its tiniest items—daisy or butterfly. Our old people could see the energy of the creative word in all motion—the power of the first *Fiat* still sweeping through creation—always lasting, because they knew the Word to be Eternal and Infinite. Each particular created thing served as a spur to their minds to make contact through its prototype with the Mind whose creative Word made all things. The ancient Irish built themselves a willow cabin at the gate of heaven itself, and their souls longed to dwell within, contemplating and hymning the ideal beauty—prototypes of every natural created form in its Source—the Divine Intelligence.

'But the question remains: are these, our beautiful Irish melodies, to be let die? The tradition at present is in a lamentable state. We need someone strong—with authority and the true appreciation—to save our musical tradition from extinction. The Church's tradition in Plain Chant was championed by Leo XIII and Pius X. Who will champion our cause?'

At the *Aeridheacht*—the open-air concert—in Fitzgerald's Park towards the end of the week, all the prize-winning choirs, solo singers, dancers, harpers and pipers took part. Father O'Flynn sang, and he concluded the evening by reciting *On Fontenoy* by Davis and *My Dark Rosaleen* by James C. Mangan. He received a tremendous ovation.

'I was full of hope,' said Father O'Flynn, 'when that glorious *Oireachtas* came to an end, that our dream of a Gaelic Ireland would be realised in the not too distant future. Never before or since did I feel that the prophecies of Mangan's poem were so true, so vital and so near to fulfilment, as in that August of 1919.'

> *Tis you shall have the golden throne,*
> *Tis you shall reign and reign alone,*
> *My Dark Rosaleen.*

6

Troubled times

CANON O'SULLIVAN, the administrator at the North
Cathedral, invited a few priest friends to supper and cards at the
presbytery in the autumn of 1920. His guests included Father
Christy O'Flynn, and his friend, Father James O'Callaghan;
Father Mick Roche, who was home on holidays from an
English diocese; Father O'Shea, one of his own curates; and the
guest of honour—a parish priest who had formerly been a
Professor of Theology in one of the major seminaries and
whom they called 'the Doc'.

At supper there was the usual clerical conversation; the
recent diocesan changes; the death of a parish priest; the
Bishop. Inevitably, the political situation, stormy and confused
as it was, came up for discussion: Arthur Griffith and Sinn
Féin, de Valera and Dáil Éireann; the I.R.A. and the Black
and Tans; Lloyd George and Terry MacSwiney's hunger
strike; the intended visit of Archbishop Mannix; the acts of
violence that were becoming more and more frequent.

'Yes—the times are very troubled, indeed,' Father O'Shea
sighed. 'And how 'tis all going to end beats me.'

'What do you think of the situation?' asked the canon of
'the Doc', as they settled around the fire after dinner, with
pipe and glass. 'You're the genius among us.'

Though they frequently pulled his leg about his doctorate,
they greatly respected his opinion.

'What is happening now,' said the Doc, 'is bad, and it
could be full of danger for the Church. I see all this violence,
this destruction of life and property, as the inevitable fruits of
a false political philosophy. When I was in Paris ——'

'I knew we'd end up in Paris sooner or later,' interrupted Father O'Shea drily.

'Let him go on,' said their host, Canon O'Sullivan.

The Doc resumed. 'When I was in Paris I got interested in French politics and in particular in the Revolution period. I'm now convinced that the philosophy that advocates the use of violence to achieve political freedom is false. It is false to human nature, to man's social nature. It is also contrary to the Catholic mind, which is traditionally the mind of peace. You have only to look at the way things have gone with the Church in France since the Revolution to realise how deeply she has been wounded and devitalised. Secularism and anti-clericalism have barred her from the schools; she has lost the working classes, and the grass is growing up through the floors of her churches. I witnessed the expulsion of the religious orders in 1903. All this, I am convinced, flows from revolutionism. Not only has it weakened the Church in France, but of its own nature it is a doctrine that tends to extremes. Karl Marx advocated world revolution by means of violence as the road to his perfect society. Atheism is an essential part of Marx's revolutionary doctrine. "Religion is the opium of the people." Here you have the fully grown monster of revolutionism. God help the Church where this teaching is put into practice, as it appears to have been since the Bolshevik revolution in Russia recently.'

'O *doctor optime,*' groaned Father O'Shea, 'will you come back from Russia and tell us simple priests what all these -isms mean to us here in Ireland?'

'Well, the Church is the same the world over,' the Doc went on. 'What injures her in France and Russia will injure her here. And I think I can recognise behind all these ambushes, burnings and murders the same false political mind that sanctioned the atrocities in France during the Revolution and in Russia today.'

'You mean this revolutionism?' asked Father O'Shea.

'I do.'

'Then would you enlighten us a little more on this "monster" as you call it, and tell us how in the name of heaven our lads came to be mixed up in it?' put in Father Roche.

'Well, let me put it to you this way,' the Doc said. 'Two men went to France in the height of the Revolution —Wolfe Tone and O'Connell. Both saw the same thing. They reacted very differently. Tone rejoiced and enthusiastically adopted the precepts and practices of the Revolution. O'Connell was horrified and rejected both. They returned to Ireland.

'Wolfe Tone was, as you know, an Ulster Presbyterian. He did not have the Catholic mind, and from what I know I think it is true to say that he lacked the vision of what Christy there calls *Sean Éire* —the old Gaelic mind. He preached revolutionism as the way to freedom. His teaching bore fruit in the rebellion of 1798. You know how it ended; it was suppressed by the superior power of the English. The Act of Union in 1800 deprived us of what semblance of a parliament we had. Wolfe Tone died in prison —but his political doctrine lived on through the nineteenth century, nurtured by a tiny group in each generation. Robert Emmet in 1803; Mitchel and Young Ireland in 1848; the Fenians in 1867. And in our own day, Pearse and his men claimed to be in the same tradition. Their aim is to set up an Irish Republic, independent and seperate from the British Empire. Pearse would have the Republic not only free but Gaelic as well. It is worth noting that the Church opposed all these physical force movements. In her eyes they were secret oath-bound societies plotting to overthrow by violence what is called "the lawful authority of the state". Her experience on the continent taught her that these societies are frequently anti-clerical as well as anti-government.

'Fenianism in the last century showed signs of this, and you all know how strongly the Bishops reacted.'

' "Hell is not hot enough nor eternity long enough to punish these rebels," ' Father O'Callaghan quoted for his friends the closing words from a sermon preached by the Bishop of Kerry in 1867.

'That about sums it up, James,' said the Doc, 'and anyone who joined these movements was excommunicated. This, of course, created a tension between the Church and revolutionary nationalism. Now that everything is in the melting pot, we can only wait and see how this tension will be resolved.'

'Whatever about the Fenians, you can't accuse Pearse and his men of being anti-clerical,' cut in Father Roche. 'Those men of Easter Week were loyal to the Church as well as to their country.'

'I'm afraid I can't agree with you there, Mick. The fact is that Pearse and his men who fought in Easter Week were disloyal to their Chief of Staff, Eoin MacNeill, by deceiving him and by disobeying his orders; they were unfaithful to one very important article in the I.R.B. Constitution, namely, not to go to war with England without first gaining the approval of the majority of the Irish people, and since the Decree of Pius IX condemning the I.R.B. in 1870 had not been revoked, they were—objectively at least—disobeying the supreme authority in the Church.'

'MacNeill was a ditherer,' interjected Father Roche—'he'd achieve nothing—and who, I ask you, in his sane senses, would hold a plebiscite in 1916 to find out if the people were ready to throw off the English yoke? Revolutions do not work that way.'

'MacNeill didn't dither,' replied the Doc, 'but in his wisdom he would have held the Volunteers together till the war ended and then used them most effectively to bargain with Britain. To my mind,' the Doc continued, 'Pearse was more a poet than a politician. His poetic mind gave to Tone's revolutionism a kind of mystical overtone. You know what he said about the shedding of blood in the cause of freedom. To my ears it sounds like blasphemy. You will have noticed too that Pearse refers to Wolfe Tone, Mitchel, and Davis, and Lalor as "the four evangelists of Irish freedom". This use of religious terms in a political context leads to confused thinking. It is bad for both politics and religion.

'The Easter rising ended a failure; Pearse and his men foresaw it would fail as a military campaign. He realised that the English held the trump cards in the game of violence: more men and bigger guns. But it appears now that the English overplayed their hand; for by executing many of the leaders of the rising they made them martyrs—another word from the religious vocabulary—and the people were roused from their political lethargy as they had not been aroused since the days of Parnell. A series of blunders on the part of our English rulers—the threat of conscription, for example, in 1918—led up to the landslide victory of Sinn Féin in the elections of 1918. True to the spirit of revolutionism Dáil Éireann, in its first session in January 1919, declared that a state of war existed between the Irish Republic and Great Britain. De Valera, representative of the military wing of Sinn Féin, became President of Dáil Éireann in April 1919. The tiny Irish Republican Army took to the gun to rid the country of British forces, and so we have this War of Independence conducted by means of ambushes, raids, murders and burnings.'

'How else do you expect our lads to fight?' asked Father Roche, testily. 'Do you expect a handful of men and boys armed with rifles and shotguns to come out into the open to be mown down by British machine-guns? Have you any sense of proportion?'

'I do not expect them to act otherwise than they are doing,' replied the Doc calmly. 'I do not question their bravery or their sincerity. But the point I am making is that once again they have played into the hands of the British by resorting to violence. 'Tis their game. They are experts at it. Look at the Black and Tans! We cannot hope to beat them.'

'This is no time to be sitting on the ditch making points, when the country is fighting for its freedom,' went on Father Roche warmly. 'I've a young brother out with the boys— and only I've got a Roman collar round my neck I'd be with them too. 'Tis easy to make points when there's none of your own flesh and blood in danger.'

'Easy now, Mick—no need to get excited!' said the Canon.

'If I may get a word in, Doc,' said Father O'Flynn, 'you mentioned that Pearse was a good poet but a poor politician. I hold he was a good poet and a clever politician. For see what his poetry has done for his political doctrine! Pearse preached the doctrine of Wolfe Tone—but with a difference. Consciously or unconsciously he has baptised the naked revolutionism of Tone by clothing it in symbols—the Christian symbols of redemption. He talks of the people being its own Messiah, of the people scourged and crowned with thorns, dying and rising again immortal. This is the poet in Pearse preaching a political doctrine in terms that can be understood by even the children on the street.'

'You have a nice point there, Chris,' replied the Doc—'but no amount of Christian symbolism can make what is false, true, and I'm very much inclined to think that Wolfe Tone's doctrine is false.'

'My dear Doctor,' cut in Father O'Flynn, 'just look at the facts for a moment! We've played the game the peaceful way from O'Connell to Butt, to Parnell, to Redmond, and we lost. They wore their tongues thin talking Home Rule in Westminster and hoping that a Liberal Government would grant it. They might as well have stayed at home. We played the game of revolution from Tone to Young Ireland to the Fenians, and to Pearse in 1916, and we were beaten. But in December 1918, we played once more the peaceful way, this time in a free democratic election according to the rules laid down by the British and under their surveillance. We won, hands down.

'De Valera, President of Sinn Féin, enjoys a majority in Dáil Éireann not equalled by any ruler in Europe or the U.S.A. today. But the score did not please Lloyd George, he could not take his beating. So Westminster denies the legitimacy of Dáil Éireann, and reverting to their own game of soldiers the English roll up the guns to shatter the Irish Republic. To fail to defend by force of arms what we have established by a free democratic vote, and to relinquish without protest what is justly ours, is to proclaim ourselves cowards in the eyes of the world and unworthy to be masters in our own house.'

'Hear, hear!' cried Father Roche, and the others joined in the applause.

'What I'd like to know,' said Father O'Callaghan, 'is this. If the cause is as just as Chris makes it out to be, why have the Bishops refused formally to acknowledge Dáil Éireann as the legitimate government of Ireland when requested to do so by de Valera? Could you answer me that, Doc?'

'I think the Bishops were wise with the wisdom of the serpent in refusing Dev—or rather it would be nearer the mark to say in postponing their decision. You see, the Bishops are caught between two fires—two governments, the British and Dáil Éireann, each claiming to be the only legitimate government of Ireland. In this confused situation, I imagine their lordships will wait till the smoke of battle dies down before they say anything decisive. Nor can you blame them for their caution in the matter, for the Church's experience of revolutions and republicanism has not been a very happy one. She has lost heavily in France—as I've pointed out—and in other countries where it prevailed. Therefore, she is suspicious of it. You can understand then why the Bishops here are slow to give Dáil Éireann their blessing. They will have to get clear proofs that the republicanism of Dáil Éireann is better disposed to the Church than the republicanism of the French.'

'I see,' said Father O'Callaghan. 'With the Bishops 'tis a case of the devil they know being better than the devil they don't know.'

'Exactly,' said the Doc, 'and until they are sure of Dáil Eireann they're not likely to acknowledge it formally as the legitimate government of Ireland—thereby rejecting the English claim.'

'All this fear of Sinn Féin,' cut in Father O'Flynn, 'seems to me to be groundless. The leaders and their associates come of good Irish families that have ever been loyal to the Church. It is not likely that they will treat her here as she was treated in France. What they need now above all is someone or something to make them "respectable"—just as Hennebry advised me to make Irish traditional music "respectable" by wearing a tall hat.'

'And how do you propose to do that, Chris?' asked Father O'Callaghan.

'I'd suggest that the Pope confer the highest papal honour on the President of Sinn Féin at once!'

They all burst out laughing.

'That would certainly make Dev and Sinn Fein "respectable" as you say,' commented the Doc, 'but it would infuriate the Orangemen in the North. Their cry "Home Rule is Rome Rule" would appear to be verified in that event.'

'If you had a free hand, Doc, how would you set about gaining independence for Ireland?' asked Father O'Shea.

'The way of the other man—O'Connell,' the Doc answered without hesitation.

'Oh! Not O'Connell!' groaned Father Roche. 'He and his methods are out of date long ago.'

'Out of fashion—yes; but out of date—no. To my mind O'Connell's methods of peaceful and reasonable discussion will never be out of date among civilised peoples.'

'You'd find it hard to convince Sinn Féin of that, Doc,' Father Roche said.

'Here's my proof,' said the Doc. 'O'Connell had the Catholic mind, and he was in the old Gaelic tradition. His experience in France led him to reject violent revolution as a means to political freedom. His reaction was, I would say, more typical of the average Catholic Irishman of his day—and of our day—than that of Tone. When O'Connell came home he worked by peaceful constitutional methods for two things, Catholic Emancipation and Repeal. He succeeded in uniting the whole country as no one before him or since has succeeded.'

'What about Sinn Féin—haven't they succeeded?' It was Father Roche again.

'They have succeeded only partly. There is the problem of the Ulster Unionists, you know, and it remains to be seen how Sinn Féin will handle that.'

'What was the secret of O'Connell's success?' asked Father O'Callaghan.

'That's the question to ask!' said the Doc. 'Where you have a Catholic community loyal to their Bishops—as you had in Ireland in the days of O'Connell and have today, thank God—then one thing should be very clear to a keen politician. With the backing of the Bishops he can unite the people and lead them successfully to action. Without the Bishops that is an impossible task, and we have the example of Parnell to prove it. In Ireland the trump card in a politician's hands is the Bishops. You see, the Church is a society in which unity is already achieved. The Church is one. That is her first mark. With the politician unity is always one of the most difficult aims to be achieved, and when achieved it is a tremendous problem to maintain it. The Bishops backed O'Connell; O'Connell echoed the minds of the Bishops in political forms. He had the whole Catholic population behind him. And he led them successfully to Catholic Emancipation. And the card with which he beat the British was the Bishops.'

'But he failed to win Repeal,' put in Father Roche. 'Your argument seems to collapse there.'

'He did—but did you ever ask yourself why he failed?'

'I did. And I'll tell you the reason why. The British guns at Clontarf unnerved him; he retreated before them and justified his cowardice by saying that no nation was worth the shedding of a drop of human blood.'

'You are being less than fair to O'Connell, his motives and his methods. He was not unnerved by British guns but very wisely he refused to play the British game of violence. And see what he preserved by his refusal. The unity of the country remained intact—a unity that has now been well and truly shattered by Lloyd George and company. Look at Ulster— Carson and his men armed to the teeth and resolved to resist to the last ditch Home Rule or union with the South. By O'Connell's refusal, peace was preserved. These were the very conditions that were so important to the Irish Church as she emerged poor and weak from centuries of persecution. Under these favourable conditions she developed rapidly—going from strength to strength all through the nineteenth century and up to our own time. The Bishops were free to give their undivided attention to the problems of reconstruction on all levels of the Church's life. To take but one point—education— see what they've achieved! Denominational religious education in all the primary schools of the country; the parish priest manager of his school; and an arrangement with the government whereby they pay all the teachers' salaries, and by far the greater part of the building cost and maintenance of the schools.

'Secondary education has gradually been provided for by the religious orders, again under the control of the Bishops; and they have made a good shot at solving the problem of university education—though here they have so far failed to reach their ideal. All this means that the Catholic mind of our people is saved for the present and guaranteed for the future. The Bishops could do no more.'

'Tell me, Doc,' asked Father O'Flynn, 'if the Church could draw such advantages from the system of primary education, why did Pearse condemn it as "the murder machine"?'

'Well, Chris, for one thing the Bishops and Pearse viewed the system from different angles. Pearse saw it as a British machine designed to destroy the political and cultural minds of the Irish people. And Pearse was right, for it did just that. We have not produced a first-class Irish Catholic political thinker since O'Connell. Unable to think correctly in politics, we have fallen into the error of adopting the false political philosophy of revolutionism. By making English the sole language of the class-room it has succeeded in cutting the main avenue of approach to the minds and hearts of our ancestors— the Irish language. Douglas Hyde and his friends saw the great cultural loss this was to the nation, so they founded the Gaelic League to restore the language. However, I'm afraid they're a century too late.

'But even here, in the Irish becoming an English-speaking people, the Church has gained another advantage: her priests now going abroad to England, America and Australia to serve there on the missions have no language problem. So you can say that while the system of primary education has gone a long way to killing the political and cultural mind of the people, thanks to the wisdom and diplomacy of the Bishops it has not killed their Catholic mind. Looking at the system from the point of view of an idealistic nationalist like Pearse, one can condemn it as "the murder machine." But we cannot but admire the realistic approach of the Irish Bishops to primary education in the nineteenth century. Accepting with qualifications the system offered by the English government in 1833, they grasped the nettle firmly, fought hard for what they wanted within that system, and got it. Having secured the religious education and the Catholic mind of the nation at the grass-roots level and later at the secondary school level, they were prepared to put up with the political and cultural disadvantages of the system. Nor can you very well blame them; for whatever way you look at it, the Bishops' primary responsibility to God and to their flock is not the political and cultural soul of the nation, but to build up the kingdom of God in Ireland. And this you must admit they have done fairly well. Again and again they have drawn advantage and profit to the life of the Church from situations that, viewed from other angles, seem hostile to the best interests of the nation.'

'Well, Chris,' said the Canon, turning to his friend, 'we all know you have very strong views on the Irish revival. What have you to say to the Doctor?'

'To me,' said Father O'Flynn, slowly and reflectively, 'Ireland is the Job among the nations of the earth. In the Golden Age she overflowed with riches—spiritual and secular. Lavishly she gave to Europe when Europe was feeding on husks; graciously she welcomed to her shores those who sought the light of her learning. Then, like Job, she suffered a series of calamities. Danes, Normans and English in turn attacked and despoiled her of almost all her riches. She saw her churches and monasteries looted; her schools of learning—Clonmacnoise, Ardmore, Armagh, Moville, Monasterboice and a hundred others—burned to ashes. That which England abandoned under Henry VIII, she set out savagely to destroy in Ireland—the Catholic religion. It was a conflict between a people fallen from the way of objective truth into the error of subjectivism and a people determined to be loyal to the objective truth even unto annihilation.

'In that unequal struggle our ancestors let everything go:

all their worldly possessions, titles, lands, property, school and church buildings, and their treasures of sacred art. Deprived of political leaders, her Bishops and priests proscribed, Ireland for three centuries sat like Job on the dunghill; the mocking of her English masters in her ears, nothing left but her sores and her faith in the God of Abraham.

'Her friends from O'Connell on have exhausted patience itself in striving by all lawful and peaceful means to regain her right to live her own life according to her own ancient and noble traditions. But her enemies have persistently and arrogantly denied her that right. Exasperated by the procrastination and the blatant double-dealing of her English masters, her sons have resorted to arms. Justice must react when faced with injustice. If it does not then 'tis no longer a virtue. The salt has lost its savour. To me Easter 1916 was another Thermopylae. It has roused the country from its political lethargy, given new hope to the people, and was the necessary prelude to the peaceful and overwhelming victory of Sinn Féin in the elections of December 1918. It has given us Dáil Éireann, our first free and independent legislative assembly in seven hundred years.'

'And what are you going to do with your freedom?' asked the Doc.

'For me this political freedom means the longed-for opportunity of restoring to the nation the mind, the heart and the vision of Sean Éire—on a nation-wide scale,' Father O'Flynn replied. 'For ten years now I have worked at the Irish language, our poets and our traditional songs. In the Gaeltacht areas of Ballingeary, Ballinskelligs and Dun Quin I have spent all my summer holidays close to the hearts of these people, assimilating their traditions. I have tasted and seen that this old Gaelic culture is sweet and a thousand times more wholesome than the poor scutch-grass British way of life we unhappily adopted during the nineteenth century. When I look at *Sean Éire* and then at the Ireland of today I can only say, like the ghost in *Hamlet*: *"O what a falling off is there!"* We are inferior in everything to our ancestors.

'Pearse was right. The "murder machine" has done a thorough job. It has killed the Irish language, the one sure avenue of access to the minds and hearts of our noble forbears. It has robbed us of their grand, open, creative approach to life. It has given us a distaste for all things Irish and native. It has severed us from our finest traditions in living, in learning and in religion. It has bred in us an inferiority complex by holding before us, as the ideal of civilised living, the loyal, successful English gentleman, and by reminding us in a hundred different ways that in his eyes we are only "Paddy-and-the-pig"—a Caliban among men. Were it not for Douglas Hyde and the Gaelic League we had lost for ever the vision of our glorious past. Hyde saw that if we are to develop normally as a people we must stop this pitiful imitation of foreign ways and manners; we must take our eyes off the English model and fix them on one from our own tradition. We must rediscover ourselves and be ourselves.

' *"To thine own self be true,"* said Shakespeare. That is the starting point of all genuine national development. No progress except along the road of truth.

'While granting much of what you have said, Doc, about the progress of the Irish Church in the last century—I strongly disagree with you on several points.'

A surprised murmur and shuffling among the audience greeted this statement.

''Twas old Aristotle observed that whatever in nature seeks its own perfection tends to return to its origin. If we, as a people, are seeking sincerely a renewal of our traditional Gaelic and Catholic way of life, and if our hope of attaining that end is not to be groundless, then we must go back to our origins, *Sean Éire,* to draw nourishment from our own best traditions. This reorientating of our minds after the distortion they have suffered in the nineteenth century is, as far as I can see, of no small importance to the life of the Irish Church.

'The Church, like her divine Founder, sows the seeds of revealed truth in the hearts and minds of the hearers. Your argument appears to have overlooked the fact that the seed of truth depends for its fruitfulness—under God's grace—on the quality of the soil in which it is sown. It was our divine Lord himself—*moladh le'n a ainm naomhtha*—who pointed out to us the futility of sowing good seed in poor soil—stony ground or thorny patches. The soil is the mind and heart of the people. "By their fruits you shall know" the tree and the quality of the soil.

'When I look at *Sean Éire*, I see a people filled with love for and loyalty to truth—the objective truth—in life, in learning and in art; a people keenly sensitive to beauty—which is the splendour of truth—in nature and in art. The pagan Irish adored the rising sun—and small blame to them, for is it not a creation of surpassing power and beauty? The Irish word for both "south" and "right-hand" is *deas*; the word for both "west" and "back" is *siar*. These two words give me a picture of a people with its back to the west, its right hand to the south and its face to the east; a people enraptured by the beauty of the rising sun. These qualities of mind and heart of our ancestors formed the rich, warm humus in which St. Patrick and his missionaries sowed the seeds of divine truth. They did not find it hard to speak to such noble minds of the Creator of the sun and the source of all the truth and beauty that their minds had patiently extracted from the universe of created things about them. On hearing the fuller truth from the Christian missionaries they leapt with joy into the arms of Mother Church, and there for fifteen centuries they have nourished their spirit.

'If the conversion of our ancestors to Christianity in the

fifth century was so rapid and so whole-hearted, if the seed that Patrick sowed produced so rich a harvest of sanctity and learning that by the end of the seventh century missionaries set out to spread the light of faith in Scotland, England, Wales and Europe, the reason I think lies—after the grace of God—in the quality of the soil of *Sean Eire*. The good seed of the gospel fell on the good soil of their hearts, and in due course it brought forth a harvest of Christian living that expressed itself in a fine, free, open, personal approach to God, to nature and to the neighbour. It expressed itself in a zeal for learning—the sacred scriptures especially, which our ancestors lovingly adorned with all the art and skill at their disposal. It expressed itself in their communal worship of God in their many monastic settlements; it expressed itself in a deep consciousness of the fatherhood of God and in a corresponding attitude of childlike simplicity and trust, in an uninhibited joy in the works of his creation. This was the Ireland of the Golden Age—the island of saints and scholars—a people who were the balm of Europe when Europe lay stripped and bruised by the barbarian; a people who were the light of Europe when Europe stumbled and groped in the darkness.'

'Hear hear, Chris!' Father Roche shouted, clapping his hands. "Tis a shame we haven't a soap-box for you, but I'm afraid 'tis not *Sean Éire* you're describing at all—but the garden of Eden before the fall of Adam.'

'Pipe down, Mick,' said the Canon.

'Sorry, Chris—apologies from a West Briton.'

Father O'Flynn went back to his *Hamlet*: ' "*Look on this picture—and on this!*" I grant you that our Bishops have done a very good job in the schools and have gained—as you say—out of our political and cultural losses. But the fact remains that the Irish mind is today politically and culturally deficient. And I hold that this deficiency is now reflected in our attitude to the service of God and the neighbour. Our post-Emancipation

Catholicism shows some striking contrasts with the Catholicism of men like Columcille and his contemporaries of the Golden Age. In place of their free, open and confident approach to life and to the service of God, I find today in many people a narrow, cautious and fearful living according to rules and regulations. Gone is that spontaneity and that personal quality that gives zest to living, and to the service of God and the neighbour.

'In our public worship in the Mass, as well as in our daily lives, the sense of community has been replaced by an individualistic spirit that was not part of the mind of *Sean Éire*. There the king stooped down and saw all the majesty in the child, the child looked up and saw all the simplicity in the king. Today, the people go to Mass to save their souls, formerly they offered sacrifice to praise God.

'In the nineteenth century the fabric of the Church in Ireland has been rebuilt: cathedrals, churches, convents and monasteries. But in all these buildings there is not a trace of originality in architecture, design or decoration. Everything is an imitation of English and continental models. How unlike *Sean Éire*, whose designs in the illuminated manuscripts, in the high Celtic crosses of Monasterboice and Clonmacnoise, and whose workmanship in chalices and other sacred vessels, can still evoke the admiration of artists the world over. St. Gall exchanged melodies with St. Gregory in the seventh century. In our churches today one hears only the imported English hymns, like, "O Mother I . . ." Sentimentality has replaced the true emotions of *Sean Éire*. Religion has become the occupation of our women. In *Sean Éire* it was the men who led. We who were a people rich in sacred songs and melodies have now handed over all church music to Germans, Belgians and French organists, who for the most part are ignorant of our beautiful native idiom in music.

'In the religious instruction in our schools today, the

catechism has largely replaced the gospels of *Sean Éire*. We regard the Bible as "the Protestant book". I have had personal experience of this attitude, for one side of my family was Protestant. The child who can repeat pat the answers in the catechism is praised for "being good at religion". In *Sean Éire*, the child was put in contact with the mind and the heart of Christ by means of the New Testament: the parables, the miracles, and the sayings of Christ. From the heart of the teacher to the heart of the child the image of Christ and the love of Christ were conveyed with deep religious feeling. Love begot love and sympathy led to imitation.'

'Whisht!' said Father O'Shea. 'Is that Shandon striking nine?' They all listened to the booming bells. 'Holy smoke, lads, 'tis ten o'clock! The whole night is gone on us arguing the toss about politics—and we're as wise as ever!'

'Chris,' said the Canon, a broad smile on his face, 'I can see you were ripe to burst into song when Shea interrupted. Give us a bar of something to end the proceedings and then we'll deal out the cards.'

All endorsed the host's request and turned their attention to Father O'Flynn.

He stepped back from the group round the fire, put out his chest, tossed back his head, and sang in Irish *Mo Róisín Dubh* with all the tenderness, power and sincerity that only he could give it.

They applauded loudly when he had finished.

'Good man, Chris—I wouldn't doubt you!' Father O'Shea said.

'*Arís! Arís!*' shouted Father Roche. 'Give us another spasm!'

'For the love of Mike, haven't we had enough of *Sean Éire* for one night?' cut in Father O'Shea. '*Sean Éire* or Shangri-la—they're all the same to me.'

'I suppose we've had enough,' said the Canon. ''Tis time we cut the cards. Shea—deal 'em out there for partners.'

They sat around the table and the host poured a generous jorum into each man's glass. Then began a noisy game of Forty-Five.

Father O'Flynn did not play cards; neither did he drink nor smoke. But he liked to watch others play cards and to observe their different expressions of hope, bluff and satisfaction in winning a trick. He observed the group at the table for a few minutes.

The Canon tapped him on the shoulder and beckoned him aside. They sat by the fire, heads close together.

'Chris,' the Canon began, in a whisper that could not be heard by the group at cards. 'Just to put you on your guard— 'tis getting round that you're mixed up in some skulduggery up in the Asylum. Well—you know how the Bishop comes to hear about these things. It wouldn't do you any good, I imagine, if he were to find out. For your own sake be careful. Ireland has enough martyrs these times. No need for you to jump into the arena.'

'So that's the way the wind is blowing?'

'That's the way, Chris.'

'I see,' Father O'Flynn said thoughtfully, knowing well what he referred to.

It was this: the British military and the R.I.C. had begun the practice of taking prominent citizens from their homes and keeping them in custody—citizens known for their sympathies towards the Sinn Féin government—and using them as hostages to bargain with the I.R.A. Some of these citizens, who had been forewarned of their impending capture, went 'on the run', and several of them Father O'Flynn had hidden in his rooms at the Asylum. There was, therefore, a certain amount of side-door and backstairs activity going on at night near the chaplain's quarters. In collaboration with one of the nurses he fed them and bedded them, and saw that the coast was clear when they wished to come or go. That was the height of his skulduggery, his 'rebel' activity.

The card game was coming to an end. The Doc said he'd better be going—it was after eleven.

'Yes—we'd all better be off,' said Father O'Callaghan. ''Tis dangerous around the streets at night these times.'

'Wouldn't ye take a cup of tea before ye go?' asked the Canon. 'I told the girl to bring it up at half-ten. She must have forgotten it.'

'Tea—at this hour of the night?' Father O'Shea made a wry face. 'I wouldn't sleep a wink after it.'

The Canon smiled and took the hint.

'A wee *deoch-an-dorais!*' he said handing glasses to his guests.

'Here's to Wolfe Tone and Sinn Féin!' said Father Roche.

'Here's to O'Connell!' said the Doc.

'Here's to *Sean Éire!*' said Father O'Flynn. They clinked their glasses, drained them and the guests stole quietly out of the Presbytery.

Next morning, soon after breakfast, Father O'Flynn put on his black leather coat, his gauntlets and goggles, kicked the starter of his Red Indian motor-bike, and disappeared down Blarney Street in a cloud of dust. Up Mallow Lane he sped, and arrived at Farranferris, the Bishop's residence.

'I'd like to see the Bishop,' he said to the secretary, 'if it is convenient to His Lordship.'

The Bishop was not engaged. Father O'Flynn was shown into his study.

'Well, Chris?' greeted the Bishop, as the virile young priest strode into the room, knelt, kissed the Bishop's ring, and then rose and stepped back a pace or two.

'My lord, before anyone else has the pleasure of informing you, I have come to tell you straight that I'm for de Valera; I voted Sinn Féin last December and I've subscribed to the loan in support of Dáil Éireann.' He drew a slip of paper from his pocket and handed it to the Bishop.

After such statements a silence is inevitable; and there was a silence—a long episcopal silence. The Bishop walked back to his desk and read the slip of paper.

'Government of the Irish Republic
5 per cent Registered Certificates (1919) (Internal)
Received from An tAhair Seamus O Floinn
Tig na nGealt, Bothar na Laoi, Corcaig
the sum of Five Pounds
Signed: Michael Collins,
Minister of Finance.'

When he had finished he placed it on his desk. He looked at the priest.

'Sit down, Chris; sit down, man,' he invited in his calm, deep voice, for Father O'Flynn had adopted a stance that seemed to indicate that he intended to get out of the room as soon as he had made his political confession.

There was a chair in front of the Bishop's desk. Father O'Flynn sat down reluctantly. He looked up at the strong immobile face of the Bishop who appeared to tower above him as he stood motionless behind the desk, regarding him through his rimless glasses.

'You're very active,' began the Bishop, implying that activity was one of those things unbecoming to the clerical state.

'How do you mean, my lord?' The priest was puzzled.

'I mean you're in a lot of things—aren't you? The Gaelic League and those choirs you bring to the *Feiseanna*. You're becoming quite a figure in the Gaelic revival.'

'I try to do my bit for the revival of our noble traditions.'

'You might be overdoing it,' commented the Bishop. 'You might also ask yourself the question I sometimes ask myself: Whether all this Gaelic revival activity is not just a fanning of dying embers rather than a sowing of living seeds. Anyway, these are troubled times, Chris, and we need to keep calm and detached if we are to see things clearly.' Then, more urgently: 'What do you think of all this violence, Chris?'

'Well, that's a big question, my lord.' Father O'Flynn was playing for time. 'One could approach the question by beginning with violence in nature—a thunderstorm, for example——'

'Don't you mind your thunderstorm now. What I mean is, what do you think of these ambushes, burnings and reprisals we read of in the papers every day—the use of that kind of violence for political ends?'

Father O'Flynn did not claim to have made any special study of the morality of peace and war, or the use of violence for political ends. It was not surprising, then, that he was stumped by the Bishop's question. He was feeling very much as he felt twelve years before when sitting for his oral examination in moral theology in Maynooth, with Professor Coughlan sitting opposite him putting the questions. He rummaged in his memory among some of those textbook problems which were neatly solved by the principles governing the action of two effects. But he could find nothing to answer the Bishop's question. However, he ventured boldly:

'I don't like violence in any shape or form, my lord, but—'

'It is not a question of liking it. It's a question of justifying it. Can you justify its use in the present circumstances, and if so upon what grounds?'

'The violence now with us, my lord, is not of our making. It was thrust upon us. I need not remind you, my lord, that only last year the hierarchy described the British regime in this country as "the rule of the sword, utterly unsuited to a civilised nation." Now they have drawn the sword, I am convinced that we cannot refuse that challenge.'

'How can you justify that?' asked the Bishop.

'The General Election of 1918 was the first opportunity that the people got of expressing their will since the events of Easter

Week 1916. In that election, which was run according to the rules laid down by the British themselves and supervised in all its stages by government agents, the people of Ireland expressed their will in a very decisive, orderly and peaceful way. They elected Sinn Féin as the lawful government of the country by an overwhelming majority. Mr. de Valera, the President of Dáil Éireann, now enjoys a degree of support unequalled by any other prime minister in Europe or even in the U.S.A. But the British turn round and deny the legitimacy of Dáil Éireann, and have set out to suppress it by force. That is the supreme injustice. And if we as a people fail to defend what we have established by our votes and know to be the lawful government of Ireland, we're not worth our salt. And so, my lord, I repeat, I'm for de Valera and Sinn Féin, and my sympathies go out to all those brave fellows who are trying to defend what we willed to be: Dáil Éireann and a free Ireland.'

There was another silence. The Bishop walked over to the fireplace and stood with his back to it.

'Our sympathies,' he said, 'if unenlightened by clear principles can lead us astray. If a man wants to enter another man's castle, he may do so in one of two ways: with a key if he has one; by violence if he lacks one. The key is cut to fit the lock; it is effective; insert it in the lock, a gentle twist, and it opens the gate. The man takes possession of the castle. But if he lacks a key and the gate is locked and barred, he has to resort to violence: the battering-ram. That is crude, brutal and destructive. The key is wisdom; wisdom is the way of the Holy Spirit. When men lack wisdom they resort to violence, and violence is close to the gates of hell. Where it prevails the Church invariably suffers. Wisdom is the gift of the Holy Spirit. Patience is its constant companion. In due season they bear much good fruit. We ought to pray much to the Holy Spirit these days. Think on that now, Chris.'

He walked over to the priest. Father O'Flynn stood up. The

Bishop looked at him. Both knew where they stood.

The Bishop offered his ring. The priest knelt and kissed it. As he stood up the Bishop said:

'Remember, Chris, what St. Augustine said about the office of a Bishop: "It is onerous, painful, and at times exceedingly dangerous." I can assure you it is all three these days.'

Father O'Flynn was about to leave.

'Put that in your pocket, Chris,' said the Bishop, handing back the receipt. 'You never can tell what it may do for you if things turn out as you hope they will.'

'Thank you, my lord,' said Father O'Flynn, pocketing the receipt and letting himself out.

'You're not in any trouble, Chris?' suggested the secretary as he saw Father O'Flynn to the door. 'In trouble? Isn't the whole country in trouble!' Father O'Flynn replied, and jumping on his motor-bike he headed home to his mother.

His parents' home at Ballyvolane was only a few minutes' ride from the Bishop's residence. He rode round the back of the house and parked his bike in the yard. Monica, his youngest sister, came to the door and greeted him.

'Jimmy! But we weren't expecting you till Wednesday! There's nothing wrong, is there?'

'Nothing at all. I was just passing by and thought I'd drop in to see Mama.'

Mrs. O'Flynn was now over seventy, but very active and very much in command. She was helping to prepare the dinner in the kitchen when her son appeared in the doorway.

'Will you look at the cut of him?' she exclaimed, eyeing his dusty coat and the goggles in his gloved hand. 'How often have I told you not to be roaring round on that thing?' Clearly, she was in one of her humours. 'Monnie—get the clothes-brush till I brush his coat.'

Her daughter went out to the hall to fetch the brush.

'What brings you home at this hour of a Monday morning?'

his mother asked, for he usually came home on Wednesdays and Sundays.

'I was just up with the Bishop and I thought I'd drop in as I was so near,' he said, acting casually.

'You were where?' She saw through his acting.

'Up with the Bishop.'

'On that yoke out there in the yard—and in that rig-out?' She was horrified at the thought of her son appearing before the Bishop in such an unbecoming costume. 'And what, may I ask, were you doing up with the Bishop on a Monday morning?'

'I went to tell him straight out that I'm for de Valera and voted Sinn Féin.'

'You did not!' she said incredulously.

'I did that—and he listened to me too.'

'How dare you speak to the Bishop like that!'

'Isn't it better to tell him myself than to have some busy-body tell him?'

'Nonsense! I warned you, Jimmy, to keep out of politics. You'll be lucky, boyo, now if you're not sent to the wilds of Muintevarra or some other God-forsaken place in West Cork with no one but the crows for company and the broad Atlantic for a view. Hasn't the poor Bishop troubles enough without you adding to his load—with your Sinn Féin and de Valera on a Monday morning! You have no more sense than the unfortunate lunatics you're supposed to be looking after up in the Asylum.'

There was no answering this. Wisely, Father Jimmy held his tongue and reflected on how mild a man the Bishop was. Curious about the Bishop's reaction to her son's political manifesto, Mrs. O'Flynn suggested: 'I suppose the Bishop gave you your answer?'

'He said that violence was close to the gates of hell—that it was not the way of the Holy Ghost.'

'And he's dead right.' His mother backed the Bishop one hundred per cent. 'And if I were the Bishop, I'd order you to get rid of that motor-bike outside there—for it kicks up a racket like the gates of hell. That's not the way of the Holy Ghost either! I'm for de Valera!' Mockingly she repeated the phrase. 'What's the world coming to?'

Monica returned with the clothes-brush and gave it to her mother.

'Stand up till I brush the dust off your coat!' she ordered her priest son as if her were a boy of seven. And he obeyed her as he had always obeyed her, since he was a child.

She brushed his clothes vigorously and kept up her commentary. 'All this, of course, comes of your going around the country in your tall hat singing Irish come-all-yes at them Gaelic League Feeshes—or whatever they call them. Look at the cut of your suit! 'Tis time you got a new one. I saw a nice bit of black serge down in Grant's last Friday. Go down and get measured at once—'twould be more in your line than Sinn Fèin or de Valera—and be here for your dinner at two o'clock on Wednesday.'

Satisfied that her son was now fit to walk out into the world again, she kissed him on the cheek and said:

'May God give you sense, Jimmy. Forget about Sinn Fèin and de Valera. Say your prayers, mind your job, and keep an eye on your promotion—or God only knows where you'll end up.'

He waved good-bye as he sped down the drive.

'And get rid of that infernal machine!' she shouted after him.

7

'A great lift up'

'Top o' the morning, Jer! Alleluia!' Father O'Flynn greeted his fellow-chaplain in the Asylum a few weeks later, waving a letter in his hand.

'What's the alleluia for at this hour of the morning?' asked Father Jer Fehily, who was finishing his breakfast.

'For the good news in this letter. I'm off—and you'd never guess where.'

'By the sound of you,'tis hardly to Muintevarra.'

'You're as bad as my mother. There's no Muintevarra about that!' And he handed Father Jer the Bishop's letter.

'To the North Cathedral,' read Father Fehily. 'By Jove, Chris, that's a great lift up—congratulations! And you'll be there till you get a parish out of it, you know.'

'I hadn't thought of that—but it suits me all right.' He took the letter from his friend and looked at it again.

'I wonder why his Lordship appointed me curate at the Cathedral?'

'Well, I suppose he considered that you'd understand the people there, and they'll all look on you as one of their own.'

'That's true.'

'Of course,' added Father Jer thoughtfully, 'the Bishop could have other reasons too.'

'For instance?'

'If he had any idea of the skulduggery going on here— you know what I mean—and wished to put an end to it, then he is going the right way about it—to move you out of the Asylum.'

'And put me in the North Presbytery,' said Father O'Flynn, seeing the point, 'with eight other priests, so that every twist and turn I make will be as obvious as the fish on Shandon!'

'Exactly. Bishops can be subtle as well as simple—that's their job,' remarked Father Jer.

'Simple or subtle, I'll have great fun telling my mother about this—for she had me booked for the headlands like yourself.'

In the same batch of diocesan changes, Father O'Flynn's friend, Father James O'Callaghan, was appointed curate at Clogheen, the chapel of ease in the North Cathedral parish.

It was a week of general rejoicing for Father O'Flynn and his friends.

When Father O'Flynn took up duty at the North Cathedral at the end of October 1920, there was a Novena for Peace in progress. Pope Benedict XV had written to Cardinal Logue of Armagh:

'We exhort English as well as Irish to calmly consider whether the time has not arrived to abandon violence and treat of some means of mutual agreement.'

In Dublin Kevin Barry, the eighteen-years-old university student, was under sentence to be hanged for taking part in an ambush in which an English soldier was killed.

In Brixton Jail the Lord Mayor of Cork, Terence MacSwiney, died on hunger strike on 25 October. The *Daily Telegraph* wrote: 'The Lord Mayor of Cork condemned himself to death for the sake of a cause in which he passionately believed, and it is impossible for men of decent instincts to think of such an act unmoved.'

The remains arrived at the Custom House Quay in Cork on 29 October, and a company of Volunteers escorted the coffin to the City Hall. There MacSwiney lay in state, and Cork gave every honour to its dead Lord Mayor. Dr. Cohalan, the Bishop, wrote in a letter to the *Cork Examiner*:

'Was Lord Edward's death in vain? Was Robert Emmet's death in vain? Did Patrick Pearse and the other martyrs in the cause of Irish freedom die in vain?

'Terence MacSwiney takes his place among the martyrs in the sacred cause of the freedom of Ireland. We bow in respect before his heroic sacrifice.'

On Sunday, 1 November, the remains were brought to the North Cathedral, and there the Bishop celebrated the Requiem Mass.

It was Father O'Flynn's first solemn function at the Cathedral.

During the month of November 1920 the I.R.A. stepped up the fight and ambushes, followed by the inevitable reprisals, were now a daily occurrence. They reached a peak point on Sunday, 21 November, known as 'Bloody Sunday.'

On Saturday, 11 December 1920, the I.R.A. ambushed a lorry of English Auxiliaries at Dillon's Cross in Cork city. One soldier was killed and eleven wounded, and the attackers got away safely. That night, as a reprisal, Auxiliaries and Black and Tans—many of them drunk—looted and burnt the main business centre of Cork and also the City Hall. It was estimated that three million pounds' worth of damage had been done.

On Sunday, 19 December, the Bishop, Dr. Cohalan, commented on the situation after High Mass in the North Cathedral.

'Murder is murder, whether committed by the agents of the Government or by members of the Volunteer organisation, and it is the duty of a Bishop to denounce murder and arson and all crimes from whatever source they come. And, today, in the presence of the destruction of our city, I ask you to consider reasonably the subject of the murders, of the arsons, of the kidnappings and ambushes with which unfortunately we have got too familiar.

'It is a safe exploit to murder a policeman from behind a screen; and until reprisals began there was no danger to the general community. But even leaving aside the moral aspect of the question for the moment, what has the country gained politically by the murder of policemen?'

His Lordship considered that nothing had been gained by such activities. He said: 'No, the killing of the R.I.C. men was murder and the burning of barracks was simply the destruction of Irish property.'

Referring to reprisals, the Bishop said:

'I might say that reprisals began here with the murder of Lord Mayor MacCurtain; and now it is like a devil's competition between some members of the Republican Army and the agents of the Crown in feats of murder and arson. . . .'

Shortly after this the Bishop issued a decree excommunicating anyone who took part in an ambush, or in a kidnapping, or otherwise became guilty of murder or attempted murder or arson.

'As far as Catholics are concerned, the last word has been spoken,' the *Cork Examiner* commented.

8

Ambush and reprisal

SATURDAY, 14 May 1921, was the Vigil of Pentecost. Father O'Flynn walked up and down his room reading over some notes he had jotted down during the week, trying to put together his sermon on the Holy Ghost.

Shandon chimed four o'clock. He decided on his theme, sat down at his desk and began to write. He had written a few lines when a terrific explosion rocked the room. Springing up, he rushed to the window. The people on the street below were running in all directions for shelter. He heard the sharp crackle of rifle fire coming from the Blackpool area.

Father O'Shea, in shirt and trousers, hair tousled, appeared in the doorway.

'What in the name of God, Chris, was that? I was having a nap when it lifted me off the bed.'

'I'm not sure—an ambush, I suppose. They'll be looking for a priest, surely, and I'm on duty.'

He took the holy oils from a safe, put the ritual in his pocket and looked around him.

'Where did I put that stole?'

'I'll get you mine.' Father O'Shea disappeared from the doorway and returned in a moment holding a stole. Father O'Flynn took it from him and threw it over his shoulders as he ran downstairs.

Just then a messenger arrived at the presbytery and propped his bicycle against the wall. He pushed through a huddle of people who had taken refuge in the hall.

'Come quick, Father O'Flynn!' he panted. 'There's been an ambush—they're all blown to smithereens!'

'Who?'

'The R.I.C.'

'Good enough for 'em—a pack of spies!' muttered someone.

'Where is it?' asked the priest impatiently.

'Down in O'Connell Street, Father—opposite Quarry Lane,' the messenger told him.

Father O'Flynn ran across the street and into the church to get the Blessed Sacrament. When he reappeared he said to the messenger: 'I'll take your bike,' and off he sped.

In O'Connell Street, an armed patrol of R.I.C. had been carrying out a methodical house-to-house search. Four constables entered each house, and four remained outside. These latter were bombed by members of the I.R.A., who then escaped out the Commons Road.

In less than two minutes, Father O'Flynn arrived on the scene.

'Over here, Father,' shouted the sergeant when he recognised the priest, and he led him into O'Connell Street.

Father O'Flynn was horrified by what he saw. Four policemen were writhing on the pavement, moaning and clutching their wounds. Their rifles had been blasted out of their hands. The air reeked of explosive, and glass from the shattered windows littered the deserted street. The priest, overcome with feelings of nausea and pity, grasped the sergeant's arm and paused for a few moments. Slowly recovering himself, he knelt beside one of the constables whose face was streaked with blood. The lower part of the body had taken the full blast of a bomb. The poor fellow was a mangled, bloody mess.

'This is the priest—I'm going to anoint you,' Father O'Flynn said aloud.

'Excuse me, Father O'Flynn,' the sergeant interrupted, 'but he's not one of yours—he is a Protestant.'

'Father O'Flynn . . .' the dying man gasped, clutching the priest by the sleeve, 'don't leave me . . . don't leave me . . .'

'Of course I won't.' The priest clasped his hand, and was shocked to recognise him as a constable from Shandon Barracks whom he knew well. With his free hand he took a crucifix from his pocket, held it before the eyes of the dying man and spoke the Holy Name in his ear. Then he took the pyx containing the Blessed Sacrament from his pocket and made a large sign of the Cross over the man on the ground. The man sighed; his head fell back and the fixed eyes stared up at the priest. He was dead.

Father O'Flynn stood up and looked round.

'They're all Catholics,' the sergeant assured him, nodding at the three men on the ground.

Father O'Flynn went over to one of them. He was in great pain but quite conscious. The priest prepared to administer the last sacraments. A woman ventured out to assist him. She brought some water, a towel and a pillow which she placed under the policeman's head.

Just then a lorry filled with Black and Tans roared along the Watercourse Road and swayed into O'Connell Street. Jumping out, they began shooting wildly up and down the street. Several bullets struck the wall above Father O'Flynn's head and flakes of plaster fell on the ground beside him. He did not move, but continued administering to the man. Lorries of regular English soldiers arrived. The Black and Tans ceased their shooting. A house-to-house search began at once. All males were ordered into the street, their hands above their heads. They stood in sullen silence, ringed by bayonets.

An English officer, revolver in hand, accompanied by the R.I.C. sergeant, approached the priest.

'Pretty mess you've got there, Padre,' he said.

Father O'Flynn ignored him and continued with the prayers for the dying: *'Go forth Christian soul out of this world . . .*

'I'd cut it short if I were you, Padre. The fireworks are likely to start again.'

The priest prayed on.

The strident clanging of a bell attracted the officer's attention. Presently an ambulance drove up and stretchers were placed on the pavement.

It was then that 'Dusty' Murphy, a coal-heaver, staggered on to the scene.

'Where's the b— Black and Tans?' he shouted, spoiling for a fight.

Suddenly he found himself facing the English officer and four soldiers with fixed bayonets. Taken aback, Dusty halted, swayed and scrutinised the foe. Then peeling off his coat, he hurled his challenge:

'Drop them b— guns and I'll beat the lot o' ye!'

The officer, without taking his eyes off Dusty, ordered his men: 'Keep him covered, this may be a decoy.'

'Drop your guns and put up your mitts!' Dusty was sparring up to the officer.

'Give him the lead, Tommy!' barked a voice from the lorry.

The captain levelled his revolver at Dusty.

'Hold it, Captain!' shouted Father O'Flynn, springing to his feet and placing himself between Dusty and the officer.

'This is a harmless poor fellow, the worse for drink as you can see, but he's no decoy—I give you my word for that.'

The officer lowered his revolver and looked at the priest. 'You've got guts, Padre. You've saved that blighter's life. But you'd better get him out of here—quick; the men are on edge.'

Father O'Flynn picked up the coat. 'Here's your coat, Dusty. Hop it home out of this—like a good man.'

Dusty was so amazed at seeing Father O'Flynn appear before him that he was speechless.

'At the double, man!' urged the priest, and thrust the coat into Dusty's hands.

At last Dusty understood. He struggled into his coat, straightened himself up and gave a shaky salute.

'Fader O'Fling—you're my captain—I obeys your orders!' He wheeled round in a wide arc, and lunged off up the street. The officer grinned and put away his revolver.

'Father O'Flynn, you're all destroyed with blood!' exclaimed the woman who had been helping him.

The priest examined his clothes. The knees of his trousers were soaked in blood; the front of his coat was heavily stained; his hands and the cuffs of his sleeves were spattered with blood.

Some children had come out on the street. Curious, they watched the wounded men being strapped to the stretchers and they waved after the ambulance as it drove off to the North Infirmary.

The officer approached the priest. 'I'm giving you an escort, Padre,' he said. He beckoned, and four soldiers with fixed bayonets stepped forward smartly. They flanked the priest, two on each side.

'No need for this!' remonstrated Father O'Flynn. 'There's no danger to me—I'm here among my own people.'

'Those four policemen were also among their own—and you saw what their own did to them.'

'At any other time,' replied the priest astringently, 'I'd give you your answer; but just now I've the Blessed Sacrament on my person—the King of kings. Let him be judge who is to blame for what has happened here today.'

'Padre, I'm not an R.C. myself—never had much time for religion—but I admire guts in any man. As a tribute to your courage, as much as for your safety, I'm having you escorted home.'

The officer saluted. The priest turned away, with the soldiers on either side. They had gone a few steps when the children flocked around them and barred the way—thinking the soldiers were taking their priest to prison.

'Go away, go away and leave the priest alone,' they chanted. Father O'Flynn turned to the officer:

'Captain, you see I've my escort now. Please recall your men.'

The officer gave a command. The soldiers returned and Father O'Flynn, surrounded by children, walked back to the presbytery.

The next morning, Pentecost Sunday, Father O'Flynn, having conducted the children's Mass, walked into the sacristy.

'Did you hear the bad news, Father?' the clerk asked him.

'What news?'

'They say Father O'Callaghan was shot this morning.'

'Father James?' He was appalled.

'Father James O'Callaghan—your old friend.'

Father O'Flynn was stunned into silence.

'How did it happen?' he asked after a few moments.

'I don't know any more than I've told you, Father. 'Twas some women going into Mass told me what I've told you.'

'Is he dead?'

'I don't know, Father.'

Father O'Flynn took off his surplice and went across to the presbytery. There he met Canon O'Sullivan. Had he heard the news? He had—and that Father O'Callaghan had been brought to the North Infirmary by ambulance early that morning. He was on his way to the hospital to find out what had happened.

As Father O'Flynn was obliged to preach at all the Masses that morning and to assist the Bishop at confirmation after last Mass, he could not go to the hospital until much later.

'While I was preaching at the next few Masses,' he said

afterwards, 'I found myself listening to my own words and they seemed to sound terribly unreal and remote from what was happening all round us that Whit week-end.

'The Holy Spirit—source of divine life and divine love in the Church—comes and dwells in each of us as in a temple. . . . The respect we owe to each other as temples of the Holy Ghost! . . . And all about us men were profaning those temples —murdering their fellowmen!'

At the North Infirmary, Canon O'Sullivan learned what had happened to his curate.

When Father O'Callaghan had been appointed curate to the church of ease at Clogheen in October 1920, there was no accommodation for him. The Canon had told him to look for lodgings. Alderman Liam de Roiste and his wife offered him a room in their home in Upper Janemount. It was very suitable and he accepted the offer.

Mr. de Roiste was a marked man, being a representative of the Republican Government in Cork. His home had been raided by the police several times, but luckily each time he was absent. On these occasions the police had met Father O'Callaghan and were perfectly aware that he was staying there as a guest.

'Don't you think 'tis dangerous?' Father O'Flynn had suggested to his friend.

'Not at all,' Father O'Callaghan replied. 'The police know that I am there as a guest. I'm quite safe.'

Between three and four o'clock on Pentecost Sunday morning, about twenty policemen and Black and Tans surrounded Mr. de Roiste's house. A loud banging on the front door awakened Mrs. de Roiste. She looked out the bed-room window.

'Is this where Mr. Roche lives?' shouted a drunken voice.

'This is Mr. Roche's house, but he is not at home,' she replied, hurriedly withdrawing from the window. She knocked up Father O'Callaghan and advised him to escape through the back way.

'Tell them I'm a priest and your guest,' he said. 'They would not dare to shoot a priest.'

'They're too drunk to reason with. They have come for murder—I know it,' she insisted.

A shot was fired at the lock on the front door. It held.

Then the panels of the door were battered in.

Father O'Callaghan went to his bedroom window. Several bullets shattered the glass. He was shaken, but unhurt.

A tall man in civilian clothes, a scarf across the lower part of his face, came into Mrs. de Roiste's bedroom. He had a revolver in his hand and was very drunk. He lurched towards her brandishing the gun. She struggled with him, forcing him to drop the gun. Picking it up he stumbled out of the room and down the stairs. She came out on the landing and saw another man challenging Father O'Callaghan.

'I am a priest and only a guest in this house. Mr. de Roiste is not here,' Father O'Callaghan was protesting.

Without another word the man fired. The priest fell to the ground. Mrs. de Roiste, horrified, saw the man fire two more shots at the priest and then run down the stairs.

'I am shot . . . I am dying,' said the priest as Mrs. de Roiste knelt beside him. She had him removed to the North Infirmary where he lay dying, but was perfectly conscious. When questioned he said he recognised his attacker as a Black and Tan policeman whom he had often seen near Shandon Barracks.

It was well on in the afternoon when Father O'Flynn arrived at the hospital. In the hall stood a tragic group; the distraught widow of the constable who had been killed in the ambush of the previous day and her four small children. Deeply moved by this sad sight, Father O'Flynn sympathised with the woman. She thanked him for his attention to her dying husband. Presently he left them and walked along the corridor to the room where Father O'Callaghan lay. At the door he met some sorrowing relatives. He had a word with them and went into the room.

Two nuns were reciting the rosary. On the bed lay Father James, his eyes closed, and he was fingering a rosary beads. Father O'Flynn sat beside him and clasped his hand.

'James,' he said. The dying priest looked up at him.

'Chris,' he replied, his eyes filling with tears.

They could say no more—for Father O'Flynn was now on the verge of tears. He continued to hold his friend's hand firmly in his own. After a little while he joined the nuns who had begun the litany of the Blessed Virgin:

Lord have mercy on us.
Christ have mercy on us.

Father O'Flynn said the invocations close to his friend's ear. Father O'Callaghan's eyes were closed, but his lips moved in prayer.

Holy Mary, pray for us.
Holy Mother of God, pray for us. . . .
    Gate of Heaven, pray for us. . . .

Gate of heaven! . . . Gates of hell! The Bishop's words flashed across Father O'Flynn's mind: 'Violence is close to the gates of hell. Where it prevails the Church invariably suffers. . . .'

He looked at his dying friend. How true—how tragically true, he reflected. This innocent priest murdered in reprisal for yesterday's ambush in Blackpool—an ambush that now meant stark tragedy for that poor woman and her children in the hall.

'*Seat of wisdom, pray for us,*' the nuns continued to pray.

'Wisdom is the gift of the Holy Spirit,' the Bishop had said. 'Those who lack it resort to violence. . . .'

This priest and that policeman . . . both victims of a callous and senseless violence.

How very much to the point seemed the Bishop's sermon last Christmas: 'And now it is like a devil's competition between some members of the Republican Army and the agents of the Crown in feats of murder. . . .'

Father O'Flynn noted that his friend's breathing became fainter.

Comforter of the afflicted, pray for us.
Help of Christians, pray for us.

Father O'Flynn took up the litany from the sisters:

Queen of martyrs, pray for us.
Queen of peace, pray for us.'

The relatives came into the room and stood around the bed. The murmur of prayer grew louder—

Lamb of God, who takest away the sins of the world, spare us, O Lord. . . .

At five o'clock, Father O'Callaghan died. Father O'Flynn released the limp hand he had been holding, slipped into the corridor, and wept like a child.

9

Easter dues

I t was Easter, and Spring had come to Bailey's Lane. Brilliant sunshine gilded the crumbling yellow tenements with a fleeting beauty. The morning thrilled with the singing of larks, linnets and thrushes that lined the yellow walls in their cages. Father O'Flynn was on his rounds collecting the Easter dues. He stopped at the first house in the lane and knocked.

'Good morning, Father O'Flynn! 'Tis early you are today.' Nora O'Brien greeted him.

'The early bird catches the worm,' said the priest with a smile.

'Come straight in, Father—I've two fine worms here for you!'

He followed her into the kitchen. She went to a cupboard, took out a jam-jar, and turned it upside down. Two half-crowns jingled on the table.

'There's two nice worms for you, Father.' She took the coins off the table and handed them to the priest. He put them in his pocket, made a note in his book, and left.

Next door lived a widow and her daughter, Madge. The priest knocked and entered.

'You've come in the nick of time, Father,' the widow greeted. She called to Madge in the back room. 'Where's the Easter dues, Madge?'

'Under St. Anthony.'

The widow went over to the statue on the mantelpiece, tilted it slightly, and took two two-shilling pieces from under it. She handed them to the priest and explained: 'There's two shillings from Madge and two more from me.'

The priest noted the amount in his book and thanked her.

'Didn't I say something would happen?' Madge joined the priest and her mother in the kitchen.

'What do you mean?' asked the priest.

'Whatever look I gave at St. Anthony and we going to bed last night, I said to me mother: "He's not looking himself tonight—wait and you'll see—something will happen!" '

'And what happened?' The priest was amused.

'The alarm never went off—we're mad late for work.'

All three went out into the lane. Madge banged the door behind them; her mother made sure it was locked.

'Good-bye, Father—we must fly!' she said, and off down the lane with the two of them.

The priest consulted his book. Someone rapped at a window. He looked up, and saw a face disappear. A moment later Annie Crowley opened the door and beckoned to him. He went over.

'Don't tell me you're passing the door, Father O'Flynn, without calling for the dues!' She was pretending to be vexed.

'Where there's no work I take no dues, Annie.'

'But there is work, thanks be to God—and good wages coming into this house.'

The priest followed her in. 'I thought Connie was idle for weeks?'

'He was indeed, Father, but back to work he went on Tuesday week and we're on our feet again, thanks to yourself.'

'Me! But I did nothing.' He was bewildered.

'Sit down there, Father, till I explain to you.' She offered him a chair, and he sat down. 'Do you remember what you said at the Women's Sodality last month?'

The priest hesitated. 'Was it something to do with home-made brown bread?'

Annie burst out laughing. 'You spoke about brown bread all right—and the bakers won't thank you for what you said. And you spoke about faith.'

'Oh yes—of course. The faith that moves mountains.'

'And you told us about the poor little woman in the gospel who said "If I but touched the hem of his garments, I'll get me wish and be cured".'

'I did indeed.'

'A few days after that I was down to me last copper. No money, no work, and no hope of work. Poor Connie walked Cork looking for a job—any class of a job—but couldn't find one. I was passing the North Chapel and dropped in to say a prayer. I lit a candle with me last penny and prayed to the Sacred Heart to direct me what to do. I sat up on the seat staring in front of me. It was then I thought of the little woman in the gospel. If only I could touch the hem of his garment he'd get work for Connie! But how was I to do that?

'Then I remembered seeing yourself after the seven o'clock Mass on a Sunday taking the ciborium from the high altar down the steps along inside the rails and over to the Sacred Heart altar. I made me plan. On Sunday morning after the seven Mass I knelt at the Sacred Heart altar. When you passed by carrying our Lord in the ciborium I put out me hand, and touched your vestments, and prayed with all me heart, just like the woman in the gospel. You never noticed. Next morning I went to Mass, 'count of it being Lent. When I came back to the lane and pushed in the door—there was a letter on the floor. I picked it up. It was for Connie. I shouted into the room to him: "Con boy, there's a letter here for you!" He jumped out of the bed with the shock. 'Twas from Mr. McCarthy in Haughton's. You can read it yourself, Father O'Flynn.'

She opened a drawer in the table, took out a letter, and handed it to him. He opened it and read it aloud:

'Dear Mr. Crowley,

Re your enquiry for a job here some weeks ago, I have been instructed to inform you that there is now work for a man in our saw mills owing to the unexpected departure of one of the men to England. If you are interested please report to the foreman this evening and arrange to be in to work tomorrow. . . .'

'This is certainly an answer to prayer!' The priest folded the letter and handed it back to Annie.

'Well, Father, we were so delighted at the news that Connie danced around the kitchen in his nightshirt and got ready to report at once to the foreman. I took the letter, and down with me to the chapel and read it out to the Sacred Heart himself.'

Annie went over to the dresser. 'Look, Father! Thanks be to God, we've full and plenty again!' she said, pointing to a row of coins on the shelf. 'There's the rent book and fifteen shillings rent—we were two weeks in arrears; there's six shillings society money—we were five weeks in arrears; that's just a shilling for the gas—and here'—she picked up a half-crown and handed it to the priest—'is the Easter dues.'

'Your story is worth a thousand pounds,' he said, putting the half-crown in his pocket.

'You're welcome to it, Father—I'm only sorry it isn't more—for after all 'twas you and your sermon at the Women's Sodality that put the ball rolling.'

The priest clasped her hand and looked at her hard.

'O woman, great is thy faith!' Then he left.

'Happy Easter, Father O'Flynn!' Matty Murphy tipped his cap as the priest rounded the corner of Flaherty's pub.

'Happy Easter, Matty!' Father O'Flynn returned the greeting. 'You're out early today.'

'The early bird catches the worm, Father. Would you have 'ere an ould bob or two—times is very bad?'

'I never met you yet, Matty, but the times were very bad. Tell me, did you ever see good times?'

'Faith and I did, Father, but 'twas a long time ago. I remember and I a young fella striking out along the road after Mass on a Sunday morning and heading for Johnny Broderick's pub down in Glanmire, with six coppers jingling in my pocket. After a fine three-mile walk in God's fresh air, I arrive *bona fide* at Broderick's. I puts tuppence down on the counter, and Johnny serves me in a pewter mug as fine a foaming pint as ever left a brewery. I drink slowly—taking me ease. Out again into God's fresh air and I strolls up along to Tivoli and in I goes to the station. I puts down a penny at the hole in the window and gets a ticket for the train to Cork. The train to Cork, Father O'Flynn, for one penny! You wouldn't get the ticket for threepence today, not to mind the train. I gets out on the platform at Cork with all the big nobs, all the Yanks off the liners at Queenstown—they call it Cobh since the change-over. Some of the lads at the station spot me. "What's Matty doing in among all the Yanks? Has he got a job on the liners?" But I pretend nothing, Father—pretend nothing only head off down along the river by the Sand Quay—Pope's Quay they call it since the change-over. There's Doodle Addy, the ferry-man, waiting in his boat at the bottom of the steps. Down the steps to Doodle Addy—a halfpenny, and he rowed you across the river. There was an eating house on the other side—down the Coal Quay—and there for tuppence I got me dinner—small meat and spuds, bread and a cup o' tea. After that I walk home full of good grub. Now, Father O'Flynn, look what you got for sixpence: a walk in God's fresh air, a fine pewter pint, another walk, the train, the boat and your dinner—and you still had change in your pocket! That's what I call decent times: today a fella would need five bob to get half that.'

Father O'Flynn enjoyed the story and took the hint. He put his hand in his pocket and he gave Matty two half-crowns.

'Here's your Easter dues,' said he, and he continued on his rounds.

'A packet o' candles . . . a bar o' soap . . . Two onions—I'll pick 'em myself . . . and . . . let me see what else?'

Molly Sweeney, a stout, heavy woman in a brown shawl, was reeling out her messages over the counter to Mrs. Buckley, known to all as Mrs. B., the owner of a wholesale and retail grocery, fruit and tobacco store, when she spied someone across the street. She waddled to the door of the shop, screwed up her beady eyes and peered intently at the figure in black.

'Is that Father O'Flynn knocking at Callaghan's?' she asked.

'Who else but his lordship looking for his Easter dues,' replied Mrs. B., looking through the large shop window.

'It must be awful demaning for the poor priests to have to go round like that knocking at doors and holding out their hands for money, like—like the tinkers. There's the door open now—fat lot he'll get there—catch stingy Dinny parting with a bob—that miser would change a penny for two ha'pence before going in to Mass. I thought so—here he's out again. He's knocking at Mahony's now. That crowd won't even answer the door—didn't I tell ye! He's walking away. Isn't he a handsome man, God bless 'im!'

Mrs. B. made no reply. Unlike Molly, she was not an admirer of Father O'Flynn.

'All that Irish Ireland stuff, rubbish! He'd be better off saying his prayers,' was her usual comment when Father O'Flynn's work for Irish culture was the topic of conversation.

During Molly's running commentary she had opened the wooden drawer of the till, selected a new crisp English pound note, folded it once, slipped it into a square white envelope, addressed it: 'Easter Dues, Mr. and Mrs. D. Buckley—with compliments,' and placed it on the shelf behind her between two tins of kippered herrings.

Molly dragged herself back from the door and stood again at the counter. 'There's something else I want,' she said, 'and 'tis gone out of me head. . . .'

She scanned the shelves behind the counter. 'There they're staring me in the face!' She pointed at the tins of kippers. 'Himself loves them, along with a few onions.'

Mrs. B. took down a tin of kippers and placed it on the counter. 'Is that all for today?' she asked.

'Isn't it enough for one day, seeing the price of things?'

'What about bread?' suggested Mrs. B.

'I'd forget me head only 'tis tied to me,' Molly laughed. 'Give me two pair.' She emptied out some more money from her purse on the counter.

'Ye're eating more bread—your usual is three loaves,' remarked Mrs. B.

'I only eat a bit of a crust myself,' Molly said. 'The children will eat two of the loaves between them. My husband and the daughter will eat another one, and my son Johnny will eat the fourth.'

'Will he eat a whole loaf?' asked Mrs. B. surprised.

'And why not? What's a loaf o' bread in a boy's mouth and he working all day on the docks?'

Mrs. B. began to make up the parcel, keeping an eye out for the priest across the way. She was a woman of medium height, with a rather full and plump figure; white hair tastefully styled, that showed up to advantage her handsome, clear-cut features. She wore a black frock to give the effect of slimness. By way of contrast, a white lace collar encircled her neck and was fastened at the front by a large brooch on which the image of Queen Victoria stood out in bold relief. She had been married twice, but had only one child, George, a son by her first husband. George was a doctor and practised in Liverpool. Her second husband, Dan, was not over robust. He suffered from attacks of asthma, and kept—or was kept—in the background.

Some said that Mrs. B. was a proud woman and that she put on airs. Others said no—but that she was in fact a superior person. Be that as it may, all agreed that she was a good business woman, had an independence of mind, a natural dignity and a remarkable beauty of feature that put her in a class apart. The neighbours respected and admired her.

'Where's Johnny working these days?' she asked Molly as she unreeled some string to tie the parcels.

'He's working up in the North Chapel—cleaning the gutters.'

'The North Chapel. I couldn't tell you how long it is since I was up there. 'Tis so dark and cold—and then there's the crowd pushing and shoving and children running all over the place—'tis impossible to pray there. Dan and myself go down to the Dominicans in St. Mary's every Sunday. 'Tis so clean and bright and well heated in winter, and the priests there are such nice gentlemen.'

Father O'Flynn was well aware that the Buckleys never went near their parish church, but attended St. Mary's instead. He had strong ideas about that.

Mrs. B. saw the priest approaching. 'Will you look at Father O'Flynn and he trying to walk like Shakespeare?'

The sarcasm was not lost on Molly. 'What's wrong with walking like Shakespeare?' She rushed to the defence of both the priest and the immortal Bard. 'He was a great man, by all accounts.'

'Father O'Flynn has the children of the parish driven mad with his Shakespeare,' said Mrs. B. testily. ''Twas only yesterday that Mrs. Foley was saying here in the shop that 'twas the small hours of the morning when her Maureen arrived home from Kinsale, where the priest had them acting Shakespeare.'

'From what I hear,' parried Molly, 'the parents are very grateful to Father O'Flynn for all he is doing for their children. Weren't they all as proud as punch to see their own doing Shakespeare in the Opera House last year?'

'Those children would be better off doing their lessons at

home, instead of wasting their time at that tomfoolery in the
Opera House. The man has no sense. God be with the older
priests—there was none of your Irish Ireland or Shakespeare
about them. They knew how to keep their distance.'

'He's coming in,' warned Molly. 'I'd better be off.' She
picked up her few messages, wrapped them under her shawl,
and made for the door.

'No need to knock here for the dues, Father O'Flynn,' she
said, winking at the priest as he passed her in. 'They're waiting
for you up there on the shelf in a nice white envelope.'

'Trust the Buckleys,' said the priest. 'Always independent.'

'Independent?' echoed Molly, turning around and facing the
shop. 'In the time of Noah and the Flood, the Buckleys had
their own boat!' And off with her down the street, laughing.

The priest laughed too. He enjoyed a good joke. Mrs. B.
smiled. She rather liked the compliment.

'Isn't she a grand old soul?' said the priest. 'Always in good
humour, full of poetry and wit.'

'Molly is not the worst of them,' Mrs. B. replied. 'She's
honest and straight and pays her way, which is more than can
be said for a lot of them.'

'God help 'em—they have a hard enough old life,' sighed
the priest. Then, changing the topic, he stepped back from the
counter and paused dramatically for a moment as he looked
admiringly at Mrs. B. 'Mrs. B., 'tis younger you're looking
every day.'

Mrs. B., suspicious of this palaver, replied curtly: 'One
tries to keep the best side out, your Reverence.' Returning the
compliment, she added: ''Tis well the clergy are looking.'

Things were going better than the priest had hoped. 'How's
Dan?' he enquired, for he had a soft spot for her husband,
knowing him to be the lesser half in the Buckley *ménage*.

'He was grand up to yesterday, thank you, but last night he

got a fit of coughing and I was up all night with him. He's resting at the moment, poor dear.'

'Asthma?' said the priest.

'Asthma,' she confirmed. 'There are times in the winter when he can hardly get his breath. He gets caught here'—she touched the brooch with the image of Queen Victoria—'and nothing seems to relieve him.'

'Did he try Friar's Balsam?'

'The doctor wouldn't hear of it. "Quackery," said he. He gave him a box of pink pills to take whenever he feels the choking coming on.'

Pink pills, my hat!' said the priest. 'Those fellows know nothing about breathing. Friar's Balsam in boiling water and a towel over his head—that's the remedy.'

There was a pause.

'We're thinking of selling out, you know,' resumed Mrs. B.

'You're not!' exclaimed the priest. 'And where are you thinking of going—Montenotte?'

Mrs. B. detected a delicate nuance of sarcasm. 'No,' she replied, with a smile of satisfaction, 'the hills would be too much for Dan. We're looking for a house in Blackrock.'

'Oh—I see,' said tne priest. 'A place on the level.'

Just then a pipers' band came swinging down the street, preceded, followed and flanked by a horde of children.

'Buy an Easter lily—wear an Easter lily!' cried a young girl clad in kilts to the passers-by on the footpaths. Some pretended not to hear; a young man stopped, dropped a coin in the box she held before him, picked a paper lily and pinned it on his coat. Outside the shop the band had halted.

The street had filled with people. A tall fellow in a leopard skin adjusted the harness that held the big drum in position on his chest; the pipers behind him cleared their throats, spat, and fitted the pipes to their lips; the row of drummers at the rear drew drumsticks from their belts and poised them over the drums that swung gently by their sides. Out in front the national flag was unfurled—green, white and orange.

'Oh my God!' exclaimed Mrs. B., forgetting the presence of the priest. 'They'll wake poor Dan with the racket.'

'Buy an Easter lily—wear an Easter lily!' The young girl in the kilts bounced smilingly into the shop and offered the box to Mrs. B.

'No Easter lilies here, thank you! We're sick and tired of collections. There's not a week passes but there's a flag day for something or other. I'm sick of 'em all.'

The girl turned towards the priest. He took a half-crown from his pocket and put it in her box. She smiled and pinned a lily on his coat. 'Thank you, Father,' she said, and left the shop.

Outside, all eyes were on the band. The standard-bearer shouted; the drummer beat his big drum three resounding blows; the kettle-drums rattled out their chorus; the pipers blew, their cheeks puffed out, and the skirl of pipes rent the air. The band marched off, the flag flew high, and the cheering children followed.

The priest listened as the music of *Napper Tandy* faded in the distance. Mrs. B. had plugged her ears with her fingers. When she judged it safe, she took away her hands and said acidly: 'Thanks be to God, they don't smell as bad as they sound! The corporation should put an end to that piping and drumming in the public street. There's no consideration for the ratepayers.'

Then, turning round, she took the envelope from the shelf. 'Here's the Easter dues, your Reverence—I presume that's why you called?'

'You've hit the nail on the head.' He tried to be good-humoured about it, and took the envelope from her. He noted it was not sealed. A new English pound note peeped from it.

'Thank you,' he said, for it was double the usual offering.

Not wishing to leave at once, he switched the conversation.

'Business is rather quiet.'

'Quiet?' repeated Mrs. B. 'Business is a thing of the past. Since the change-over all we do is huckster. Look at the shop—empty! Tariffs on everything. We can get nothing now without permits or licences. Apples, oranges, bananas, chocolates, soap—there's duty on everything. As for the Irish stuff they want us to stock, I wouldn't soil my shop with it. Rubbish—that's what it is.'

The priest was turning the envelope in his hands and trying hard to control his feelings.

Mrs. B. went on. 'I remember when we had this shop open till ten and eleven on a Saturday night, the street alive with people, and fistfuls of silver changing hands. Today we could close the shop at six o'clock and not lose a shilling's worth of business. That's what your Easter lilies did.' She pointed at the priest's lapel. Then, touching lightly the brooch at her throat, she continued nostalgically:

'Ah, God be with the British, and the old R.I.C.—they were gentlemen, not like our own crowd—Dutch tomatoes fourpence a pound and barrels of Danish bacon.'

Boiling over with rage, and for the moment bereft of words, the priest glared at Mrs. B., whipped out the English pound note, and held it high.

'British Empire?' he said, scornfully.

Then he tore the note into very small pieces, placed them on the palm of his hand, and blew them down along the shop.

"Tis gone!' he said. And turning on his heel, he strode out into the Irish Free State.

At the presbytery door someone was knocking. Silence. No answer. A small, worn hand pulled on the brass knob. A bell jangled in the kitchen. Silence. No answer.

'They must be all dead,' the old woman said to the little

child by her side. She reached for the heavy black knocker again. The banging echoed in the hall.

On the first floor a window shot up, and a head jutted out like a gargoyle on a Gothic cathedral.

'Well?' it rasped. It was Father D.'s housekeeper, known as 'the Ramrod' to all regular callers at the presbytery.

'I want to see Father O'Flynn,' the old woman shouted up.

'You can't—he's not on duty,' came the sharp reply.

'He'll see me all right if you tell him who's here.'

The Ramrod hesitated, eyed the caller critically, then withdrew her head and shot the window down.

'A pity her head wasn't under it!' muttered the old woman. She settled herself on the doorstep, holding the child by the hand. She was a wiry wisp of a woman. Her frayed black shawl had slipped off her head as she was looking up at the window, and revealed a thin, yellow, heavily-lined face. Her hair was grey, parted in the centre, neatly combed and tied in a bun at the back. She was toothless, and her gums showed when she spoke. Her soft blue eyes revealed a kind and sympathetic soul. Just now they flashed with indignation.

The hall door opened. The Ramrod towered above her, big-boned and domineering.

'He's out!'

'I'll wait over at the chapel till he comes back.'

She walked away with the child. The door banged behind her. She sat on the steps of the church, playing with the child. Shandon chimed two o'clock.

Father O'Flynn rounded the corner in a hurry. The old woman spotted him, rose, and made across the street to catch him. His housekeeper had taken the day off, and had arranged with the Ramrod to give him his dinner. He was well aware that on the stroke of two his dinner would be on the table. It was up to him to be there. He headed hard for home.

'Happy Easter, Father O'Flynn!' greeted the old woman.

'Happy Easter, Aggie!' replied the priest, going in the gate.

'I won't keep you a minute, Father—for I know you're in a hurry.'

The priest stopped. 'There's a lovely little girl.' He bent down and took the child's hand. But she hid her face in the old woman's skirts.

Father O'Flynn knew Aggie Mullins well. She lived in a cottage in a little poke of a place off Cattle Lane. She was a widow these five years, and had had a large family, but they had all gone to England and were no help to her.

'Who is the lovely little girl?' He was curious about the child.

'God help her, Father, but that's a little mistake me daughter made—the one that went to Birmingham.'

The priest straightened up and looked at Aggie. Then he clasped her hand in both his own. 'That's the most charitable statement I've heard this many a long day,' he said.

'Thank you, Father.' Aggie blushed a little, for she rarely received praise or admiration.

'But tell me, how long have you the child?'

'Since she was six weeks old, Father. Handed her over to me in her little wrappers, she did. "I'm off again tonight in the *Innisfallen*. I'll send you something every week," said she.'

'And she did?'

'She did in her hat! I haven't had sight nor sound of her since, and that's more than four years ago. That's the modern generation for you, Father O'Flynn! There's no nature in 'em.'

'Imagine leaving a lovely child like that!' remarked the priest.

Both looked down at the little girl.

'She has a look of her poor mother round the eyes,' he continued.

'She has—for all the good 'twill do her. But you should have seen her the day I took her!'

Father O'Flynn attempted to cut short the conversation and get home to his dinner, for he now sensed that he was in for a day-by-day account of the child. But in vain. Aggie barred the way, standing with her back to the gate.

'. . . a sixpenny doll out o' Woolworths was bigger'n her— no cutting on her at all—a frightful dawny child. The first year she'd gasterenteritis. Day and night I walked the floor with her and she coughing up every lung in her little body. After that she got pneumonia and had to spend six weeks in St. Finbar's. The paving stones were wore out with me trotting over and hither every day. Over there the doctor had a look at her and said she's vision in both eyes.'

'You mean the child was suffering from double vision?' the priest asked.

'Isn't that what I'm after saying—double vision in both eyes?

' "We couldn't let that go on, Mrs. Mullins," said the doctor. So he gave her drops and said she was very near getting glasses.

'Last week all her head broke out and I had to take her to the dispensary. The doctor took a look at her and said he'd have to cut the whole head off her. Shaved her clean, he did. That's why she has that woollen cap down over her ears. God help her—she's only the leavings of hospitals.'

Aggie bent down, wiped the child's nose, and adjusted the woollen cap on her head.

'Say "God bless you, Father," to the priest.' She shook the child. But the child only buried her face more deeply in the skirt.

'Good-bye now,' said the priest. 'I'm mad late for dinner.'

'Wait a minute, Father O'Flynn!' Aggie grasped him by the sleeve. 'I haven't spoken to you at all yet.' She took an envelope out of her apron and waved it before the priest. 'Father O'Flynn, it's the cause of confession to me.'

'What's this?' he asked.

'That's a bit of a note you gave me for the St. Vincent's—for all the good it done me!'

'Didn't they give you any help?' asked the priest.

'Help, how are you! Wait till I tell you.' She wrapped her shawl more tightly round her head and body so that nothing but the flashing blue eyes and the pointed chin were visible. 'I went up to Mr. Duffy on Tuesday night as you told me. He met me coming down the stairs. "Oh, it's you again!" says he. "You're late—the meeting's over!" "Mr. Duffy," says I, "I'm no beggar—me own family dragged me down to where I am." "Well—what do you want?" says he—a little more respectful.

' "Here's a bit of a note," says I, "writ by the holy anointed hand of Father O'Flynn himself. Now if you are a gentleman and stand for religion at all, you'll do what the Lord's anointed bids you."

'I handed him the note, Father O'Flynn. He didn't even open it—you can see for yourself.' She handed the envelope to the priest, who examined it and noted that it was still sealed.

' "Mrs. Mullins," says he, handing me back the note, "I told you before that we've so many married women with large families to help that we can't visit single people like you."

' "Begging your pardon, Mr. Duffy," says I, "I'm a woman what was twice married, reared ten children—not counting the three that died—and with the death of me second husband, the late James Mullins, that leaves me twice a widow. So there's nothing single about me."

' "You're wasting your time, Mrs. Mullins," says he, "coming up here. We have our rules."

' "You and your rules!" says I, "and the widow and orphan starving!"

'What kind of religion is that, Father O'Flynn?'

'Ah—there must be some mistake, Aggie.'

'There's no mistake at all, Father—'tis the gospel truth I'm telling ye. They're helping them that don't deserve it—that are getting help from all around: the relief, food and clothes and money, and coal-bags filled with coal, but others are left cold and desolate, looking at empty grates.' She began to weep, and fumbled for her bib to wipe her tears.

'Me poor woman, no wonder you'd weep.' The priest tried to console her.

'Men do be callous-hearted,' she sighed.

'Don't bother about them any more—we'll fix up everything between us. Come in here for a minute, and we'll see what we can do.' He linked her arm into the presbytery and put her sitting on a chair in the waiting-room, while she eased her sorrow with tears.

"Wait there and I'll be back in a minute.'

He left them, climbed the stairs, and entered his room. He glanced at the table. Yes—there it was, sitting on the table: his dinner, now a cold and soggy mess of meat and vegetables. He sat down and wrote two letters. On his way out, he took a small Easter egg off the sideboard.

Down in the waiting-room he handed the letters to Aggie.

'Bring that over to Mr. O'Sullivan, and you'll have two coal-bags filled with coal delivered on your doorstep tonight. And give that to Stasia Cahill, and you'll get ten shillings' worth of groceries every week for the next month. If you want anything else for yourself and the child, you know where to come.'

Stooping down, the priest gave the Easter egg to the child.

'Say "Thank you" to the priest!' Aggie shook the child.

'Thanks!' whispered the child shyly.

Father O'Flynn saw them off at the door. The old woman grasped his hand and kissed it.

'I love the bones of ye, Father O'Flynn!'

She smiled up into his face, and took the child by the hand. They walked down the path. At the gate they turned and waved to the priest.

'Happy Easter, Father!' Aggie shouted.

'Happy Easter, Aggie!' He waved back.

They went off. He went up to his room to his neglected dinner.

10

The Loft

'WHAT goes on in the Loft, Chris?' asked Canon Coughlan, the administrator at the North Cathedral.

'Come and see, Dan,' invited Father O'Flynn.

'I'll drop down some night during the week. Is it in order if I bring along a friend or two—just for moral support?'

'Bring whom you wish, we'll be honoured by your visit.'

They parted at the presbytery gate and Father O'Flynn walked along Cathedral Street. He noticed Matty Cronin standing at the corner of Flaherty's pub.

'How's Matty?' he enquired.

'Taking the air, Father O'Flynn—and trying to avoid the funeral expenses!'

The priest laughed at Matty's joke.

'I thought you looked gloomy as I crossed the street,' remarked the priest.

'Why wouldn't I,' said Matty, 'seeing how the times were never so bad?'

'There's a lot of unemployment, all right,' commented the priest. 'But cheer up, there's news of a new factory opening shortly in Blackpool.'

'The new factory! The new factory, God help us!' said Matty contemptuously, casting his eyes to heaven. 'Work for little girls, Father. No place for a man there. Factories, how are you!' Matty dismissed the subject and the priest went on his way.

'There's no point in arguing with a fellow like Matty, or trying to persuade him he's wrong,' said Father O'Flynn to the class in the Loft. 'But how superbly he expressed his contempt! There was great raw material for the actor. I caught the perfect cadence of cynical contempt from Matty when he said: "Factories how are you! . . . work for little girls!"

'Take that sentence now, Jim!'

And James Stack—'Stackie'—the eighteen-year-old Iago, took the phrase from the 'priest'; for thus he was affectionately known to all connected with the Loft.

'Factories how are you!' He repeated it with as much contempt as he could muster.

'No, that won't do—you're elocuting beautifully, but you're not getting the emotion correct. Listen again.' The priest stood up, impersonated Matty at the street corner, and gave powerful expression to the phrase: 'Factories how are you! Work for little girls!'

'The whole man must become alive with feeling. Watch the eyes, the sneer on the face and the curl of the lip.' He repeated the phrase. 'Do you get that? Try it again now.'

Jim tried again.

'You're very near to it now,' encouraged the priest. 'Keep at it. Let the emotion do the work—it must come from inside. Right. Now take the lines in Iago's speech—"*One Michael Cassio, a Florentine*". Iago despises Cassio; his first speech is full of contempt. Try now to wed Shakespeare's lines to the feeling of contempt you've evoked in yourself.'

Jim spoke the lines, beginning:

> *And what was he?*
> *Forsooth, a great arithmetician,*
> *One Michael Cassio, a Florentine,*
> *A fellow almost damn'd in a fair wife;*
> *That never set a squadron in the field,*
> *Nor the division of a battle knows*

> *More than a spinster; unless the bookish theoric,*
> *Wherein the toged consuls can propose*
> *As masterly as he: mere prattle, without practice,*
> *In all his soldiership.*

'Good man—put it there!' And the priest clasped the boy's hand. 'You've got the feeling of it now. Work on it at home and have the emotion of it stronger for the next night. Notice the phrase: *"Mere prattle, without practice"*—and think of Matty's words: "Work for little girls!" Exactly the same emotion.'

A knocking at the door below. The class was silent and listened. It was odd. Nobody ever knocked at the Loft—they just walked in.

'See who that is, Gussie,' said the priest. And Gussie Healy, the hon. secretary, disappeared down the steep stairs. He shouted up in a moment:

'Distinguished visitors to the Loft!'

All stood up and looked towards the well of the stairs. Presently there emerged the Canon, followed in succession by Father Jerry O'Mahony and Dan Corkery, lecturer in English at the University. Gussie brought up the rear.

Father O'Flynn shook hands with all three, and welcomed them to the Loft. When he had introduced them to the class, he had chairs placed by the fire for them.

'Don't mind us at all, Father,' said the Canon. 'Carry on as if there was nobody here.'

'We'd like you to ask questions,' said Father O'Flynn. 'We could learn something about ourselves from that.'

'Do you want us to display our ignorance?' The Canon laughed, pulled his chair near the fire, sat down, and folded his arms. Dan Corkery took out a notebook, and Father Jerry lit his pipe.

Father O'Flynn walked to the other end of the room and, turning, addressed the class.

'I feel our visitors must be disappointed with the Loft. 'Tis poor and ill-equipped. But poverty of means does not necessarily imply poverty of ends—as the gospels prove. There we read of the highest spiritual ends being achieved by the use of means most humble—water, bread and wine, the Eucharist, the Mass, the sacraments, the apostles, the beginnings of the Church.

'The end of all our work in the Loft is to ennoble youth by putting them in contact with truth. Shakespeare in his dramas had truth that ennobles.

'The head of a match found in the corner of a waistcoat pocket is a poor thing indeed. But it is a live thing, and could create an inferno. The most vivid painting of an inferno could not excite the life there is in the head of a match. Truth, no matter how small, is precious, because it is life-giving. It has the power to enrich the mind and develop personality.'

'Tell us, Father,' asked the Canon, 'why did you choose Shakespeare as your text?'

'We have installed Shakespeare as headmaster in the Loft,' replied Father O'Flynn, holding up a volume of Shakespeare, 'because here we have gathered for us in these dramas a whole world of humans in their classic types. Shakespeare's plays are packed with the truth about human nature. And Shakespeare makes it clear that human greatness and nobility of life come of a mind fed on truth. Equally, he teaches that to depart from the way of truth brings disaster. We use Shakespeare in the Loft to arrive at a better understanding of what we are—and to widen our sympathies with our fellowman.

'*Ailneacht in Uachtair*—Seek Beauty—is your motto, I note,' said Mr. Corkery. 'Why beauty, Father, may I ask?'

'Why beauty? As truth is one aspect of reality and most needful for our development, beauty is another aspect of reality—and needful too. Where the truth is expressed and presented to us in a beautiful form then it has an added attraction for the human spirit. Shakespeare expressed the truth about the human heart in poetic dramas of excelling beauty. Truth, adequately expressed in an artistic form—that is what I understand by the term beauty.

'Seek is an apt word too. In summer do we not see the people in their thousands crush into trains and buses and off to the seaside or countryside, to catch a glimpse of beauty—the beauty of sunlight on landscape or seascape—and to bask in its health-giving rays? What country nowadays does not advertise its beauty spots? Tourists flock there to satisfy their hunger for beauty. Silently they feast their eyes upon it. Beauty speaks directly to the human spirit. Immortal longings are allayed a little.

'Were we not made for beauty? To enjoy hereafter, in a better world than this, the Beatific Vision? Do we not hope that some day we shall find ourselves in the fresh fields of paradise standing before the throne of God and enraptured by the beauty of truth itself?

'*Ailneacht in Uachtair*—Seek Beauty—is an apt motto. Plato was a pagan, yet he saw in creatures vestiges of the Creator—something of the truth, goodness and beauty of God. We read in *Ecclesiasticus*, xvii, 7. that the Creator put into the heart of man an eye to see the wonders of his works. Plato trained that inner eye of the soul with loving care. Nature taught Plato. He pursued beauty ardently; he rejoiced in truth. His motto is ours: *Splendor Veritatis*.

'Does that answer your question, Dan?'

'Very well indeed, Father. Thank you.'

'Back to work now!' Father O'Flynn ordered; and the class of about forty boys and girls, who up to this had listened quietly but with varying degrees of receptivity, now sprang to life. They broke up into five or six groups, each occupying its own place in the room. They were the principal actors in six different plays of Shakespeare.

Father O'Flynn, standing in the middle of the Loft, asked, 'Where is Marullus?'

'Over here, Father,' Kevin O'Shea answered. The priest went over to the group doing *Julius Caesar*.

'Now, Kevin, begin: " *Wherefore rejoice . . .*" '

Kevin opened his text at the beginning of the play, and started. After ten lines the priest, who had been listening carefully, interrupted him.

'No! You're declaiming now. That won't do at all. Do you know what you're saying?'

'I'm giving out to a Roman mob.'

'That's too vague, and you can forget about Rome for the moment. You've got to get at the specific human emotion that animates Marullus and from which the whole speech takes fire. What is it?'

'Anger,' said Kevin.

'Anger it is. We're dealing in this speech with the human emotion of anger, and there is a strong dose of contempt there also. Could you give me now a short everyday phrase that the man in the street uses to express his anger?'

Kevin came up with a few, but none of them satisfied the priest.

'When I was coming down here to-night,' he said, 'I saw Mr. O'Mahony putting up the shutters on his shop. He's a cranky sort of man, as you know. A couple of small boys were passing by. I overheard one of them say: "Come on and we'll take a rattle off ould Mahony." They started to shout and jeer at him. He got very angry, and, shaking his fist, he threatened them: "How dare you—you young blackguards! Clear away at once, or I'll get the guards!"

'There's the raw material you're looking for, Kevin. "How dare you!" Repeat that phrase now, and put feeling into it.'

Kevin repeated the phrase, giving it stronger and stronger expression.

'Now you're getting somewhere. You've come in contact with a reality—the live human emotion of anger. It only

remains now to develop it. To help you do that, take those
three questions in the middle of Marullus' speech:

> *And do you now put on your best attire?*
> *And do you now call out a holiday?*
> *And do you now strew flowers in his way*
> *That comes in triumph over Pompey's blood?*
> *Begone!*

'Answer each question with the phrase: "How dare you!"
putting into it all the feeling of indignation you are capable of.
Then you'll have your finger on the pulse of Marullus—you'll
have generated in yourself the specific human emotion that
gives life to the whole speech. Watch!'

The priest did the speech with tremendous power and
sincerity.

'Now, Kevin,' he encouraged; and with new confidence
Kevin tried to put the lesson into practice.

'Good man! But mind you don't imitate me. It must come
from within yourself. I thought I noticed a few hollow
inflections where you had lost the feeling. Work at it, and we'll
have it again tomorrow night.

'Now, Eddie—Mark Antony's speech over the murdered
Caesar.'

Eddie Golden, a tall, fair, clean-cut youth, stepped out from
the group. He had already served five years' apprenticeship in
the Loft, and had assimilated much of the priest's method. He
was proving himself an actor of unusual sensitivity and power.
Nature had given him a beautiful voice, which he was developing carefully under the direction of the priest.

'Now, Eddie—up on the stage!'

Eddie mounted the small platform at the end of the room.
He put his book aside, as he had the part pat. Down on one knee
he knelt, slowly removed an imaginary cloak from the

imaginary corpse of Caesar, gazed long at his murdered friend, and then began:

> *O pardon me, thou bleeding piece of earth*
> *That I am meek and gentle with these butchers. . . .*

After four or five lines, the priest interrupted him.

'That's going fine, Eddie. Now we can aim at perfection. Stand down a moment.'

Master and pupil changed places.

'Look up here a minute, please,' the priest called to the class. They gathered round the tiny stage.

'We're at a very beautiful thing here—Mark Antony lamenting the death of his friend. Here Shakespeare gives us his version of an Irish *caoine;* nature's way of expressing sorrow in tears. This speech of Antony's should be preceded by a long pause—just as you did, Eddie—not because a pause is effective here but because the emotion dictates it. As Antony looks on the mangled Caesar, sorrow wells up within him. When that emotion spills over in tears, then—and only then— will the words come naturally.'

The priest demonstrated to the class. He went down on one knee. Silently he gazed at the ground before him. His eyes filled with tears. They trickled down his cheeks. Softly the words crept out:

> *O pardon me, thou bleeding piece of earth*
> *That I am meek and gentle with these butchers!*
> *Thou art the ruins of the noblest man*
> *That ever lived in the tide of times.*

The priest had become a picture of living sorrow. On the next line: '*Woe to the hand . . .*' he modulated into a new key. Sorrow gave place to menace. Standing up, he threatened the world:

> *A curse shall light upon the limbs of men . . .*

Crest upon crest the passion grew in power and intensity, reaching the climax on:

Cry "Havoc" and let slip the dogs of war.

Then it glided down into the trough, and simmered there with:

That this foul deed . . .

The class applauded. The priest stepped down. The Canon and his friends cried: 'Bravo!' Dan Corkery made a note in his book.

'Now, Eddie—try it,' invited the priest.

''Tis very hard to do it after you, Father.' Eddie mounted the stage. The class continued to attend, for Eddie was one of the leading artistes among them.

'Could you give us tears now, Eddie, before the words?' the priest coaxed.

Eddie knelt, gazed, and to the intense delight of all, the tears brimmed in his sad eyes. He began the speech in a warm, tender tone. The class hung on every accent, inflection and pause. When the mood changed to menacing, Eddie gave a more controlled performance than the priest. He ended. Priest and class applauded.

'The pupil is as good as the master,' said Father Jerry.

'Don't be afraid to play the second part of the speech with abandon,' advised the priest. 'The intensity of the sorrow must be followed by an even greater intensity of the emotion that grows out of it—menace and the thirst for vengeance—if you are to be true to the natural movement of the emotion.

'Before we pass on, I would like to draw your attention to a passage in the gospels where the same thing occurs.

'Our divine Lord was perfect man. He had the human emotions that we have, and in *Luke* xix, 41, we see him suffer sorrow and anger in the sequence we have just been studying in Shakespeare. Christ looked down on the city of Jerusalem from the Mount of Olives "and seeing the city he wept over it." These tears of Christ expressed the sorrow of his Sacred Heart for his fellow countrymen, the children of Abraham. They would reject him, cast him out and crucify him. They would bring down upon them the wrath of God, his Father. They and their city would be destroyed utterly in A.D. 70 by the Roman general Titus. "*There shall not be left a stone upon a stone.*" Then Jesus went up to the Temple and, finding it full of buyers and sellers, his sorrow turned into a flaming righteous anger. He took a scourge and drove out the buyers and sellers. "*My house is a house of prayer, and you have made it into a den of thieves.*" The peace that reigned in the Temple when Christ taught there!

'We are made in the image and likeness of God. God made man showed us this very convincingly in his tears over Jerusalem and in his just and mighty anger in the Temple.'

The class dispersed, several having taken down notes of what the priest had said.

Father O'Flynn now called the group studying *Macbeth*. Here he found Peadar Houlihan and Clare Lee. Peadar was very happy in his part, and had been working hard at it. Not so Clare. She had her heart set on getting the part of Rosalind in *As You Like It*. That delightfully feminine and witty role appealed to her. But it was Katherine Hickey whom the priest had chosen to play Rosalind, and Clare was given Lady Macbeth. It was, of course, one of the great Shakespearian roles, but that ambitious, domineering woman and her terrible black moods did not appeal to Clare. Besides, she felt that the priest had chosen her because of her height. She was conscious of being a tall girl. She had already played Goneril, King Lear's cruel and heartless daughter, and she objected to having herself identified with such repulsive types. There was only one compensating factor—Peadar Houlihan was a very nice fellow!

'Out on the floor with the Macbeths!' said the priest. 'I

asked you to get up that wonderful scene, Act I, Scene 7: "*If it were done . . .*" This is the turning point in Macbeth's life. Shakespeare shows us in this scene that it is only touch and go whether he will turn to the left or to the right. Alone, he has a good look at things. He examines carefully the issues at stake, balancing the disadvantages with the advantages. He sees that while he can wish and dream and plot and plan for power, unless those plans are in conformity with the facts of existence then reality will cut and bite him for disrespecting her laws. Macbeth is an exquisite poet, and in his soliloquy his rich endowments of imagination and emotion ally themselves with his reason, judging soberly the facts. He resolves against the murder.

'Lady Macbeth enters, and by the sheer force of her personality she dislodges her husband from his firm resolution. She uses intellectual violence to win him over: mockery and sarcasm. He capitulates.

'This is first-class drama, Shakespeare at his best. Here his art-mirror reflects accurately, powerfully and beautifully nature's workings.

'Come on now, Peadar—"*If it were done . . .*" '

Peadar Houlihan, tall, dark, with a high forehead, pale complexion and large expressive eyes, took the floor and began the soliloquy;

> *If it were done when 'tis done, then 'twere well*
> *It were done quickly . . .*

After six or seven lines, the priest interrupted Peadar.

'Remember what I told you about that jerky rhythm of those first few lines. It was not for nothing that Shakespeare put all those monosyllables there. You are giving them too smooth an utterance. Staccato is the way. Besides, you have in this speech a series of run-on lines; that creates a free rhythmic structure—just as in traditional Irish melody. You must choose carefully the point towards which the rhythm moves.'

'Sorry to interrupt, Father,' said Dan Corkery, 'but you did invite us to ask questions.'

'Certainly, Dan—go ahead!'

'Now that you're at it, would you tell us what you understand by rhythm in the present context?'

'First let me remind you of what you already know. Shakespeare used the iambic as the unit of his verse. He got it from Marlowe. It is the one-two rhythm. To me, that is significant, for that is the pulse of the human heart. As Shakespeare was *par excellence* the poet of the human heart, it is very fitting that he should use its pulse as the unit of his verse. The heart-beat is normally imperceptible. But notice how people express themselves when stirred by strong emotion. The angry woman shouts at her child: "I *told* you *not* to *put* the *bucket there!*" She speaks in iambics. If she had a stick in her hand she would beat out that rhythm with it. Here the emotion makes transparent for the moment the rhythm of the human heart. The iambic is its natural rhythmic form. For the actor, then, rhythm is the expression by the animated body in look, gesture, attitude and movement, in the tone, inflection and cadence of the voice, of the movements of the human spirit that seeks strongly to communicate with the fellow-man. Rhythm is the emotion in action. The emotion carries the movements of the spirit.

'Take the actor. His body, eyes, and so on remain the same; but the form—of the spirit within—moulds it now one way, now another, according to what it wishes to say.

'The fundamental utterance of a specific human emotion is the beginning of the rhythm. In great art the specific human emotions find their adequate expression. Where this is achieved you have a classic—poem, drama or song. When an actor succeeds in giving perfect expression to the emotions and rhythms of the part he is playing, you have a classic performance. The human spirit has received a form in words, lines, gestures, tones, and so on of the actor that speaks in a manner that is universal and immutable. Does that answer your question, Dan?'

'Perfectly.' Mr. Corkery made a few notes.

'All that I have been saying becomes quite clear from examples. Watch this.'

Father O'Flynn sat down and at once assumed an attitude of deep depression and lassitude, and from that state he went through the whole gamut of moods, right up to hilarious joy, without ever uttering a word. It was one of his virtuoso pieces. All applauded his excellent performance.

'Do you see what I mean by rhythm in drama now?' asked Father O'Flynn.

''Tis as clear as daylight—after that,' Dan Corkery said.

'This scene from *Macbeth* will further illustrate the same point,' Father O'Flynn went on. He turned to the class.

'Now, Peadar, give us of your best—go right through the soliloquy and I'll comment quietly to our guests.'

Peadar began: '*If it were done . . .*'

The priest commented: 'Wishful thinking of an agitated mind and an uneasy conscience. Jerky rhythm—staccato and in spurts. "Oh, if only . . ." and—hump the next life!'

'*But in these cases . . .*' Peadar continued.

The priest went on: 'A more sober examination of the realities of life: reason asserts itself. A smoother line, a calm rhythm, a slower tempo.'

'*He's here in double trust . . .*'

'Emphatic mood,' said the priest. ' "Suppose I do it?" asks Macbeth, "what will the world say?" It will be horrified. Imagination and emotion now paint the picture. Macbeth's conscience speaks through both. Rhythm now assumes the dignity, majesty and power of a deep Atlantic swell. Macbeth is carried on its tide. His wishful thinking and vain ambition evaporate under these pressures.'

> *I have no spur*
> *To prick the sides of my intent, but only*
> *Vaulting ambition, which o'erleaps itself*
> *And falls on the other.*

'Well done, Peadar!' congratulated the priest. 'You had every nuance of that correct.'

He turned to Dan Corkery. 'All these different attitudes that Peadar gave us in the course of that soliloquy were simply rhythmic expressions in look, gesture, stance, cadence of voice and so on, of the emotions within. The rhythms derive their shape and movement from those emotions. And the emotion is the carrier of the movements of the spirit of Macbeth.

'Now, Clare, we'll give Peadar a rest and I'll do Macbeth for the moment.'

Clare walked to the centre of the floor, book in hand.

'Do you need the book?' The priest was disappointed. 'I thought I asked you to have it by heart?'

'I hadn't time, Father,' said Clare.

'Well, we'll go ahead with it.' And the priest, playing the part of Macbeth, began:

'*How now? What news?*'

Clare went on, and they spoke the lines in turn:

'*He has almost supp'd. Why have you left the chamber?*'

'*Hath he asked for me?*'

'*Know you not he has?*'

'*We will proceed no further in this business . . .*'

The priest, as usual, gave a fine performance. It should in fact have been easy for Clare to play back to such good acting. But no. Her next lines:

> *Was the hope drunk*
> *Wherein you dressed yourself? Hath it slept since? . . .*

were spoken listlessly and without conviction.

'What's wrong, Clare?' asked the priest. 'You're like a lump of water, girl. You're only reading the words. It's emotions we want, the emotions of scorn and mockery. Come on, now!'

'*Was the hope drunk . . .*' Clare repeated the lines, but the priest was not satisfied.

'No—that won't do at all! What are you supposed to be saying?'

Clare was silent.

'You're taunting your husband. "Are you a man or a mouse?" Take that phrase now, Clare, and put your heart into it.'

Clare repeated the phrase, but it was clear that her heart was not in it.

'Remember your Goneril!' said the priest, encouraging her to emulate her former triumph.

Clare did not like to be reminded of her Goneril.

'Look—I'll do it for you,' said the priest, beginning to get impatient with her. He did the whole speech, beginning: '*Was the hope drunk*' down to '*the cat i' the adage.*' Then he pointed out: 'Look at all those questions: "*Was the hope drunk?*" . . . "*Hath it slept since?*" . . . "*And wakes it now?*" . . . "*Art thou afraid?*" ' And he ended by mimicking a cat miaowing.

The class laughed at his interpretation of the cat. But Clare was on edge.

'Now try it!'

She did the speech again. The priest was dissatisfied, and his patience was running out.

'Leave it alone. We'll go on to the next speech:

> *What beast was't then . . .*
> *That made you break the enterprise to me?*

This demanded even more emotional power. The priest was in a stubborn mood, and got Clare to do it over and over again. He made her repeat each phrase after him. Clare was exasperated, and repeated the lines listlessly for the tenth time: '*What beast was't then . . .*'

'Ah—what beast, my hat!' the priest exploded, and flung the book on the ground. It slithered across the floor and stopped near the Canon's feet.

The room was silent. All eyes were on Clare and the priest.

'You're wasting your time, Father!' she shouted with temper. 'I will not play Lady Macbeth!'

'You will play Lady Macbeth, or I'll—'

'I will not!'

'And why not?'

'Because I will not—that's all!'

'How dare you!'

'How dare *you*!'

'*Prithee, peace. We will proceed no further in this business.*' Gussie intervened to avert a disaster.

'Oh—shut up, you!' Clare hissed at poor Gussie. She whipped her coat off the bench, pranced across the floor, swept past the visitors, and disappeared down the stairs. She was in revolt against Shakespeare, the priest, the Loft—and especially against herself for being tall and masculine, and so like Lady Macbeth.

The door banged below as she made her exit.

It was the priest who broke the silence.

'Boys, oh boys! What a Lady Macbeth! All the emotional power and expression that Shakespeare needs—and she was trying to prove that she couldn't do the part!'

'Shall I run after her and bring her back?' asked the peacemaker, Eileen Curran.

'No—let her off. She'll take a while to cool down after that. She'll be back after a week or so.'

The Canon rummaged in his pocket, took out a handkerchief, and blew his nose. Father Jerry tapped the ashes from his pipe into the fire. Dan Corkery put his notebook back in his pocket. It seemed that their visit to the Loft had come to a dramatic conclusion.

'Boys, oh boys! What a Lady Macbeth!' repeated the priest, joining his guests by the fire.

'By jove, Chris, we got more there than we bargained for in the line of dramatics,' said Father Jerry, smiling wryly.

'We got the reality,' said Dan Corkery.

'Life and drama rarely run smooth,' Father O'Flynn confessed.

'I suppose 'tis hard to keep the real emotions from getting mixed up with the dramatic emotions, seeing that one is the raw of the other—as you explained to us,' commented the Canon, perceptively.

'True, Dan. And when they do, 'tis like a spanner thrown in the works—everything stops. But she's a fine girl—she'll be back again and all will go well.'

' "How dare you! How dare you!" ' Father Jerry was relishing the fatal phrase. 'Well, that's one bit of Shakespeare I've picked up tonight. And, I must say, I like the way your theories all worked out in practice. "The woman in her expression of anger is less restrained and more elemental in her fury than the man!" I hope she's not waiting for you, Chris, to eat your heart outside in the Butter Market!'

They laughed at Father Jerry's joke.

'By the way, Jerry,' said Father O'Flynn, 'it wasn't Shakespeare who said "How dare you." That's only the raw material. What he said was: "*Hence home, you idle creatures!*" '

'And I think we'd better be heading that way now,' said the Canon. 'There's Shandon striking half-past ten.'

In a brief speech the Canon thanked the class and encouraged them in their good work. Then he and his friends left.

The priest and his pupils knelt before the statue of the Sacred Heart and recited a decade of the rosary, as was the custom each night before going home. It was Gussie who led the prayer. With unconscious humour he began:

'Let us offer this decade for peace in the world . . .'

The prayer finished, they all stood up and began to depart.

'As I've the Sodality on Friday night I'll be down late,' said the priest. 'So instead of a rehearsal I'll say a few words on *Macbeth*. Tell those who aren't here tonight, Gussie. Home now—and no dilly-dallying on the way.'

'Good night, Father!'

'Good night!'

'Good night!'

The boys and girls jostled down the stairs and out into the crisp, starry night.

Such was the Loft in 1928. It began quite simply five years earlier. Father O'Flynn, at the end of his weekly class in Irish singing at the North Monastery, invited any boys who were interested in acting to meet him that night in the Presbytery. He also invited a few girls he had seen in a Christmas play at St. Vincent's Convent. About ten boys and six girls turned up. The first class met in the choir room at the North Cathedral.

'*What bloody man is this?*' was the first line from Shakespeare the priest asked his pupils to say. Each of the boys tried it in turn. Because their 'ths' sounded like 'ds' he gave them a sentence to practise: 'I told him to his teeth that there was no truth in his throat.' It became the classic test of every pupil that subsequently joined the class.

One of the boys at that first meeting found difficulty in pronouncing 'what'. He was young Jack Curran. Father O'Flynn immediately paid special attention to this boy, and gave him another line to say, this time from *Twelfth Night*: '*Why I your purse?*' It became clear at once that Jack Curran had an impediment of speech. He found great difficulty in pronouncing any word that began with a vowel or open consonant. Far from dismissing him as unfit for the drama class, Father O'Flynn encouraged him, and promised him that he would do all he could to cure him of his impediment, and that one day he would play a leading role in Shakespeare.

Father O'Flynn took Jack several times a week for many months. He taught him how to breathe correctly; how to produce a continuous sound by humming; how to get a grip on the explosive consonants B and P; and finally how to pronounce the open consonants—'*Why—I—your—purse?*'

Jack was a quiet and sensitive boy. The others in the class watched his progress with interest, a progress that was not achieved without difficulty. Eddie Golden, who was Jack's contemporary, said that he saw him pausing for several minutes, and sometimes drivelling from the mouth, before he got out the line, slowly, very slowly: *Why—I—your—purse?*'

'It was not so much the techniques which the priest used,' Eddie said, 'but the wonderful sympathy and personal interest he showed in the boy; the encouragement and praise he gave to his every little effort and success, that seemed to work the cure.'

Jack eventually played the part of Sebastian in *Twelfth Night*, with its famous line '*Why I your purse?*' His sister Eileen played Viola. It was Jack's first triumph.

Father O'Flynn, who never did things by half, now put before his young pupil the challenge of playing *Hamlet* on the stage of the Opera House. After many months of rehearsal Jack was ready. His slim figure, his thoughtful eyes, his deep resonant voice, fitted the part well. Father O'Flynn rented the Opera House for one night in 1926, and Jack Curran played the Prince of Denmark to a crowded house.

All the members of the class followed his every word on the stage that night.

'We were all so anxious that Jack should get through without faltering,' said Mirette Mangan, 'that it seemed to me that the whole class was playing the part that night.' Mirette was a lady-in-waiting at Elsinore. 'Each of us felt it as a personal triumph when Jack got through the play without a slip and spoke his final line: "*The rest is silence*".'

Now that he could speak correctly, he joined the Dominicans —the Order of Preachers—and was ordained a priest at Rome in 1933. Father O'Flynn was present at the ordination ceremony with Jack's sister, Eileen.

It was the first of many such cures Father O'Flynn effected over the years.

Among the first members of the Loft were: Tom Vesey, Roland Hill, Jim Stack, Jack Curran, Jack O'Connor, Harry Weldon, Frank Flanagan, Dan Skidd, and Dan and Jim Buckley. They were soon joined by others: Teddy, Gussie and Jerome Healy, Leo Griffin, Eddie and Geoffrey Golden. The girls included Eileen Curran, Alice Power, Kathleen Collins, Rita Coughlan, Rita O'Neill, Rose Dennehy, and Annie and Kathie Hickey.

From the two reservoirs of St. Vincent's Convent and the North Monastery, steady streams of talented girls and boys flowed into the class. Father O'Flynn taught them poems, dramatic recitations, songs—solos, duets and trios—and did a few scenes from *Twelfth Night* and *Richard III*. The children loved it, and advertised the class to their friends. It was a school that was not a school. Soon the class had grown so big that Father O'Flynn rented a room over a cobbler's shop in Clarence Street. There the work continued. They now became known as the North Parish Shakespeare Society.

As the pupils became proficient, the priest secured engagements for them at charity concerts in the city and in the large towns all over County Cork. For transport, a char-à-banc was hired. Father O'Flynn and his pupils usually assembled outside St. Mary's Hall. When the char-à-banc arrived they piled in with their cases of costumes and props. Father O'Flynn usually sat in front beside the driver; his pupils behind appreciated his tact!

In January 1926 the priest rented a large L-shaped room over a sweet factory off Mulgrave Street, near the old Butter Market and under the shadow of Shandon steeple. This was at once named 'the Loft'.

Here the class gathered around the priest four nights a week to learn to act Shakespeare from one whom they all recognised as a master in the art.

That summer the pupils of the Loft played *Richard III*, *As You Like It* and *Twelfth Night* in the grounds of University College, Cork, for the benefit of a group of teachers who were taking a Summer Course there. It was their biggest undertaking since they started. In 1927, Father O'Flynn sent Tom Vesey to London to purchase five complete sets of costumes— one for each of the plays they had planned to produce in the Cork Opera House. The costumes cost over three hundred pounds. The money was borrowed from the bank and it was guaranteed by the O'Flynn Bros., victuallers. All Cork went to the Opera House that week in May 1927, to see the Loft do six plays of Shakespeare. It was a resounding success and Cork took the Loft to its heart.

The Linnet

I T was a gloomy afternoon in late November. Father O'Flynn
was sitting by the fire in his sitting-room, engrossed in one of
his favourite authors, John Ruskin. The book was *Modern
Painters*, Vol. IV. He was reading the chapter headed Turnerian
Picturesque.

The passage he was now perusing he found to be of particular
interest, for he had begun to underline certain sentences with
his pencil. '. . . *observe how the higher condition of art . . . depends
upon largeness of sympathy. It is mainly because the one painter
has communion of heart with his subject and the other only casts
his eye upon it unfeelingly, that the work of the one is greater than
that of the others.*'

Father O'Flynn followed carefully Ruskin's distinction
between the lower picturesque and the higher, noting that the
lower picturesque ideal is eminently a heartless one, and the
lover of it a merciless artist. He read on: '*What is it to him*
(the lower picturesque artist) *that the people fester in feverish misery
in the low quarter of the town, by the river? Nay, it is much to him.
What else were they made for? What could they have done better? . . .
What is it to him that the old man has passed his seventy years in
helpless darkness and untaught waste of soul? The old man has at
last accomplished his destiny, and filled the corner of a sketch,
where something of an unshapely nature was wanting . . . Poverty,
darkness and guilt bring in their several contributions to his treasury
of pleasant thoughts.*'

Footsteps sounded on the stairs. A call? He hoped not. A
knock on the door.

'Someone to see you in the hall, Father,' the housekeeper said. 'I think 'tis urgent.'

'I'll be down right away,' he said.

Placing the book on the table, the priest went down the stairs, his heavy tread echoing along the empty corridor.

In the unlit hall he did not at first recognise the figure in the black shawl. Then it spoke.

'Father O'Flynn, will you come down at once and put the fear of God in Danny? I'm scalded from him.'

It was Polly Buckley, a decent little woman from Chapel Lane with four of the nicest children in the parish. Her husband Danny was a drunkard. That was her misfortune.

'Is he on it again?' the priest asked as they went into the waiting-room.'

'Again, Father?' Polly's tone was one of mock surprise. 'He never stopped since the drag-hunt in Blarney over a month ago. You can imagine what 'twill be like coming up to Christmas unless someone puts a halt to his gallop. Me heart is broke from him. And to add to me trouble, one of the children is very sick.'

The dull light coming in through the large window fell upon Polly's head and shoulders. She was young—only twenty-five —but the bloom of youth had gone and a haggard look had replaced it, like a mask on a child's face. She was old before her time. She looked appealingly at the priest. He noticed there were tears in her eyes.

Father O'Flynn knew Polly and Danny well. He had married them seven years ago in the church across the street. Mingling with the onlookers outside the church after the ceremony, he had overheard a few shawlies commenting.

'Isn't she gorgeous—and so young, God bless her!'

'Sure, they're all lovely when they're young. Look—she's laughing . . . God help her!'

Polly made an excellent wife and mother. Her four little

children were a credit to her, and she kept her tiny house in Chapel Lane, with its one room downstairs and its two rooms upstairs, spick and span. It was only last week that Father O'Flynn had remarked as he stood in her kitchen: 'What a lovely neat little home you have! 'Tis a credit to you, Polly.'

'Pity good for me, Father O'Flynn,' she sighed, 'when himself crawls in here on a Friday and Saturday night, drunk as a lord. And if I say as much as one word to him he'd smash every ornament in the room.'

'And you still carry on?' The priest looked at the brave little woman with sympathy and admiration.

'I do, Father—hoping and praying that something will happen to change his ways.'

The priest looked round the room at the ornaments that were in danger of being smashed every week-end. On the mantelpiece squatted two ugly pug-nosed china dogs and two gaudily-coloured flower vases with bunches of nondescript artificial flowers stuck in them. Two pictures hung upon the wall; one was a coloured print showing a priest on horseback giving a last absolution to the Munster Fusiliers at the Rue de Bois; the other was a portrait photograph of Polly's parents sitting side by side. The strong square face of the woman— innocent of any make-up, hair parted in the centre and swept back under a small black bonnet—was looking straight out. Her husband beside her had a round, cheerful face with bushy eyebrows, a bristling moustache, a bow tie and a high stiff collar. A bowler hat was tilted rakishly on his head. Oblivious of his better half beside him, he too was looking straight out.

On the dresser shelf stood a small gilt frame, and in it a photo of Danny and Polly. 'Took outside Kennefick's pub in Crosshaven,' Polly nostalgically explained. It was their honeymoon. Over the fireplace hung an oblong bevelled mirror.

In a niche in the wall stood a statue of the Sacred Heart. Before it, on a bracket, a little red lamp glowed. Various nooks and corners round the room enshrined statues of the Blessed Virgin and the saints—'chalky gods' the people called them. They were made somewhere off the North Main Street by an Italian plaster artist, and were peddled from door to door all over the city and county of Cork by a dark-skinned foreigner whom the people referred to as the Smoked Irishman.

No doubt Ruskin the aesthete would have been pained by this collection of 'the lower picturesque' in Polly's parlour; so was Danny, but for different reasons. In his cups he was an iconoclast. He had already smashed one of the pug-nosed dogs, but Polly had managed to stick it together with seccotine. She also had to replace the glass in the picture of her parents; and the bevelled mirror, which he had shattered into smithereens with the poker, she replaced with a new one which it was her good luck to win at the merry-go-rounds in Crosshaven. But now all was in danger again, for Danny was on the beer and in one of his shattering tempers.

It was, then, no cultivated literary taste that made Polly now exclaim, in the priest's waiting-room: 'Father O'Flynn, I'm scalded from him!'

In these days of the professional social worker, Polly's request to 'come down at once and put the fear of God in Danny' would no doubt have been treated with all the caution, reserve and tactful investigation that such a thorny problem demanded. But now that problem was Father O'Flynn's. It was to him that Polly looked for a solution.

'Does Danny know where you are?' he asked her.

'He's so stupid with drink, Father, that he wouldn't notice Blarney Castle if you put it down on the kitchen floor before him!'

'Good,' said the priest thoughtfully. 'Go back to the house and slip in quietly. Pretend nothing. Make him a strong pot of tea, and I'll be along in half an hour.'

Polly went home, and the priest went up to his room. He sat again by the fire and opened the book where he had placed the marker. He began to read.

'*Yet for all this, I do not say the lover of the lower picturesque is a monster in human form . . . Generally speaking he is kind-hearted, innocent of evil, but not broad in thought; somewhat selfish, and incapable of acute sympathy with others . . .*'

His mind wandered from Ruskin to the Buckleys in Chapel Lane. . . .

That unfortunate poor girl, married to that drunken bully . . . who understands no other language than that, he thought, looking at his own powerful clenched fist. I've asked him, time and again, to give up the drink, but no good. . . .

The priest resumed his reading. '*Therefore, even the love of the lower picturesque ought to be cultivated with care, wherever it exists; not with any special view to artistic, but to merely humane education . . . it will lead to a truer sympathy with the poor, and better understanding of the right ways of helping them; and in the present stage of civilisation, it is the most important element of character . . . which can be cultivated in youth; since it is mainly for the want of this feeling that we destroy so many ancient monuments . . .*'

Unable to concentrate, the priest closed the book, got up from the fire, and stood with his back to it. He thought: If only I could find one wholesome spot in Danny . . . just one good natural feeling for grace to work on. . . .

He drifted over to the book-case, vaguely searching for a solution. He scanned a few of the titles. The Greek philosophers, Socrates, Plato and Aristotle; Roman culture and civilization; the Renaissance painters. No help from these! St. Thomas Aquinas, Descartes, Shakespeare, Dinneen's Irish Dictionary— they all looked cold and uninspiring in their leather bindings. He turned away and walked to the window. He heard a chattering of sparrows outside in the eaves that ceased as abruptly as it had begun.

'Birds!' he said aloud, and smiled as a ray of hope lit up the darkness. Danny used to be keen on the birds, catching them, breeding them, training them; larks, thrushes, linnets and pigeons. He had noticed several bird-cages in Danny's house last week, but they were nearly all empty. Danny had only one bird for some time past—a linnet.

'Father O'Flynn, the heart lifts up inside me when I hang out the cage in the morning and hear the sweet roll of me linnet,' Danny had enthused. 'I love to be up on Spangle Hill or the top of Grawn, hiding in the corner of a meadow, and one of the lads over opposite trying to get a fix on a lark that would be about to drop out of the blue sky and the white scuds into the long flowery grass. . . .'

Yes, there was poetry in Danny, and that could save him; and a nobility of mind and emotion lay buried somewhere beneath the debris of his drunken, dissolute life. But how to make those noble emotions triumph? That was the problem. For Danny had tried and failed many times in the past. He had taken numerous pledges, had sworn by Father Mathew's Statue that he'd never touch another drop. But the seasonal hazards—St. Patrick's Day, the August bank holiday spent in Kennefick's pub at Crosshaven, the drag-hunt at Blarney in October, and above all 'the Christmas times'—proved too much for his resolutions.

The priest recalled Polly's words: 'I'm hoping and praying that something will happen to change his ways.'

The clock on the mantelpiece chimed five. Time was up.

'*We must do something and I' the heat,*' the priest quoted to himself. He put on his biretta and strode down the street towards Chapel Lane.

He knocked on the low narrow door, and Polly opened it at once.

'God save all here!' greeted the priest. 'I just called in to bless the sick child.'

'She's over here in the pram, Father.' Polly preceded him to the corner. He blessed the child.

Then, turning round, he looked at Danny, whose bleary eyes blinked back at him from where he slumped over the table, holding a large mug of tea in both hands. The priest was silent. To the befogged mind of Danny that silence was accusing, offensive. He resented it. Polly, standing by the pram with arms folded, looked on. At last the priest spoke.

'Drunk again, Danny?'

Danny looked away from his steady gaze, and peered at the tea-leaves in the recesses of the mug.

'I am,' he muttered sullenly. 'And what about it?'

'How dare you speak like that to the priest!' cut in Polly. 'Give it to him, Father O'Flynn!'

On Polly's plea for action the priest stepped forward and seizing Danny by the lapels of his coat he jerked him to his feet. Looking straight into his glazed eyes, he said:

'Danny, God has blessed you with a grand little wife and four lovely children, but you have been acting the blackguard and are unworthy of them.' Then, shaking his clenched fist before Danny's flushed face, he went on: 'Do you see that? If as much as one drop of drink goes down your throat between now and New Year's Day, you'll get the full force of that between the two eyes.'

'That's the stuff to give him,' said Polly.

Drunk though he was, Danny was shocked into an acute sense of his danger. With his own eyes he had seen what the priest could do with a half-hundred weight, tossing it twelve feet over a bar without even taking off his coat.

'Do you promise me to stay on the waggon 'till New Year's Day?' demanded the priest, shaking Danny in his grasp.

'I do, Father,' he blurted out reluctantly.

'Are you sure you do?' urged the priest, giving him another shake.

'I am, Father'—a little more respectfully.

'To make doubly sure, be up at the presbytery tomorrow night at eight o'clock when you are stone cold sober, and you'll take a pledge and keep it until after Christmas.'

'He'll be there all right, Father,' assured Polly.

The priest relaxed his grip and Danny slid down on to the chair.

'Get him to bed now,' advised the priest.

Just then the little red lamp before the statue of the Sacred Heart caught his eye. He looked at Danny, who was staring stupidly at him, and then at the lamp. Over he went to the niche in the wall, bent down, and blew out the lamp and walked back to the door.

There was a horrified silence, as they looked at the smoking lamp. Even Polly was struck dumb.

Turning to Danny, the priest said: 'Not until you take the pledge and mean to keep it will that lamp be lit again. Don't forget—to-morrow night at eight o'clock!'

The tiny door closed behind him. Danny began to cry.

The next evening, as Shandon bells chimed eight o'clock, Danny, dressed to the nines and freshly shaved, was escorted to the presbytery door by Polly. She rang the bell and, leaving him on the doorstep, she crossed the street and went into the church to say a prayer that all might go well.

Father O'Flynn came to the door to see a caller out. Then, turning on Danny a winning smile, he said: 'Put it there, Danny!' He grasped Danny's hand in both his own. 'I knew you were a man of your word. Come in, and we'll do our business in private.'

They went into the waiting-room. Danny sat on the edge of a chair, and the priest stood with his back to the door. Admiring Danny all spruced up, he declared: 'Danny, you look a new man already.'

'I don't feel a new man at all,' muttered Danny, nervously fingering his cap and casting his eyes on the ground.

'I know well you don't,' said the priest. 'You must have the father and mother of a hangover, and that is a very sore thing indeed.'

Encouraged by this sympathetic comment, Danny shed some of his awkwardness and ventured: 'You don't know the half of it, Father. Just now I've a splitting headache, and to tell the truth, I'm hanging.'

'And what other way could you be after—but we'll say no more about that.' Father O'Flynn spoke in a kindly tone. 'We've forgotten the past, and we're looking to the future, and that future will be full of happiness and love, for Polly and yourself and the children, if we could only keep our pledge— even until after Christmas.'

'There's going to be no until after Christmas about this pledge, Father O'Flynn,' said Danny in a strange, courageous voice. 'I'm taking the pledge for life!'

The priest was astonished for a moment by this unexpected declaration.

'For life? That's a long time to go without a drink, Danny. You might be biting off more than you can chew there. After all, we did fail to keep some short-term pledges in the past. It might be wiser to——'

'Excuse me, Father—but 'tis for life or nothing this time, and I'll tell you why.'

'Is it the Sacred Heart lamp?'

'That's part of it, but by no means the whole story.'

'Tell me,' said the priest, for he was now very curious indeed to learn the cause of Danny's conversion.

'You know yourself, Father O'Flynn, that I'm very fond of birds.'

'I do indeed—and a noble trait it is.'

'Well, I've a little bird below, as you know, Father—a linnet that I sprigged myself out in Spangle Hill. That little linnet have the sweetest roll in all Blackpool. 'Twould do your heart good to hear him sing. I let no one near that linnet, Father; I always cleans the cage meself and feeds him, and every night I waters him. Well, last night—as you well know, Father—I was in no condition for that job. You were hardly out the door when Polly bundled me off to bed, and I was snoring before I thought of it. I woke up in the coal black of the night, and the first thing that came into me head was: water for the bird! I forgot to water the linnet! He'll be parched with the thirst below in the heat of the kitchen. I nudged Polly.

' "Did you give any sup of water to the bird last night?"

'I needn't tell you, Father, she wasn't in the best of humour.

' "What are you talking about," said she, "at two o'clock in the morning? Go to sleep or you'll wake the children!"

' "Did you give any water to that poor little bird?" I had to find out, Father.

' "Hadn't I bird enough," said she, "trying to put you to bed, without bothering me head about water for the linnet?"

'Well, Father, I had to get out of bed and feel me way down the steep stairs into the kitchen below. Father O'Flynn, I'll never forget the darkness of that kitchen—desolation—no Sacred Heart lamp; we're not staying another night in that house unless you come down and light the lamp that you blew out.'

'We'll go down together in a minute,' promised the priest. 'But go on about the bird.' He was fascinated by Danny's tale.

'In that pitch darkness I poked around looking for the bucket of water that herself leaves ready for the morning. No trace of the bucket.

' "Where's that bucket of water?" I shouted up the stairs.

'Father O'Flynn, I couldn't repeat all she said.

' "You and your bucket—at this hour of the morning. 'Tis out in the back yard," said she.

' "Is there any water at all in the kitchen?" I shouted again.

' "There's water in a bottle there on the dresser," she said. "Shut up or you'll wake the children."

'Well, Father, I fumbled around until I found a crockery bottle on the dresser. God only knows how I found the cage and poured in the water. Back I went to bed.

'At six o'clock Polly woke me up. "Come here," said she. "What water did you give to the bird this morning?"

' "The water in the crockery bottle on the dresser," said I.

' "Oh my God!" said she. "That's holy water! There's salt in that—'twill kill the poor bird!"

'Father O'Flynn, the heart stopped inside me. Me poor little bird poisoned with holy water! Down the stairs I crawl again in the cold grey dawn of the morning, and stand beneath the cage looking up at me poor little bird. There he was up on the perch, with his little head under his wing. I talked to him. "Tweet tweet tweet!" Not a stir out of him, Father. I try again. "Tweet tweet tweet!" and this time I rub me finger along the bars of the cage. Out he draws his head from under his wing, cocks his little eye, and looks down at me, as much as to say: "You're a nice pal, aren't you? What kind of water was that to give a bird last night?"

'Next thing, he stands up straight on the perch, sticks out his chest, clears his throat, and sings the first verse of *Faith of Our Fathers*.

'Now, Father O'Flynn, you know all about theology. Was that a miracle or the effects of drink?'

The priest walked to the window, his back to Danny to hide a smile. At length, he turned to Danny.

'Kneel down there, Danny, like a good man, and say these words after me.

'I solemnly promise . . . the Sacred Heart . . . and you, Father O'Flynn . . .'

Danny repeated each phrase after him, taking the pledge for life. As he was getting up off his knees, they heard Polly in the hall.

'I thought ye'd never be finished,' she said, as the priest opened the door. 'I said two rosaries while I was waiting.'

'And your prayers have not been in vain, for I think something has happened at last that will make a new man of Danny,' the priest assured her, smiling.

'What would that be, Father?' Polly asked.

'He'll tell you himself.' And off they went.

Early in the New Year, Father O'Flynn met Polly and Danny walking arm in arm along the street.

'Where are the pair of you off to now?' he asked them.

'We're off to see the pantomime at the Opera House,' Polly said. 'And we were just saying that we must call in to thank you.'

'For what?' asked the priest.

'For the lovely happy Christmas we had, Father. 'Twas the first time since we got married that Danny saw Christmas sober. You should have seen him—down on his hands and knees on the kitchen floor playing trains with the children!'

'Father O'Flynn,' said Danny, shyly, 'I never thought Christmas could be so lovely.'

'Well, now that you've seen it sober once, please God you'll see it sober for ever,' said the priest.

'He will, Father—thanks to you and to the Sacred Heart,' said Polly gratefully.

'And to the linnet,' added the priest as they parted.

12

The Loft again

IF you happened to be the first to arrive at the Loft you had to get the key—a massive one weighing five or six ounces at least—from the letter box across the lane. The door to the Loft was heavy, old and loose, and its lock was as massive as the key.

Opening the door, you looked up a steep stairs that led to the first floor, where the Loft itself was located. Instinctively you gripped the shaky handrail on your right and hoisted yourself up. On your left, through a wooden partition, percolated a syrupy odour, 'not poppy nor Mandragora' but the unique distillation of various concoctions used in the making of boiled sweets in the factory on the ground floor.

When you reached the top of the stairs your head emerged out of the floor like a man coming up from a well. If you paused to get your breath, you viewed a panorama of polished knobs and shiny heads of nails. Above you, the roof was unsheeted and the rafters were black with age.

You find yourself standing at one end of a large L-shaped room, that is poorly lighted by a few small windows. The rough unplastered walls are painted with a pink distemper, rather faded.

Beside you in the end wall is an old and worn fire grate; above it on a mantelpiece stands a statuette of Shakespeare. The furniture in this part of the Loft consists of a few wooden forms and a few kitchen chairs. At the opposite end of the long room you see the small stage, less than two feet high and surrounded by a plywood proscenium. There are no drapes or curtains to conceal the grim back wall. Turning into the toe of this L-shaped room you notice that this section is much brighter because of the skylight. It is also better furnished. That long deep press against the wall was specially made for the costumes. On top are some large wicker baskets—also for costumes. You can still read the faded labels: 'Foxe's Theatrical Costumiers, London.'

There was tremendous excitement that night in 1927 when seven of these baskets containing five complete sets of costumes for five plays of Shakespeare arrived in the Loft. The opposite wall is festooned with shields, helmets, spears, swords and other theatrical props. That long chest on the floor is called 'the coffin.' It contains tights and cloaks. That glass-fronted press in the corner contains rings, bangles, clasps and other small props. That statue of the Sacred Heart was placed on top of this press on the night that Father O'Flynn consecrated the Loft and its members to the Sacred Heart. The table and chairs are for the committee which holds its weekly meeting here. Although he was president of the Cork Shakespearean Company, Father O'Flynn rarely presided at the meetings. It was Gussie Healy, his second-in-command, who usually took the chair. Gussie's common sense, his tact and his unfailing good humour steered many a stormy meeting to a peaceful conclusion.

Questioned on where he got his method of teaching, Father O'Flynn replied: 'From the gospels'; and explained: 'Infinitely above all teachers is Jesus Christ, who is the way, the truth and the life. One thing is to be noted: he revealed his mind by the spoken word and by his actions. He did not use books nor did he command that they be used. It was to the ear he addressed his message. Through the ear and into the hearts of the hearers his divine words travelled. The dynamism, the accents, crises and cadences of his voice fell on their ears and inflamed their hearts with love and loyalty for the Son of Man. In action he exemplified his words—the people saw him doing the truth in charity. Miracles won the multitudes, but those who did not hear the Word and keep it soon forgot the miracles. The ear is primary in the work of tradition. Truth carried alive into the heart by the voice of sincerity has power to move one to do good. We hear angels more often than we see them. But in our schools today all the emphasis is on the book, grammar, words—lifeless things—while the ear and the heart are neglected. Our educational planners seem to have lost sight of the impact that noble emotion has on the hearts of children.

'But in the Loft, the ear and the heart hold pride of place. Even Shakespeare's words are secondary with us, for we concentrate on realities, on developing the specific human emotions that nature has implanted in the child with a view to uplifting it to a love of the true, the good and the beautiful. In the Loft we aim at educating the heart.'

The Loft was not exclusively a school of the Shakespearean drama. Constant in his love for 'Dark Rosaleen' and loyal to the ideal of a Gaelic Ireland, Father O'Flynn did what he could to foster Irish dancing and music in the Loft. Once a week there was a dancing class which was attended by the younger children. Had you visited the Loft on one of these 'Irish nights' it would have been like this:

'Hello, Mr. Moynihan! Hello, Mr. O'Brien!' the boys and girls greeted the dancing master and the fiddler as they clambered into the Loft and gathered round to watch the dancers dance a fourhand reel.

Mr. Moynihan, known to all as 'Katja', was a slim little man with a head that appeared to be several sizes too large for his body. He had stripped off his jacket before the lesson began, and changed his boots for a pair of suede shoes which he carried round with him neatly rolled up in a piece of oilskin. He stood before the dancers in his waistcoat and shirt sleeves, the ends of his trousers tucked into his socks. He wore a 'spoggar'—

a cloth cap with the peak turned up. This made his pupils very conscious of his broad, square forehead. Although over fifty years of age, he was very agile and light as a feather on his feet. In his own words, he was dog-fit. It was said that in his enthusiasm to get the steps of the dance correct, he used to lie on his stomach on the kitchen floors of the Gaeltacht watching at close quarters the dancing feet of those who had the true tradition. They called him 'Katja' because his first appearance in the Loft happened to coincide with a musical comedy in the Opera House, *Katja the Dancer*.

Mr. O'Brien, a traditional fiddler, provided the music. He was a tall, gaunt, drooping man with hard jagged features and a bushy moustache. His bald dome was ringed with scraggy grey hair. He stood in the shadows a little away from Katja, looped over his fiddle with the butt-end socketed into a red silk handkerchief under his lean jaw. He fiddled away with short jabs of the bow. Now and then he peered at Katja, and all the time he tapped a foot on the floor.

'There's not a fiddler in Munster to equal O'Brien for the flowing line,' Father O'Flynn assured the class the night he introduced him. The fiddler was promptly named 'O'Brien o' Munster'.

When the reel had ended, the crowd of boys and girls clapped the dancers. One of the boys questioned Katja about some tricky steps of a slip-jig he was trying to learn. He danced a few steps to illustrate his difficulty.

'Wo—you have it all tray-na-kayla!' Katja stopped him. 'Watch it!'

Then he hitched up his trousers, adjusted his cap, briskly rubbed his hands, and gave O'Brien the beck. 'Keep well back or ye'll cramp his style.'

The fiddler cleared a space with a wide sweep of his bow. The crowd stepped back, O'Brien played up, and Katja sprang into action.

He was good, very good, and he took a conscious delight in his skill. He loved an audience. He had one now, and to complete his joy he spotted Father O'Flynn looking at him over the heads of the crowd. With a wink and a smile and a shake of his head, he danced to his heart's content. It was a treat to watch him. O'Brien o' Munster surpassed himself on the fiddle.

'Will you look at the music on that fellow's face!' whispered the priest to Gussie beside him.

'Will you listen to the tapping of those feet!'

'See how smoothly he glides across the floor!'

The dance over, the crowd applauded. Katja bowed, and the priest clapped him on the back.

'*Tadhg, a ghrádh,* you have the genuine tap!' He shook hands with O'Brien. 'You've as sweet a finger as ever slipped along the strings of a fiddle!'

He turned to the group. 'Girls and boys, that Irish jig as danced and played by our two friends here comes of the same tradition that gave us songs like *Úna Bán* and *Máire de Barra*. The men who made them knew nothing of notation. They had music in here'—he struck his heart with his fist—'and they expressed it not in notes but in rhythmic lines that move with the motion of winds and waves. To do justice to *Máire de Barra* the singer must "swim" the melodic line if he is to achieve the liquescence demanded by the underlying emotion.'

To prove his point, the priest sang the song in his own highly individual style.

'We'll be here all night if someone doesn't stop him,' whispered a voice in the crowd. Gussie took the hint.

'Father—'tis nine o'clock. We'd better get on with *Macbeth*.'

'We'll have one sweet melody from Mr. O'Brien,' he said, 'and then we'll begin. What'll it be tonight, Tadhg?'

He looked at O'Brien. The fiddler hesitated, and scratched the side of his head with his bow. '*The Cualann,* Father.'

It was a good performance, and Father O'Flynn was most

generous in his praise of the fiddler, who blushed and shuffled his feet.

'Only three places in the world will you get a liquescent line like that: in a traditional Irish air; in a Plain Chant melody; and—to give him his due—in Shakespeare's verse. Yes, Shakespeare had a line like our Irish melodies. As he mastered the craft of writing he realised that rhyme was interrupting the feeling, and the run of the feeling. He finally discarded it altogether, except to indicate the end of a scene. Shakespeare's verse became less mechanical and more subtle, swift and complex; not in the sense of mechanical arrangement, but in that it achieved a mystery of movement. It achieved liquescence —a perfect expression of the underlying emotion—as we find in many of our Irish songs.' He quoted from *Macbeth*:

> But let the frame of things disjoint, both the worlds suffer,
> Ere we will eat our meal in fear, and sleep
> In the affliction of these terrible dreams
> That shake us nightly.

'There you have a gathering up of many syllables under the great accents, and you get a wave-like motion that is similar to that in the *Cualann*, or in the slip-jig danced by our friend Mr. Moynihan.'

As if haunted by the beauty of the *Cualann*, the priest took the fiddle and bow from O'Brien and attempted to play the tune himself. After the first few bars it was painfully clear that he was no master of the flowing line on the fiddle.

'Give it up, Father, and stick to Shakespeare!' Gussie cut in.

And there the recital ended in hearty laughter. Katja turned down the peak of his cap, and carefully rolled his dancing shoes in the piece of yellow oilcloth. O'Brien o' Munster packed away his fiddle, and put on his long coat and floppy hat. The pair exchanged a few words with the priest, and left.

'If I had my way,' Father O'Flynn said, 'those poor fellows would be installed as masters in one of our musical academies and treated with honour and respect—for they have the genuine tradition. But the genuine tradition is neither recognised nor welcome in our academies today. I've got the cold shoulder myself. I'm beginning to feel like a man with a *birín breo* cupped in the hollow of his hands and breathing on it gently to keep the life in it. Our tradition has very few friends left.'

'Why is that?' Gussie asked.

'Because our minds have been poisoned by a system of education that our government has unhappily taken over holusbolus from the English. While our government is sincere in trying to forge a link between the past and the present generations, it is, in effect, undoing that link by the system of education it imposes. The culture and the mentality which that system fosters and rewards with certificates and good positions is not the culture or mentality of *Sean Éire*. It is something very different from the old Gaelic way where freedom, inspiration and fosterage were the means, and personality was the end of education. Compulsion is the way of our modern system—and that is a kind of intellectual violence. The drive for the revival of Irish is now an admitted failure. What the Minister for Education complains of as a lack of sympathy is in fact a dour antipathy to the revival of our whole Gaelic way of life. This argues a noble people fallen from their pristine national vigour. I bewail that antipathy, but I hate the idea of compulsion. It has proved itself ineffective; it has failed to bring the language as a living thing from the class-room as far as the playground. The Minister should hand in the whip . . . .'

These sentiments brought loud applause from the pupils who then settled themselves for a talk on the Bible and *Macbeth*.

Among the pupils of the Loft, there were always a number who had no talent for acting or singing. These came, attracted by the personality of the priest, to listen and learn from his many interesting and illuminating asides on all sorts of things.

'Although I had no talent whatsoever for acting, I attended regularly the class in the Loft for several years. I found Father O'Flynn a source of enlightenment and inspiration on many topics outside Shakespeare and Irish music, and I remember keeping a notebook in which I recorded many of his comments on life. Silly and giggly as some of us youngsters undoubtedly were in those days, we instinctively recognised that for Father O'Flynn it was neither Shakespeare nor Irish culture that came first—but we ourselves; that we should learn to pursue the true, the good and the beautiful in all walks of life.'

Another of those non-actors who attended the Loft has observed:

'In nature, escape means life: for the fox from the hounds, for the sparrow from the hawk, for the trout from the pike. To live as an artist, Father O'Flynn had to escape. The Loft was his refuge. There in exercising his God-given talents he not only fulfilled himself as an artist, but also greatly enriched the lives of hundreds of young people.'

13

La musique et la danse

FATHER TIM was a man of few words, a calm man, an easy man to live with. A country man, he never took kindly to the city pavements. He found it hard to understand these people of the streets and lanes around the North Cathedral, so he waited patiently for the day when the Bishop would appoint him to a quiet country parish. He was a man of simple tastes: the rod, the gun, his pipe and *The Cork Examiner*.

Unlike his fellow–curate Father Christy O'Flynn, Father Tim was no man of the arts. His musical repertoire was limited to the Benediction Service, and even that was a bother to him. High Mass was beyond him. He had come to an agreement with Father O'Flynn that when it came to his turn to sing High Mass, Father O'Flynn would go on in his place—in return for a day's duty. 'Nothing for nothing around Mallow Lane,' they said.

Father Tim was not completely out of touch with the arts. That could hardly be possible since he lived under the same roof with Father O'Flynn. Father Tim's sitting–room was situated on the first floor of the presbytery directly underneath Father O'Flynn's room on the second floor.

Father O'Flynn had a piano which he played, sometimes tolerably well and sometimes not so well. It was Professor Fleischmann, choir–master and organist at the Cathedral, who introduced Father O'Flynn to Beethoven's *Sonata Pathetique*. Father O'Flynn was profoundly grateful.

'And the strange thing is,' he remarked to Herr Fleischmann, 'I get far more pleasure out of playing it in my own tin-pot

way than listening to a perfect recording by Paderewski.' And
he went on to enthuse over the haunting beauty of the *Adagio
cantabile*.

'Ah, but what of the opening of the first movement?'
exclaimed the professor. 'Surely you were moved by those dark
mysterious chords! Those double-forte chords! There is
drama! As good as your Shakespeare!'

Father Tim in his room underneath, browsing through *The
Cork Examiner,* was indeed moved by the pounding of those
mysterious chords and the subsequent shower of quavers and
semiquavers that rained down upon him, but not in the sense
implied by the professor. He was irritated; at times he was
demented. Being a fair-minded man he would have admitted
that Father O'Flynn played the *Adagio cantabile* with much
feeling, but when he had heard it several times in succession—
for Father O'Flynn liked to savour every bar of that beautiful
slow movement—it began to pall. What little pleasure it may
have given Father Tim as background music to his reading
was soured by the foreboding that it would be followed
immediately by a staggering rendering of the final rondo.
Having taken up the piano rather late in life, Father O'Flynn
lacked that finger dexterity needed to do justice to the *presto*
passages. The result was a halting, edgy, performance. But
Father Tim, being a man of peace, said nothing. During these
recitals he stole out of his room, crossed over to the church
and read his breviary.

Father O'Flynn had a harp. On entering his room it was
the first thing that caught the eye, standing there in the corner
in its green dust-cover. It might be said without straining the
truth that Father O'Flynn played the harp tolerably well.
Now and then when he came home at night from the Loft,
he would remove the green dust-cover, lay his harp against
his shoulder, and sing to himself one or other of those delightful songs from Shakespeare's plays. It might be: *O, mistress*

mine,' where are you roving? or *Full fathoms five* . . . It might be
a more lively ditty like: *It was a lover and his lass, with a hey
and a ho, and a hey nonni no* from *As You Like It*. In itself the
performance was pleasing enough, and in all fairness Father
Tim admitted that it was streets ahead of the rondo from
Beethoven's *Sonata Pathétique*. But even the '*hey non-i-noni-
no*' was rather trying, especially at eleven o'clock at night when
Father Tim in his room below was trying to finish his breviary
for the day. On those nights when Father O'Flynn was moved
to unburden his artistic soul with some passionate Irish song of
vengeance or battle, it seemed to Father Tim that he was back
in Tara's Halls and the poor old harp was being 'tore asunder'.
But being late at night, the church was locked; there was no
escape.

One evening Father Tim was sitting by his fire, reading
that section of *The Cork Examiner* headed 'Roscarberry Notes.'
Voices sounded on the stairs speaking out loud in Irish. Someone knocked at his door and he opened.

'Good night, Tim,' Father O'Flynn said, breaking into a
disarming smile. 'Meet my friend Mr. O'Brien—the sweetest
fiddler in all Munster, no one to match him for the flowing
line.'

O'Brien stepped forward, fumbled with his violin case and
shook hands with Father Tim.

'Would you be a gentleman, Tim,' Father O'Flynn resumed,
'and do devotions for me tonight? You may chalk it up against
your next High Mass.'

'Righto, Chris,' Father Tim agreed.

'Would you like to join us?' asked Father O'Flynn. 'We're
going up to play a few tunes just now.'

'No, thanks,' replied Father Tim, ''twould only be wasted
on me, as you know.' Then turning to O'Brien o' Munster he
smiled faintly and said: 'Best o' luck with the flowing line',
and retired into his room. He spread *The Cork Examiner* on the

table, spilled out the collection from the Men's Confraternity and began to count the coppers. It was one of those routine, unspectacular jobs at which Father Tim excelled.

He could hear Father Christy with his friend walking across the room above him. A single note was sounded several times on the piano. They were tuning up. Then followed a few false starts and at last they got it going. It was a jig. At this particular period Father O'Flynn was very keenly interested in the rhythmic structures of certain Irish dance tunes. They were playing one now. But there was no flowing line; there was no sweet fiddling. It was dance music. Down through the ceiling it shot in short sharp spasms that put Father Tim's foot tapping to a rhythm contrary to that in which he was counting the coppers. He had to give it up . . . impossible to count accurately while the jig was hopping off the ceiling. He got up from the table, lit his pipe and stood before the fire.

'Tis about time somebody said something about this sort of thing, he mused—looking up at the source of his annoyance. Just then the bell for devotions tolled. He put on his biretta and went across to the church feeling irritated.

A week or two later, Father Tim returned home after a day's shooting. It had been a good day. He had six pheasants in his bag. As he came in the presbytery gate, complete with gumboots, dog and gun, he was a tired but happy man. Father O'Flynn was coming out.

'Any luck, Tim?' he asked cheerfully.

'Powerful!' replied this man of few words. Then brushing aside all painful memories of piano, harp and fiddle, he took a pheasant from his bag and said: 'Like a bird, Chris? 'Tis mud fat.'

'Nothing I'd like better, Tim—a thousand thanks—you might leave it with the housekeeper on the way in.' They parted.

Up in the Loft, Father O'Flynn had had several discussions with O'Brien on the rhythmic forms of Irish dance tunes. The subject fascinated him. O'Brien, noting his enthusiasm, remarked that to enjoy its full flavour one needed in addition to the fiddle a piper to play the cross-rhythms on the bagpipes.

'Cross-rhythms on the bagpipes?' queried the priest. 'Yes, on the bagpipes,' affirmed O'Brien and added: 'I have the very man who can do it—O'Connor of Tralee—and he is staying with a brother-in-law of mine up in Fair Hill at the moment.'

'We'll hear him,' said the priest, intrigued by the prospect of a cross-rhythm to the already intricate rhythm of the dance tune. And so it was arranged that at nine o'clock O'Brien o' Munster with his fiddle, and O'Connor of Tralee with his bagpipes, would meet in Father O'Flynn's room in the presbytery. It happened to be the very night that Father Tim had returned so happy with his bag of six pheasants. After his supper he began to sneeze and shiver. He had got a wetting when he slipped into a drain during the day's shoot, but in the excitement he had paid no attention to it. Now he felt a chill coming on, and he had a slight headache. He drank a glass of hot punch sitting by the fire, and then reached for his breviary. He had the whole of that day's Office to read. He blessed himself and tackled in to Matins.

He had just finished the first nocturne when he heard footsteps on the stairs and several voices talking out loud in Irish. It was O'Brien with his fiddle, O'Connor with his pipes, and to complete the ensemble they had brought along Katja the dancer. Up to the second floor they tramped, knocked at Father O'Flynn's door and entered. He welcomed them with open arms and they set to at once shifting the heavy mahogany table and rolling back the carpet to provide a floor for Katja. O'Connor uncovered his pipes—and what pipes! As he fitted them together he explained that they were known as the war-pipes to distinguish them from the Uileann pipes. He himself was a member of the Brian Boru war-pipers' band.

The fiddler sat on the edge of a chair and made a few

preliminary jabs with his bow; the piper inflated his bagpipes and nursed them tenderly. Katja in his shirt-sleeves stood at the ready in the middle of the floor. Father O'Flynn took out a notebook and pencil to record his observations on these Irish dances.

'What would you like first, Father—a jig, a reel or a horn-pipe?' Katja asked.

'Begin with a jig,' the priest replied.

'A jig is the expression of great joy—it has the rhythm of joy in it. You can write that in your little book,' said Katja to the priest, and continued: 'But what kind of a jig do you want?'

'How many kinds are there?' asked the priest.

'There are many kinds—but these are the main kinds: a slip-jig, a double-jig, a single and a hop. You can write that down in the little book!'

'We'll have one of each,' said the priest.

'Righto—and we'll begin with the hop,' said Katja nodding to the fiddler. It promised to be a gala night.

Down below Father Tim was finding the going very heavy as he ploughed through the psalms of the second nocturne. He felt sure that he was running a temperature. His headache had developed into a sharp pain. The room was too hot with the big fire his housekeeper had built up; he opened his soutane and took off his Roman collar. Stretched out before the fire, the cocker spaniel slept soundly. Father Tim opened his breviary at the third nocturne, sat back in the chair—and then it began.

Relentlessly the fiddle rasped out the tune, monotonously the bagpipes droned in counterpoint. Katja rapped the floor with his dancing shoes and slid like a skater across the floor, hopping in the corner, up, down, and skipping back again to the middle. Stimulated by Katja's prowess at the dance, O'Connor filled his lungs and began to improvise some shattering *glissandos* on the pipes.

'*Am briathar, is tú an buachaill, a Sheáin!*' exclaimed Father O'Flynn in admiration of the performance. Then he jotted down some observations: 'Did not that series of weak pulses leading to the strong accent resemble a diver running along a springboard, jumping on the end, and flying gracefully through the air? Ah! the vision of that flowing line! Or was it inspired by the crashing of the great seventh wave on the shore?' Here was endless food for reflection.

Squirming in his chair beneath this hail of cacophony, Father Tim was discovering new meanings in the psalms of the third nocturne:

> *You have plunged me into the bottom of the pit,*
> > *Into the dark abyss.*
> *Upon me your wrath lies heavy.*

Down upon his aching head that cascade of rasping, clattering sound continued to rain . . . and the psalmist continued:

> *And with all your billows you overwhelm me,*
> *I am imprisoned and I cannot escape.*

But there is a limit to what a man can endure, and Father Tim had reached that limit now. Escape he would and escape he could, whatever the psalmist said. He rocketed out of the chair, picked up his gun, shot out the door and up the stairs, his cocker spaniel at his heels. He knocked a loud resounding knock and flung the door wide open. The quartet froze. Over six foot tall, broad and powerful, Father Tim filled the doorway, his soutane flying open, no Roman collar, his glasses up upon his forehead like another pair of eyes and the shot-gun well to the fore.

'Do you see that?' he threatened, holding up the gun for their inspection. 'If I hear one more squawk out of any of them things,' he continued, pointing the gun in turn at the harp, the fiddle and the bagpipes, 'there'll be blue murder in this house!'

He glared at them. It was brief, to the point, and—as events proved—highly effective. He was gone. Along the corridor and down the stairs he tramped, his cocker spaniel at his heels. They heard his room door close. He stood the gun in the corner, took up his breviary from the table and concluded Matins for the day, singing in his heart with a quiet satisfaction:

Te Deum laudamus. . . .

14

Rashers

'HELLO, Lizzie!' said Father O'Flynn, walking into the kitchen.

'Glory be to God—'tis the priest!' Lizzie unbent herself from over the tub of washing, and with a sudsy hand whisked a few grey hairs from her hard, careworn face.

'I just dropped in to see poor Rashers—I heard he's not too good.'

'Faith, by the antics of 'em he can't be too bad either.' Lizzie dried her hands and followed the priest into the tiny bedroom off the kitchen.

'Cocks' Murphy was standing at the foot of the capacious iron bedstead that seemed to occupy most of the room. He saluted the priest and flattened himself against the wall to let him pass. The bed was covered in newspapers and in the midst sat Rashers. In his hands he held a sleek, red fighting-cock. Cocks bred these birds; Rashers trained them; and they shared the profits. Although confined to bed by doctor's orders, Rashers continued daily to exercise the cock by bouncing it up and down on the bed.

When Father O'Flynn entered the room the cock took fright, flapped its wings and rose perpendicularly out of the bed. Feathers filled the air.

'Cocks!' ordered Lizzie, 'take yourself and your bird out of here at once—and stop out!'

Cocks retrieved the bird and fled. In his rush through the kitchen he knocked over the tub of washing and shot through the door like a scalded cat.

'O Sacred Heart of —!' Lizzie stopped herself in the nick of time.

'Father O'Flynn,' she fumed, surveying the mess in the kitchen, 'only you're a priest of God, I'd light the lane with living language the likes you never listened to!'

Furiously she snatched up the newspapers and upbraided her husband. 'Look at the cut of that bed, you have it like a pig-sty.' Then she stormed out to mop up the kitchen.

The priest and Rashers were silent during the cock and newspaper operations. Both knew Lizzie. When she had left, Rashers spoke in a hoarse voice:

'The doctor yesterday; the priest today; I suppose 'twill be the undertaker tomorrow!'

'No wonder you're upset, my poor man.' The priest was on Rasher's side.

'Father O'Flynn, the way that one do be nagging at me day after day I'd be as well off in my grave!'

'Who is talking about graves?' said the priest. 'Lie back there now till I have a look at you.'

Rashers lay back on the pillow, and Father O'Flynn put his hand on the patient's forehead. Then he examined the eyes. They were yellow and bloodshot. The skin was copper coloured. Father O'Flynn did not like the look of things. He heard voices in the kitchen.

'The doctor's here,' Lizzie shouted. In deference to the priest, the doctor from the dispensary waited in the kitchen.

Father O'Flynn took a thermometer from his pocket, shook it, and placed it under Rashers' tongue. Then he began to take the pulse.

The doctor, becoming impatient, entered the bedroom.

'Good-day, Father O'Flynn,' the doctor greeted.

'Good-day, doctor,' the priest replied. Then nodding at the patient he continued: 'Eyes muddy, skin soggy and pulse a little rapid.' He held the thermometer up to the light. 'He's running a slight temperature too—maybe due to exercising the cock.'

'Exercising the what?' The doctor was startled.

'Let me see your tongue, like a good man,' Father O'Flynn requested the patient. But Rashers closed his lips tightly and muttered incoherently.

Lizzie interrupted. 'He's ashamed to show his tongue, Father, for 'tis like the bottom of a bird-cage and there's a whiff off his breath worse than Sullivan's quay at low tide.'

The doctor laughed; the priest was serious. He gave his diagnosis. 'Rashers has a bad dose of jaundice, and the poor old heart is not so good either.' He turned to Lizzie. 'Give him some yeast and the whites of three eggs every day and let him drink nothing but spring water.'

Lizzie nodded.

The doctor had heard of Father O'Flynn's reputation as a medico.

'Father,' he said politely, 'I don't wish to hurry you, but if you're finished with the patient would you mind if I went ahead and anointed him?'

All four burst out laughing, and Rashers showed a tongue that verified Lizzie's words.

'Oh, you ruffian, you!' The priest good-humouredly shook his fist at the doctor. 'Some day you'll be glad to have a priest.'

'Of course I will,' retorted the doctor, 'and I'll make sure they don't send me a medicine-man!' There was more laughter.

The priest and Lizzie withdrew while the doctor examined Rashers.

'They say he hasn't been to the Sacraments for a long time?' whispered the priest to Lizzie before he left.

'No need to whisper about that, Father, for the whole world know he don't go. And he wouldn't go to Mass either only I push him out the door on a Sunday morning.'

'In that case,' said the priest thoughtfully, 'I'd better call back and have a chat with him when things have quietened down.'

'You'll have your work cut out for you, Father,' warned Lizzie.

Father O'Flynn walked back to the presbytery.

They all called him Rashers, though nobody seemed to know why. Perhaps he had worked for a short time long ago in Denny's Bacon Factory. No one was sure. His parents called him Rashers; Lizzie his wife called him Rashers, and his own children called him Rashers. Few knew his real name. In his heyday, at the turn of the century, Rashers was a devotee of St. Mary's Hall opposite the church, where the League of the Silver Cross ran a gymnasium. His great strength earned him the title of champion weight-lifter.

Bored with life around the lanes, he had joined the British army, and there he was trained as a boxer. But he was too slow on the feet to do any good. However, he learned to defend himself, and when he was pensioned out of the army with a shrapnel wound in the leg he retired to Bailey's Lane and reigned undefeated champion in the Shandon area. He liked to lounge at the corner of the lane with a few of his pals, and to show off before newcomers by warning them.

'See that?' he would say, showing them his left fist—'the North Infirmary!'

'See that?' he would say, taking his right fist from inside his coat as if uncovering some terrible weapon—'Sudden death!'

He never lacked challengers, for he loved a fight and bore the marks of many a battle: a cauliflower ear, a broken and flattened nose, and a long scar under the left eye. These were wonders that he, in his simple way, delighted to show to his own children when they climbed on his knee. He attended the clinic at the North Infirmary to have the wound in his leg dressed. His calumniators spread the rumour that when the wound healed up, Rashers used to open it afresh with a razor-blade to keep his contact with the clinic and his title to the few extra shillings disablement pension.

For a time, Rashers took up droving. He frequently travelled with cargoes of cattle or pigs from Cork to Bristol, where it was his job to see that the animals were safely delivered to the buyers. During one of his visits to Bristol he got involved in a fight with a Welsh docker—'a giant of a man', as Rashers described him. He came home to Lizzie with his head swathed in bandages. He had to have an eye removed and a glass eye fitted. He spent several weeks in the 'Eye and Ear' on the Western Road. Looking at the job of restoration that had been done on her husband, Lizzie at once named the glass eye 'the fixed one' and the good eye 'the rover'.

Rashers learned to turn his loss to his advantage. When standing at Flaherty's corner listening to some of his pals, he would turn on them 'the fixed one', thus deluding them that he was paying them full attention. This left him free to scan the other side of the street with 'the rover'.

Unfit for droving, Rashers drifted from job to job, and finally retired to live on his pension and what Lizzie earned by charring. She had a hard life with him, for he had a quick temper and a fluency in unprintable language, together with a love for fighting and drink. Not for him the peaceful pastimes of racing pigeons, or sprigging larks or linnets. He was a one for the blood sports; hunting with the beagles on a Sunday, and cock-fighting at dawn up on Fair Hill. His other recreation was playing pitch-and-toss up in Skyes Lane. His losses at gambling and his drinking habits evoked from Lizzie many a scathing cascade of abuse when he returned home at night. Now and then he repaid her with a black eye or a swollen cheek—'just to let her see who's boss in this house,' he explained to her brother 'Ducker' Doyle when he came to protect his sister. Small wonder that Lizzie was hardened.

Now Rashers was near the end.

'The heart could stop any minute—'tis only a matter of days,' the doctor had warned Lizzie.

Father O'Flynn returned that evening. He spoke to Rashers about old times; the weight-lifting days in St. Mary's Hall where only Father O'Flynn himself, then a very young man, could rival Rashers' prowess at throwing the half-hundred weight.

Rashers was at ease talking to Father O'Flynn. He recounted an incident from his droving days.

'I was driving home some pigs through a street in Bristol when one of them bolted, and into a Protestant church he ran. In after him with me. There was a Service going on. I met the pig coming down the aisle and, hitting him a belt of me ashplant, I said: "Hell to your soul for a pig! You weren't long left Ireland when you lost your faith"!'

They both laughed heartily, and Rashers, feeling that he had a sympathetic audience, sang a few verses of his favourite song, *The Boys of Fair Hill:*

> *Our band is out tonight, boys*
> *Our gallant fife and drum;*
> *Let no one here insult Fair Lane*
> *Or we will make them run.*

The priest joined him in the second verse:

> *We're in by day and we're out by night,*
> *And we're always out for game;*
> *Let no one here insult Fair Lane*
> *Nor the cowards from Quarry Lane.*

Rashers was delighted to find the priest so human.

Then Father O'Flynn told him a story which began: '*A certain man had two sons. And the younger of them said to his father. . . .*' It was the parable of the Prodigal Son (Luke 15).

While the priest was telling, in his own very moving way, the parable of God's mercy and love for the wayward one, Rashers listened intently, focussing on the priest's face both 'the rover' and 'the fixed one'.

At the end there was silence. The priest took a purple stole from his pocket, and draped it over his shoulders. He made the sign of the cross over Rashers, while saying the opening prayer of the Sacrament of Penance. Then he took Rashers' hand in his own.

It was not hard for Rashers to make his confession.

'Thanks be to God that's over,' he said, lying back in the bed, as the priest folded the stole and put it back in his pocket. 'I feel as light as a feather after that,' said Rashers.

Later that evening Father O'Flynn returned, and Rashers received the Last Sacraments, Lizzie and one of the neighbours kneeling by the bed.

Each morning Father O'Flynn brought Holy Viaticum to Rashers, and in the evening he came again, and prayed and chatted with him in the dingy bedroom behind the kitchen. Rashers was growing weaker and weaker, but he obviously enjoyed speaking of old times to the priest.

'Ah, they were the days, Father O'Flynn; they were the days out by the Killeens with the pack of beagles. God be with the days!'

'On a Sunday morning,' he reminisced to the priest, 'you'd hear the bugler up at the clubhouse in Fair Hill calling all the hounds. You'd see the lads coming from all around, with their beagles, their coats shining with good condition. Connie-the-dogs and Connie Doyle and John Joe Moriarty—they were great men after dogs, Father O'Flynn—always airing the dogs out on the Commons Road. On a Saturday night Connie-the-dogs would bring home a sheep's head to the wife and say: "Put that in the skillet for the beagle," and he'd feed it to the dog himself with a glass of sherry to put condition on him. Just imagine—a glass of sherry for the dog! Ah, God be with the days, Father O'Flynn—God be with the days!'

In the kitchen Lizzie set about preparing for the end. Her married daughter Statia was often with her these last days. They bought the brown habit in Coady's little drapery shop and had it airing by the fire one evening when Father O'Flynn called in for his chat with Rashers. They asked him to bless the habit. He blessed it, and then went into the bedroom.

He was greeted with a complaint. 'Do you know what that one said to me today, Father O'Flynn?' The priest saw at once that Rashers had lost some of the fervour of his conversion. 'She said: "Can't you be looking up at the picture of the Sacred Heart, and saying aspirations, instead of grumbling there in the bed?"'

''Tis in an awkward place,' the priest said, looking up at the picture behind Rashers' head.

'Awkward is right!' said Rashers sarcastically. ''Tis the way she wants me to die of a crick in the neck.

'Will you close the door, Father—I've something to say to you—private?' Rashers winked 'the rover'.

The priest closed the bedroom door and sat on the edge of the bed. Rashers gripped his arm.

'Father, I want you to promise me something?'

'Certainly. What is it?'

'Promise me that you'll see me buried out in Garrycloyne with me poor father—and that you'll see me down into the grave with your own two eyes. For I can't trust that one where she'd put me when I'm gone.'

'Rest assured, I'll see that your wishes are carried out.'

'One thing more, Father: I want me old pal Cocks Murphy to be in charge that day. I don't want any of her crowd pushing me around.'

'You have my word for that too. I'll see Cocks when the time comes.'

A week later, Rashers died as Father O'Flynn read the prayers over him, and Lizzie held the blessed candle in his hand.

They waked him for a day and a night. The kitchen and the tiny bedroom where the corpse was laid out were filled with a steady stream of neighbours, calling in to pray and to console the widow. But the widow herself suffered a conflict of emotions.

'God forgive me, Father O'Flynn,' she admitted to the priest the night Rashers died, 'I don't feel a bit sorry that he's gone. He gave me a terrible life, as you know yourself.' She began to cry softly.

'Indeed, I can well understand your feelings,' consoled the priest. 'Are they not like an April day when we see sunshine and rain at the same time?'

'That's exactly how it is with me just now, Father. I feel I could laugh and cry at the same time.'

Whatever the conflict within her heart, Lizzie felt that in the eyes of the world, and of Bailey's Lane in particular, she must play the role expected of her—the sorrowing widow. She wore her black dress, covered her head with her long black shawl and sat in a corner of the bedroom quietly sobbing.

Ducker Doyle, her brother from Quarry Lane, came in and stood at the foot of the bed.

'You're dead, poor Rashers, you are—there's no fight in you now, boy! Going down to the grave with your cauliflower ear, eh? Who gave you the cauliflower ear, eh? Your old pal, Ducker. But who knocked out my front teeth—eh, Rashers? But no harm—poor Rashers! Ah, you gave me poor sister, Lizzie, a hard time, you did—a very hard time she had, poor girl. She have seven stitches over her eye after you. Ah, she'll remember you all right. No need of a mortuary card with those stitches to remind her. But what harm. God be good to Rashers!'

Rashers' elder sister Jule met Father O'Flynn as she was on her way to her brother's wake.

'Thanks be to God, Father O'Flynn, that you fixed up poor Rashers. I was always praying to the Sacred Heart that he'd make his peace with God before the end.'

Jule, arriving at the house, went into the bedroom, and embraced her sister-in-law.

'Oh Lizzie, Lizzie, our all is gone! Poor Rashers is gone! God help you, poor girl—'tis a cruel blow to you. You'll miss the bit of a pension, no doubt. Sure he wasn't the worst of them. A great lad to throw the weights—a great man after pigs. God rest him now! You're crying? Poor Lizzie! Don't be crying at all, girl! Sure he had a beautiful death, with the priest praying over him and yourself holding the blessed candle in his hand. Sure he died like a nun.'

Jule adjusted her shawl so that just one eye peeped out. She moved over to the dresser and took a pinch of snuff from the saucer placed there for the mourners. She inspected the corpse on the bed and, noticing the glint of candlelight in Rasher's glass eye, she said: 'Come here—don't tell me you're going to bury the glass eye with Rashers? There's no point in doing that, girl.'

'And what else would I do with it?' said Lizzie acidly from the corner.

'I thought you might keep it as a souvenir.'

'Haven't I souvenirs enough'—Lizzie touched the stitch-marks on her forehead—'without keeping that on the mantel-piece to remind me?'

Jule was nettled by Lizzie's words. 'Seeing you don't want it yourself,' she said petulantly, 'maybe you'd give it to me who'd have a care for it.'

'No! 'Tis staying where it is, and down to the grave 'twill go with him!'

Jule went over to the corpse and rested her hand for a

moment on the forehead. She looked puzzled. She turned to Lizzie who had resumed her soft weeping in the corner.

'Lizzie, girl—there's heat in him yet!'

Abruptly Lizzie stopped her weeping.

'Hot or cold,' she said sharply, 'out of this house he goes tonight!'

The gas lamps in Bailey's Lane were casting a cold lemon light as the fellows from the Harriers' Club in Fair Lane shouldered Rashers' coffin to the mortuary in the Cathedral. Lizzie, linked by her daughter Statia, and flanked by her two brothers, Ducker and Springer Doyle, walked immediately behind the coffin. All the neighbours followed, the women anonymous in their black shawls, the men bare-headed. Father O'Flynn, in surplice and soutane, preceded by a cross-bearer and two acolytes, received the remains at the church door. He sprinkled the coffin with holy water and proceeded to the mortuary chanting: 'Miserere mei Deus. . . .'

Next day, 17 March, was St. Patrick's Day. The funeral was due to leave at three in the afternoon for Garrycloyne cemetery, about six miles out along the Blarney Road. It was a squally day, with showers of needling rain and sleet and an odd ray of sunshine.

The Bishop was due to dine at the presbytery at six o'clock. Father O'Flynn was anxious that the funeral should start on time. He did not want to be late for the Bishop's dinner.

He was in the mortuary at three o'clock, and read the prayers. Four of Rashers' cock-fighting pals shouldered out the coffin and loaded it on to the hearse, which was drawn by two black horses caparisoned in all the funeral trappings. Six cabs were pulled up beside the footpath, behind the hearse. The widow, her daughter Statia and her two brothers got into the first cab, which was reserved for the chief mourners. The second cab was for Rashers' people: his two married sisters, Jule and Mollie, and their husbands and children. There was a coolness between the two sets of mourners over Rashers' glass eye. It began to drizzle, but the mourners remained lined up against the railings, except for the children who had already piled into the cabs.

Father O'Flynn strode out of the sacristy.

'What are they waiting for now?' he asked Cocks Murphy, Rashers' friend, who had emerged from the group of mourners as the master of ceremonies.

'They're waiting for some cousins from Ballinascarty,' he explained.

'And when will they be here?' asked Father O'Flynn.

'In about half-an-hour,' said Cocks.

'Get the funeral moving at once,' the priest ordered. 'The Ballinascarty people can follow us out.'

Assuming a confidential tone, Cocks posed a problem for the priest. 'In order not to delay you, Father O'Flynn, will we walk it out to Meany's first and then jog it from there to the graveyard, or should we jog it to Meany's first and then walk the rest of the way?'

The priest saw at once that the nub of the problem was Meany's, a public-house at Waterloo, half way to Garrycloyne.

'Walk it out to Meany's in this weather?' exclaimed the priest. 'Do you want them all to catch pneumonia? Get them into the cabs at once and jog it out the whole way, or we'll be burying Rashers by moonlight.'

Cocks went over to the mourners by the railings and ordered them into the cabs. 'The priest said to hurry or ye'll all catch ammonia standing there in the rain.'

In they piled, the grannies and the women in their shawls, some old friends of Rashers: beagle boys, weight-lifters, a few sparring partners, the cock-fighters and a few old comrades of the Munster Fusiliers. Satisfied that all were safely stowed, Father O'Flynn gave a final warning to Cocks and the cab drivers: 'No stopping at Meany's!' Then he got into his car and drove ahead to the cemetery.

The bell tolled mournfully. The funeral rolled slowly through the streets of Blackpool and out the Commons Road towards Blarney. Bystanders on the footpath stopped, removed their hats, bowed their heads and walked the three conventional steps with the hearse. The children waved out of the windows of the cabs to their less fortunate friends in the street. They always enjoyed a funeral, particularly when there was a long drive out to Garrycloyne or White Church. A slanting shower of sleet shut up the windows of the cabs. Inside, the mourners shivered with the cold.

After some time the procession halted. Heads looked out of the cabs.

'We're at Meany's,' someone said.

'What's wrong?' asked Cocks of the driver.

'One of the horses has a stone in his shoe. He's lame. He will have to have it taken out at the forge.'

There was a forge near Meany's pub. The lame horse was untackled from the hearse. The children got out to look at this interesting operation; the mothers got out to fetch the children, and the men got out to stamp their feet and stretch their legs. In Meany's window there was a warm, welcoming glow. In two minutes the party of shivering mourners were within, warming themselves at the big log fire.

In the meantime, Father O'Flynn had arrived at the cemetery. Muffling himself up against the weather, he slowly pushed open the heavy iron gate. He walked about in the pathless graveyard overgrown with long lush grass and nettles, looking for the grave-diggers. After a while he spotted them sheltering by an ivy-clad wall.

'Bad day, men,' greeted the priest.

'Shocking, Father.' The two grave-diggers in union lifted their caps.

'Where's the grave?' asked the priest.

'I'm afraid, Father,' the first grave-digger said, 'that there's no grave at the moment. We're waiting for the relatives to show us the place.'

'Don't tell me you haven't dug the grave yet?' said the priest, annoyed at this unforeseen crux.

'We can't dig a grave until we know which grave to dig,' explained the first grave-digger, filling his pipe.

'Rashers is to be buried with his father, Danny,' insisted the priest.

'We know that, Father,' chimed in the second grave-digger. 'But where is Danny's grave?'

The priest looked helplessly over the profusion of old headstones and crosses and the many unmarked graves.

The second grave-digger, seasoned in such matters, explained to the priest: 'There would be holy war, Father O'Flynn, if we redden the wrong grave. We can't turn a sod until we get a plan or something.'

Father O'Flynn looked at his watch. It was four o'clock. He walked to the gate and looked down the rain-swept road. Not a sign of the funeral. 'Meany's!' he muttered, starting up his car and heading back for Waterloo.

He pulled up twenty yards from the pub, and through the windscreen viewed the dismal scene. The hearse stood outside the forge, only one horse between the shafts; the six driverless cabs straggled along both sides of the road as the horses cropped the grass; the light was fading; it was raining steadily, and from Meany's came the sound of voices singing.

He got out of the car and walked towards the pub. The singing stopped as he arrived at the door. Cocks was addressing the mourners.

'In order not to show disrespect to the corpse, let there be no cheering or shouting.'

The priest heard a murmuring, a shuffling of feet and a

clinking of glasses. Then someone said: 'Bina, girl, give us a bar of an old song!'

Bina obliged with *The Bride of Liscarroll*, a mournful ballad about a bridal couple who met with misfortune on their way to the church. A storm of thunder and lightning broke upon them, killing the bridegroom and blinding the bride.

Father O'Flynn, concealed in the porch, listened. He recognised the singer; it was Bina Buckley, a well-known character from Water Lane, with a supply of ballads, grave and gay, for all occasions.

> *She's the pride of Liscarroll,*
> *Sweet Katie O'Farrell;*
> *Cheeks like the roses*
> *And teeth as white as pearls.*
> *The neighbours all pity*
> *For Katie's so pretty*
> *O how they all loved the blind Irish girl!*

Bina's voice was sweet—'the sweetest voice in all Blackpool'—but she lacked technique. She scooped up at the high notes, glided down to the low notes, and flattened on one or two of the twirls. She took obvious delight in birling the 'rl' sounds in 'Liscarroll', 'Farrell' and 'pearls'. She ran out of breath after 'o' and had to inhale deeply before finishing the line. Taking a drink from her glass, she continued:

> *What a sad and awful ending*
> *Just when everything seemed bright,*
> *She to lose her future husband!*
> *And then again to lose her sight!*

Although fascinated by Bina's singing of the ballad, the priest now noted the large yellow dial of the clock inside Meany's. It was half-past four. Unless things moved very fast indeed, he would be late for the Bishop's dinner.

A bell clanged above the priest's head as he pushed the door open.

'Cripes—'tis the priest!' said Cocks.

The singer broke off her song; men drinking at the bar looked up amazed; women at a table tried to hide their glasses under the benches. Father O'Flynn noticed that Rashers' relatives were in the large room with the crowd, while his widow, Lizzie, sat apart in the snug, with her brothers and daughter.

Standing in the middle of the floor, he addressed the crowd.

'I thought I said no stopping at Meany's?'

'Ah, don't be too hard on 'em, Father O'Flynn,' said Cocks, detaching himself unsteadily from the group at the counter. 'After all 'tis St. Patrick's Day and poor Rashers . . . and all . . . and I was just saying to them here—"No stopping at Meany's!" '

The priest saw that Cocks was under the weather, but allowed him to continue.

'We really didn't stop at all, Father . . . it was the horses—a shoe in one of the horses—I mean a stone in one of—'

'That will do, Cocks,' cut in the priest, and turning to the embarrassed crowd he said: 'You have one minute to finish your drinks and get out to the cabs.'

Seeing Bina Buckley he said: 'Bina, you went flat half-way through your song.'

'Why wouldn't I, Father, after drinking a pint of ould Meany's flat porter,' she said holding up an empty glass.

The priest strode out of the pub, and Cocks stumbled after.

Thick pint glasses were hastily tilted high on lips that drained the last drops; lemonade bottles were siphoned dry by the children, who then ran out to be first into the cabs; the women, shrouded in their long black shawls, filed out with heads bowed and in silence. The men followed sheepishly. As there was disorder among the cabs there was confusion among the mourners. They had forgotten who was to go into which cab.

The priest tried hard not to lose his patience.

'For heaven's sake, will ye get in somewhere or 'twill be dark before we know where we are!' He pushed some fumbling laggards into the cabs and shut the doors. As the last of the mourners emerged from the pub, a side-car careered along the road towards Waterloo. Seeing the funeral, the driver reined his steaming horse, and three men in oil-skins jumped down. They were Rashers' cousins from Ballinascarty. The people in the cabs got out to welcome them. Lizzie remained inside. There was talk of going in for a drink.

'Hurry up there,' said Father O'Flynn, 'or the grave-diggers will be gone home to their tea.'

They all got into the cabs again.

'Hop it up there now to Garrycloyne,' he said to the driver of the hearse, and got into his car.

Off they trotted at a smart pace. The priest brought up the rear.

At the cemetery the children tumbled out of the cabs and raced joyfully through the gates. The mourners gathered behind the hearse. A dispute arose over who should carry the coffin to the grave. Cocks arbitrated and gave judgement in favour of the four old Munster Fusiliers. They straightened themselves up as best they could, shouldered the coffin and proceeded unsteadily towards the gate. The mourners followed, headed by Cocks and Father O'Flynn.

'Where's the grave?' asked one of the men under the coffin when they came up to the grave-diggers.

'We're waiting for someone to tell us,' was the reply.

The coffin was lowered on to the ground. Cocks consulted with the grave-diggers. Then he turned to the mourners and said:

'Do any of ye know where Danny's grave is?'

Several felt sure they knew the spot.

'Then in God's name find it,' said Father O'Flynn.

At that, the mourners split up into groups and set out in different directions to find Danny's grave. But what with the long wet grass, the crops of nettles and the steady grey drizzle it proved a very unpleasant and difficult task.

'Have ye no bit of a map or plan?' asked one of the grave-diggers.

'We have,' said Cocks, the master of ceremonies.

'Well—show it to me.'

"Tis with the solicitors in Cork,' he informed them.

'Father O'Flynn,' said the grave-digger, 'that crowd are all on their ear. They won't find the grave in a week.'

Time was running out, and it was getting dark. Calling the chief mourners about him, the priest addressed them.

'Look here, if you can't find the grave in five minutes, I'll have to say the prayers and go home. You can leave the coffin under a tree till tomorrow.'

'Father O'Flynn,' whispered Cocks, 'you can't go away now after promising poor Rashers to see him down into the grave.'

The cousins from Ballinascarty blamed the grave-diggers for all the delay and now they tackled them vigorously.

The priest had to come between them to keep the peace.

Rashers' sister Jule and Bina Buckley were crawling on hands and knees over some graves nearby. Their shawls were trailing behind them and their long hair was streeling on the ground. They were looking for something Jule had placed on Danny's grave when he was buried there. Father O'Flynn was watching them with great interest. They were moaning and crying and the worse for drink. A few women went to lift them up.

'Let them alone—don't disturb them,' warned the priest. 'They're being driven by some kind of instinct to crawl over the ground like that. If Danny's grave is to be found at all, I bet you they'll find it.'

'Seeing 'tis getting so dark,' suggested Lizzie's brother Ducker, 'couldn't they dig a new grave?'

'Look here, boy,' said the priest, still keeping his eye on Jule and Bina, 'if they put Rashers down in a new grave and cover him with gold dust, up he'll rise again, and up he'll stay until they put him down with Danny.'

Suddenly Jule rent the air with a hysterical cry.

'I have it! I have it. Danny's here!'

The scattered knots of mourners hurried over to Jule, who was kneeling on the ground, and holding up, for all to see, a small weather-worn statue of St. Anthony.

'There's the crockery statue that I planted on Danny's grave —Danny's here!' she cried triumphantly.

Then, falling flat on the grave, she knocked on the ground with the statue.

'Danny boy!' she shouted. 'Are you there, Danny boy? Move over! Poor Rashers is coming.'

Father O'Flynn, having abandoned all hope of getting back in time for the Bishop's dinner, was fascinated.

'Dig there!' he ordered.

The grave-diggers threw off their overcoats and set to work with pick and shovel. Jule and Mollie were cared for by a group of women. While Rashers' relatives stood crying in a little knot at the head of the grave, Lizzie, his widow, stood silent and dry-eyed with her daughter and two brothers at its foot.

The coffin zigzagged its way towards the grave on the shoulders of the four Munster Fusiliers. Rashers was laid in the earth. Ducker Doyle held an umbrella over Father O'Flynn as he read the prayers from the ritual: '*Ego sum resurrection et vita . . .*'

Before he finished he nodded to Lizzie to conclude the

liturgy. Taking his cue, she stooped down and picked up a handful of earth. She paused for a moment, looking into the open grave. The priest noted the peculiar look on her face. A faint smile was flickering there, like the first weak rays of sunshine after a long, dark storm. The emotional conflict within was nearing its resolution. She cast the clay on the coffin. The priest prayed: '*Requiescat in pace*', half expecting the widow to respond, not '*Amen*', but '*Deo gratias*'.

Back at the presbytery, the Bishop's dinner had got off to a bad start. Whether it was the weather, or his meeting with the Lord Mayor and Corporation earlier in the day, the Bishop was not in festive form.

The Canon, who was a nephew of the Bishop's, had noted this during the morning's ceremony. He was extra careful in arranging the seating at dinner. His Lordship would, of course, sit at the centre of the long table facing the fire; on his right, the Canon himself, on his left the senior curate, who unfortunately was a man of few words. He decided to place Father O'Flynn directly opposite the Bishop; for he had no fear of Bishops, and an easy flow of conversation, and a ready supply of stories and jokes suitable for episcopal ears. The Canon was relying on Father O'Flynn to keep things going at the dinner.

'Be sure to be back in time from Garrycloyne, Chris,' he had said that morning to Father O'Flynn, for good timing helped greatly on these occasions.

The Bishop and his secretary arrived promptly at five minutes to six. One look at that solemn face confirmed the Canon's worst fears. To crown it all, there was no sign of Christy.

'Isn't it very bad weather, my lord,' chirped the Canon, taking the Bishop's coat and hat.

"Tis God's weather, Canon,' croaked the Bishop, closing

that topic of conversation for the rest of the evening. The Bishop was crusty—and he was going to remain crusty.

The Angelus rang at six o'clock. Being St. Patrick's Day, the Canon thought it fitting to say the Angelus in Irish; but through an unfortunate lapse of memory he dried up half way through. To his confusion, one of the more fluent Irish speakers among his curates chipped in and finished the prayer. The Bishop passed no remark, but proceeded to say grace—in Latin. All sat down at their appointed places. The Bishop was silent, so was the senior curate. It was up to the Canon. He ventured a safe remark.

'They say 'tis a great day for the Irish in New York today, my lord.'

'Do they?' said the Bishop.

'They do,' said the Canon, and the dialogue fizzled out.

The rest of the curates were concentrating hard on the pattern of the tablecloth, and taking their soup.

Noticing the vacant chair, the Bishop asked: 'Where's Chris?'

Glad of the opening, the Canon was about to launch into a lengthy explanation of Father O'Flynn's absence, when the door opened and in he walked.

All heads turned, and the sense of relief was palpable. Over to the Bishop Christy went, and kissed the episcopal ring.

'I'm very sorry, my lord, for being late. I was delayed beyond all expectation at a funeral in Garrycloyne.'

'Garrycloyne?' queried the Bishop. 'That's a long way out for a funeral on a day like this.'

''Twas not the length of the journey at all, my lord, that caused the delay, but what happened on the way and in the cemetery.'

The Bishop was showing interest, and the company followed suit; and in a moment Father O'Flynn was re-enacting the whole macabre incident, beginning with a most accurate impersonation of Bina Buckley singing *The Bride of Liscarroll.*

'You have that perfect, Chris,' chuckled the Bishop, leading the table in a gentle applause. 'But did you stand in the doorway listening to that song?' the Bishop asked.

'I did, my lord, because what really interested me was hearing the soul of that poor old sentimental creature pouring itself out in sympathy for "poor Katie Farrell", and at the same time giving a kind of consolation to the mourners in the pub. Of course sentimentality is a false thing if you like—the mere lipstick of true human emotion—but for lack of proper education these poor people know no other way of expressing themselves.'

Then Father O'Flynn acted the graveyard scene, and was so carried away with his own enthusiasm that he got up from the table, knelt on the floor, and imitated Jule knocking on Danny's grave with the statue of St. Anthony. And before he realised what he was saying, he had said it:

'Are ye there, Danny boy? Move over—poor Rashers is coming!'

The Canon suffered a momentary horror; the curates held their breath. How would His Lordship, Daniel of Cork, react to this?

'You should be on the stage, Chris,' was all the Bishop said, with a smile; and he neatly summed up the performance with a phrase from the *Dies Irae: 'Mors stupebit,* Chris.'

'*Et natura,* my lord,' Father O'Flynn replied, while all the table laughed in relief.

'It didn't turn out too bad after all. You saved the day, Chris,' commented the Canon later, having seen the Bishop off at the door.

Then he invited the curates up to his room for a night-cap. They heard him humming contentedly as he mounted the stairs before them.

'*O Danny Boy. . . .*'

15

Fair daffodils

IT was the weekly half-holiday at Saint Finbarr's seminary and the three senior classes were corralled in the library. The April sunshine poured in through the two large windows, on whose deep timbered ledges a few insensitive youths rasped their combs at a quick game of push-penny. The cheerful chatter might lead one to surmise that the day's work was done. In a sense it was; at least the serious work, for there was but one class to go before lunch, elocution.

Father O'Flynn's elocution class, like Herr Fleischmann's singing class, was reckoned by the students among life's least worries. For one thing, those sister arts were liberally pursued. There were no examinations, no marks. But the exam-ridden, mark-conscious student, when faced with an examless subject, invariably argues with himself: 'That which carries no marks, carries no weight. But elocution carries no marks, Ergo.' Even Socrates is silenced. To the hesitating, unsure adolescent one thing was certain, in the Leaving Certificate examination high marks meant distinction, low marks extinction, academically speaking. Being a written examination, it was the accurate pens which scored the high marks and got the first places.

It followed, therefore, as the night the day, that speaking the speech trippingly on the tongue or chanting the Plain Chant tunefully were the merest trifles compared with dexterity in the Greek irregular verbs and the use of '*ut*' with the subjunctive, as laid down in Rule 90 of Longman's Latin Grammar. Equipped with these skills, a boy could pick up a cool 400 marks—440, through the medium of Irish! When placed beside the two giants, Maths and Irish, each carrying 600 marks, poor elocution was seen in all its futility.

The significance of these facts and figures was not lost on those long-headed Cork boys. They saw that, in theory at least, full marks could be obtained in all subjects in the Leaving Certificate by a dumb candidate. What price, therefore, elocution? Why waste time perfecting one's utterance with such nonsense as 'Thirty-three thousand and thirty-three thoughtless thieves thinned three acres of thistles before tea', or that other exercise for developing resonance: 'om-m-m, om-m-m, om-m-m, *mná na hÉireann*.' A boy would be better employed stuffing his brains with mark-winning jingles such as 'Males, mountains, months, the winds, the streams and people masculine we deem', and the still more valuable mathematical formulae. These were the facts, and these the attitudes they evoked. No wonder, then, that the art of fine speech and the cultivation of refined feeling had 'fallen into abatement and low price'. In curt, unfeeling, schoolboy fashion, the teacher was rated with his subject: 'Flynnie's mad.'

That is not to say, however, that the elocution class had not its uses. It had. Just now the captain of a hurling team, aided by his henchmen, was forcefully ejecting a couple of day-pupils from a back desk. There, effectively screened by a bench of broad shoulders who were quietly but firmly warned to 'keep sitting up straight', these team builders built their team for the after-lunch hurling match, discussed *sotto voce* the strategy of the game, and tried to resolve the crisis created by Sullivan's inability to play. Small use had these match-minded men for 'thoughtless thieves thinning thistles', or for *mná na hÉireann*, if it comes to that.

Just then a big Dodge car nosed through the college gates, accelerated up the tree-lined avenue, splaying the gravel, and crunched to a halt before the library windows. The push-penny lads gave 'Nix!', slid off the window, and scurried to the back desks. Repulsed by hostile occupants, they dived for the few empty seats at the top of the class.

The bell-man pulled on the bell and deafened all ears with his ringing; the prefect held the class-room door open; the class stood in silence; a heavy footfall in the corridor; and enter Flynnie, head high, unbonneted, barrel-chested, lustre-coated, and in his hand a golden daffodil. To the top of the room he sweept like Brutus entering the Senate. Head bowed before the crucifix he prayed: '*Go mbeannaithe duit a Mhuire . . .*' The Gaelic rolled musically from his lips. 'Amen' responded the multitude in Hebrew and squashed itself three in a desk. 'The daffodil?—the daffodil?' a few of them cried. 'We'll come to the daffodil later,' Flynnie promised and he placed the flower in the window ledge.

'We'll begin with an exercise in voice production,' he said. This was the cue for 'om-om-om, *mná-na-hÉireann.*'

'The first thing is to fill the lungs with air like this.'

He began to demonstrate. Standing at ease, he let his head fall slightly forward and began to inhale deeply and slowly through the nose. He filled all the back of his lungs with air, and the lower part of his great barrel chest ballooned until it seemed his lustre coat would rip asunder. Lifting his head, he siphoned in the last few cubic centimetres of air. Then, holding his breath for a moment, he lit a match and held the flame before his mouth. Then he began:

'Om-om-om,' on a deep soft note, 'now-I-can-say-what-I-like'; up a tone: 'Om-om-om, *mná-na-hÉireann.*' Up another tone: 'om-om-om . . .' And up along the scale he climbed, powerfully omning his way, opening and closing his mouth on the O sound, and never a flicker out of the match; all the cavities in his head and face resonating with a rich volume of continuous sound sufficient to fill a cathedral.

He dropped the match on the ground as it burned his

fingers. The class applauded him roundly. When it came to *vox*, Flynnie had what it takes.

Then he asked: 'Who's the strongest boy in the class?'

A youth called Batt the Bull had won that unique distinction for himself. Batt was the Hercules of his generation, and he knew it. He took special pride in his biceps. Their like had not been seen in the school in living memory: solid as rocks of granite. Batt had in his desk a book of body-building techniques with a picture on the cover of Charles Atlas, clad in a tiger skin and flexing his muscles. The legend underneath said: 'You too can have a body like mine.' Batt was in the Charles Atlas class. All he lacked was the tiger skin.

He ambled to the top of the class with a slight nautical roll, quietly confident of his great strength.

'Place your fist there,' said Flynnie, standing with his back to the bookcase and indicating a spot at the top of his own abdomen, 'and when I tell you, press in with all your strength.' The boys at the back of the class stood up in their desks to get a clear view of this trial of strength.

Flynnie inhaled and gave the word. Batt pressed for all he was worth, putting the whole weight of his powerful body behind the fist. He made no indentation. Flynnie took another short breath, worked the muscles of his abdomen, and out shot Batt's fist. There was a mighty cheer. Batt the Bull had met his match in muscles. He rolled back to his place, blushing scarlet.

Flynnie calmed the class and spoke of the muscles of the diaphragm, their function in deep breathing and their importance in voice production.

'Now we'll try it together,' he invited.

The whole class—about sixty boys—began with Flynnie the long, deep breath. When they had filled their lungs to the brim he ordered: 'Now hold it for a few seconds.'

It was a hard thing to do. One of the boys exploded like a

bursting tyre. The class followed suit and exploded in laughter, the hearty ringing laughter of boys. Flynnie laughed too.

But suddenly all laughing ceased. The dean's familiar profile was silhouetted on the frosted glass panel of the door. Like rabbits panic-stricken by a ferret, the boys froze in the desks. The shadow passed on. The boys relaxed.

Flynnie was on their side. 'Alleluia is laughter,' he said, 'and we find it all over the liturgy.' Then he gave a few laughing alleluias, sang a verse of the Easter hymn: '*Resurrexit sicut dixit— alleluia,*' and added peals of triumphant laughing 'alleluias'. It was an amazing performance.

He continued: 'The Church wastes nothing. She gathers up all the good fragments of our poor human nature, even our smiles and our laughter, then consecrates all to God. If that is not a smile in the second prayer after the Consecration in the Mass, what is? *Supra quae propitio ac sereno vultu respicere digneris* (which he translated: 'Please loose upon these offerings a friendly smile'). 'And in heaven itself I am sure we shall make the rafters ring with the great "alleluias" of our laughter. Those who don't like it,' he went on, casting a roguish eye at the door, 'can stop outside the gates. But to come back to earth. A good hearty laugh is a tonic for the voice. It exercises the muscles of the soft palate'—he opened wide his mouth and showed his soft palate—'and gives mobility to the countenance. Usually, we're much more attractive when we smile. Of course, different people laugh differently.'

He then gave in rapid succession, vignettes of about six different types of laugh. He began with the smile, followed it with a shy laugh, then a suppressed laugh, which all recognised as 'laughing at prayers'; then an old man's cackling laugh, a young girl's giggle, the refined, cultivated, drawing-room laugh; and finally, the uninhibited 'whole-man' laughter of a Jack Falstaff in the Boar's Head tavern, complete with tears rolling down his cheeks.

It was a virtuoso performance. The boys clapped lustily and, like Oliver Twist, 'they wished there was more'. Then he taught them a prayer: 'May God give us all good humour.'

Flynnie began on a new line. 'When people are happy, they express themselves in laughter. What do they do when tired?'

'They go to sleep, Father,' answered someone.

'That's not the answer I'm looking for,' said Flynnie. 'Well? Ah, there it is—that boy down there is doing it—yawning. Come up here so that we can learn something from that fine yawn you have!'

Sheepishly, a tall gangling youth stalked to the top of the class. He had long thin hands, and just now was at his wits' end to know what to do with them. Put them behind his back? No. In his pockets? No. Fold them in front of him? No. He rested one on the bookcase and dangled the other at his side. In heartless schoolboy fashion his class-mates enjoyed his embarrassment.

But Flynnie, always kind on these occasions, walked over to the boy, took him by the hand, and said: 'What's your name?'

'Driscoll from Bantry parish,' replied the youth; and from that moment he was known as 'Bantry Parish'.

'Why, man,' said Flynnie, 'you have the blood of kings and poets in you.' Then, silencing the titter from the class, he continued, all absorbed in the pupil standing before him: 'Don't mind them at all. Their turn will come soon. Hold on to the back of that chair now.'

Driscoll grasped the chair like a drowning man clutching at a straw. Flynnie addressed the class again.

'Nature gives us the yawn, and it serves a very useful function. Even better than laughing, yawning develops the muscles of the soft palate. These muscles need developing, otherwise we shall have trouble with our speech. Culture of yawns and laughter is therefore necessary.'

This statement was vigorously applauded by the class.

'Watch now,' continued Flynnie serenely, 'and I'll show you how to yawn.'

The class was all attention. He assumed a yawning posture, bending and stretching his arms, standing on his toes, opening his mouth and heaving a succession of breaths until he succeeded in inducing the yawn *par excellence*—the very prototype of all yawns. Having reached the climax he slowly relaxed, unbending himself, and meanwhile explaining how the whole body and all its muscles are now relaxed and in perfect poise. He then turned to Driscoll and put him through the yawning sequence.

'Come on now, Driscoll—show the world what Bantry can do!' The youth attempted the yawn. He went through the actions of stretching his limbs, closed his eyes and opened wide his mouth. Flynnie, spotting something inside, gave it as his opinion, after feeling the boy's throat with his fingers, that there was need for tonsillectomy.

Flynnie concluded with this advice to the class: 'When you are very tired—completely exhausted—do that yawn as I have shown you and then lie down flat on your back on the floor. Remain there for ten minutes while the frame of your body settles itself and relaxes. This gives perfect poise, and you will be a new man when you get up.'

Flynnie paused. The boys adjusted themselves in the crowded desks, and waited in silence.

A sad smile suffused Flynnie's face; tears brimmed in his eyes. He began:—

> *Fair daffodils, we weep to see*
> *You haste away so soon:*
> *As yet the early rising sun*
> *Has not attained his noon.*
> *Stay, stay,*

Until the hasting day
    Has run
But to the even-song;
And having prayed together, we
    Will go with you along.

The boys were fascinated. They hung on every syllable. The sincerity of the man; the wistful quality of his tones on 'Fair daffodils'; the significant pause before 'we weep'; the gentle coaxing of 'Stay, stay', and in the last two lines the natural simplicity of a child talking to children charmed them.

He continued with the second verse now quietly reflective, pausing slightly after each statement as if waiting for the flowers to nod assent:

We have short time to stay, as you,
    We have as short a Spring;
As quick a growth to meet decay
    As you, or any thing.
      We die
As your hours do, and dry
      Away,
Like to the Summer's rain;
Or as the pearls of morning's dew,
    Ne'er to be found again.

When he finished, there was a warm applause. This was the real Flynnie; Flynnie at his best. Not when he was explaining, but when he was doing.

'That's a lovely little poem,' he said, 'and we should be grateful to Herrick for it. But where did he get it? He was inspired by a reality—his own personal vital contact with—the daffodils.

'Man needs nature—not only as food to nourish his body, but also as food to nourish his mind. The proper food of the mind is truth. The mind gets truth by coming into vital contact with real things—natural forms. No vital contact—

no truth—no inspiration—no creative activity. Look at this daffodil.'

He held it up for their inspection. Rippling with subdued laughter, the class strained forward with an exaggerated attention.

'See the structure of it,' he continued, indicating gracefully the parts of the flower. 'A bulb-like root, a long, slender stalk tapering to the bloom; that little knot you see there is where the plant synopsises itself; and then the star-like petals and the deep golden cup. Look at the rhythmic line of it, the symmetries and harmonies of this piece of green and golden reality. Straight from the mind of God who designed it, straight from the hand of God who made it.' Then, in a sarcastic tone: 'Nouns and verbs, how are you! See the reality!'

He noticed an unresponsive trio near the back of the class; it was the team builders. Sensing his eye upon them, they at once switched on a look of sweet, sad innocence. They, too, could act when the occasion arose.

Flynnie went on: '*Consider the lilies of the field, how they grow!* Our Divine Lord, *moladh le na ainm naofa,* asks us—commands us. What mood is "consider", boy?'

'Imperative mood, Father,' answered the boy in the front desk.

'You'll go far,' said the priest;'—then commands us to learn a lesson from the way things grow.'

Being mostly from the country the boys were all with Flynnie here. This was down-to-earth talk.

He continued: 'Now that spring is here, there is intense activity just below the surface of the earth. Everywhere the vegetable world is stirring with new life, germinating and pushing up little green shoots of wheat and oats, new grass, and a whole new generation of flowers. Prodigious labour, this growing of things! Do we hear any noise? Any shouting of orders? Banging and clanging of machinery? Hooting of factory sirens? Not a sound. It is a world of silence. But if nature is silent, she is not dumb. She speaks her message to us without words, in natural forms. Take this daffodil.' Again he held it up, and many now seemed interested. 'What does the daffodil say?'

He paused. The boys were at a loss, so he continued: 'It makes two statements. It says: "I am, and he is"—that is to say, God is. Of course every item of creation says the same thing—but each thing says it in its own way. The heavens declare the glory of God and the firmament proclaims his handiwork. How beautifully the daffodil says it!'

The class was intrigued, though a little confused by this 'talking' daffodil.

'Having said that,' said Flynnie, 'and that is saying a great deal indeed, it says more. Did not our Divine Lord say: "Consider the lilies of the field, *how* they grow." All things grow without stress or strain, worry or care. Each flower is happy to be what God made it. The daffodil does not fret because it is not red like the rose; the rose does not worry because it is not smooth and white like the lily; the shy violet does not envy the sunflower its height and glory. Do you find here any nervous disorders—emotional fatigue, hypertension, neuroses or complexes? Not a sign of them. This is a world without competition, without vanity, without envy, where each plant and flower is happy to be what it is and peacefully pursues its perfection along the lines laid down for it—from root to shoot, to blossom, bloom and fruit.

'Have we learnt that lesson? Not a bit of it. The world we have made for ourselves, a society of concrete, steel and glass, is a world where the chemist makes a fortune selling remedies for our disorders: tranquillisers, barbiturates and sedatives of all kinds—dope to deaden our pains. The daffodil has something to say—it is saying it everywhere this spring; it has been saying it every spring from the beginning, but nobody listens and nobody learns. Why don't we learn the lesson? Because we are sadly lacking in metaphysics.'

That word was new to the class; the thing it signified unknown. With that word they seemed to turn abruptly off an interesting road and enter on uncharted country.

'What's metaphysics?' asked a red-headed youth from Goleen of his immediate neighbour.

'How do I know? Ask Macker.'

Macker was the oracle of the class, a scholarship man who got full marks in Latin and Greek in the Intermediate, and was now bidding fair to get first place in Ireland in the Leaving Certificate. For all his brains, he was patient with duller spirits, and always willing to enlighten in a kindly way. Quizzed now on metaphysics, he cupped his hand before his mouth and whispered to the red-head:

'Meta means "after" or "above", and physics means "nature".' He paused: he thought, and again he spoke: 'It's something "after" or "beyond" nature. It may have something to do with God.'

The red-head nodded 'message received'; but his face expressed incomprehension. 'It might be chemistry,' he told his neighbour, 'for chemistry usually goes with physics.' They were definitely off the main road now, and heading for the bog.

'Our ancestors,' went on Flynnie, 'had a fine metaphysical quality of mind. Even the daisy growing in the field stimulated thought in them. They were able to get at the essential, the eternal thing the daisy had; and then, constructing a ladder of essences, they climbed the Everest heights of the intellectual world, and did not stop till they got at the prototype in the mind of God.'

This was the middle of the bog; the class was up to its ears in a metaphysical morass.

'The backs are all right if we can trust Goggin in goal,' whispered the chief team-builder to his colleagues. 'But what about the half-forward line? Sullivan being in the infirmary, who can we put on the "forty"?' The problem was acute and demanded a solution before lunch.

'You could try Padsna there,' came a timorous suggestion.

'That *amadán,* he doesn't know which end of the hurley to hold. No. . . .'

Flynnie was now lamenting to a class that had lost all vital contact with its teachers, its ancestors and metaphysics. Heads nodded, shoulders drooped, the boys drowsed in the comforting rays of the sun.

'We sadly lack metaphysics. We are unable to get beyond the daffodil. We stick it in a vase and say "how lovely"! And that's the end.' He put the daffodil on the desk.

'Take Ruskin,' he said, picking up *Sesame and Lilies,* which was on the English Course that year. 'Poor old Ruskin,' he continued as he searched for the passage he required. 'I could weep for him. He had so much of the truth, and yet he died without hope. Imagine Ruskin dying without hope! Why? Because he lacked metaphysics.'

This shortage of metaphysics was becoming acute. It would appear now that the British Isles were affected. Ireland was not alone in her need.

'Here it is—page 49.' The boys rummaged for the book in their desks; this was bread-and-butter stuff, prescribed examination text.

Flynnie read: '*Having then faithfully listened to the great teachers, that you may enter into their thoughts, you have yet this higher advance to make; you have to enter into their hearts. As you go to them first for clear sight, so you must stay with them that you may share at last their just and mighty passion. Passion or sensation. I am not afraid of the words; still less of the thing.*'

'Do you think we might get that bit in the examination, Father?' interrupted a keen matric man in the front desk. The class pricked up its ears at the prospect of a tip for the exam, but it relapsed at once into a semi-comatose state when Flynnie answered:

'Not the slightest chance. Ruskin is dealing here with the need for culture of the emotions—education of the heart—and that is unknown in Irish education today. Search the syllabus from top to bottom and you won't find the word emotion. Nor is the reality known to the Department officials. Education today in Ireland is reduced to sharpening the intellect so that we get mere mind functioning; there is little understanding and no wisdom. Your poor memories are over-burdened and exhausted trying to cram them with a heap of irrelevant facts, figures and formulae.'

It seemed that Flynnie had a point here, for some were nodding assent.

'But as for establishing any vital contact between the mind and God's creation that comes of the study of individual real things—a horse, a tree, or natural forms like the specific human emotions, or this daffodil here—not on your life.'

'What have daffodils to do with the Department of Education?' muttered Big Tim from Skibbereen. 'I thought the Department of Agriculture looked after them.'

'To get back to Ruskin. What does he mean when he says: "*You have this higher advance to make, you have to enter into their hearts*"? He is talking, of course, about the masters of literature, Shakespeare especially. Take a play of Shakespeare's that you know: *Julius Caesar*. You might know all the lines off by heart, you might be able to parse and analyse every sentence and word in the play; you might be able to give the central idea—vile phrase—of each speech or scene, and understand the different political themes and the dramatic structure of the piece. When you have all that much, Ruskin says you only half know it. You have yet to learn to feel with the characters, Brutus, Cassius and the rest; to sympathise with their moods.

'And this you can only do by a cultivation of the specific human emotions. Yes, emotion—'tis not respectable to speak about it in our time. *"Passion or sensation. I am not afraid of the words; still less of the thing."* That is how Ruskin puts it, and he was dead right. But we are afraid of it, so we ignore it; we try to forget it. Result: the heart of the youth of the country is *"an unweeded garden, things rank and gross in nature possess it merely!"* Neglect culture of the emotions, and what have you? Vulgarity and depravity in private and in public life. Listen to Ruskin: *"The essence of all vulgarity lies in want of sensation! That is lack of sympathy, the inability to feel with and for one's fellowman. The emotion that moved the Good Samaritan to pour oil and wine into his neighbour's wounds. . . ."* '

Unlike Macker, Big Tim from Skibbereen was never much good at the verbs. Flynnie's concern about the contemporary shortage of metaphysics stirred no ripple in the calm waters of his spirit. A warm shaft of sunlight pouring down upon him as he lounged in the desk dissolved his powers of concentration. He slipped away gradually into that silent peaceful world of fair daffodils. Flynnie's voice faded in his ear. Tim slept. . . . The class was coming to an end. The bell-man went out to ring the Angelus.

Flynnie was demonstrating the correct pronunciation of 'th': 'You put the tip of the tongue at the back of the upper teeth: "thirty-three thousand thoughtless thieves thinning thistles . . ." '

Big Tim got a dig in the ribs and a voice in his ear said: 'Wake up, Tim—Flynnie's gone—And there's jam for lunch—Hurrah!'

16

'Mon General'

THE sun was warming the flagstones outside the presbytery with the first heat of the year. Except for a few children playing 'pickie' on the footpath beside the church, the street was almost deserted. A Dodge car parked at the kerb on the presbytery side shimmered in the sun. It was Father O'Flynn's car.

Up the steep incline of Roman Street a sturdy mare laboured between the shafts of a high, square bread-van, battering rhythmically on the tarred road with her iron shoes. A cap on his head, a pencil behind his ear, a large leather purse slung from his shoulder, Pat the van-man sat high on the driver's seat and urged the mare. On the side of the bread-van was painted a large silver cup surrounded with medals, and underneath the legend: 'PRIZE WINNING BREAD' in faded gold letters. At the back of the van a canvas bag half full of oats was swinging in time with the steps of the mare.

She stopped opposite the Presbytery gate, purely out of habit. Pat jumped down from his seat, went round to the back of the van, untied the nose-bag, returned to the mare's head, and fixed the bag over her nose. She bent her steaming neck until the bag rested on the ground, and then munched the hard black oats contentedly. An appetising aroma of fresh crusty bread floated from the back of the van when Pat opened the double doors, took out the large wicker basket, and filled it with loaves, pans, baskets and turnovers. He entered the gate leading up to the presbytery door. Father O'Flynn was coming out.

'Good day, Pat,' said the priest.

'Good day, Father O'Flynn,' replied Pat. And, not being in a hurry, he continued: 'That was an awful misfortune Stephen Callaghan met with.'

'I didn't hear of any misfortune—what happened?' asked the priest.

'He sent twenty birds up North, to Ballycastle in the County Antrim, and nineteen of them were lost in a storm over the Border on the way home yesterday.'

'That's a terrible blow to poor Stephen,' said the priest, quite dismayed. 'He was so proud of those pigeons. I'll call down right away and have a word with him.'

They parted. The priest set off for Quarry Lane where Stephen Callaghan lived. Quarry Lane was a large open space off Clarence Street, and it was backed by a high sandstone cliff that sprouted scraggy bushes from its moist and jagged surface.

In a small whitewashed yard behind his little cottage in Quarry Lane, Stephen had built his pigeon-loft. It consisted simply of a row of wooden soap boxes faced with wire mesh and fixed to the whitewashed walls. The yard was usually filled with a noisy clucking and cooing and flapping of wings.

Not so today; Stephen's back-yard was silent. The pigeon-loft was empty except for one exhausted bird that had succeeded in weathering the storm. It was practically feather-less, and nestled, half dazed, in the bottom of a box.

Stephen was lamenting his loss to his friend Connie Cremin when Father O'Flynn was shown out to the back-yard by Nonie, Stephen's wife. The priest was silent for a moment, noting sadly the empty cages. Shaking his head and heaving a sigh, he walked over to Stephen and Connie and clasped their hands in sympathy.

'My poor man, I'm very sorry to hear about the birds. A terrible loss; a cruel blow,' sympathised Father O'Flynn.

'Desolation, Father O'Flynn—desolation. That's the only word for it,' replied Stephen, and Connie nodded assent.

'God help us, 'tis a terrible trouble to you after all the rearing and feeding and training you put into those birds,' said the priest.

'Desolation,' said Stephen, loading his favourite word with a high quantum of grief. Connie again nodded.

'What happened at all?' asked the priest.

'They were all lost in a storm of wind and rain that blew up over the border. They were coming home from Ballycastle in Antrim. There's the only one of them that came home, Father O'Flynn.' He pointed to a cage on the wall.

The priest walked over to inspect the lucky bird. To his eyes it was a shabby, mean-looking thing with hardly a feather left.

'She's a marvellous bird, Father O'Flynn, she came all the way from Ballycastle, through storm and all, and arrived safely in her cage.' Just then a plump pigeon of beautiful plumage flew into the yard and alighted on one of the boxes. Innocent of the ways of pigeons the priest said: 'If this little bird could come home from Ballycastle surely that fine-looking bird there could fly from Glasgow?'

'Glasgow?' Stephen broke into a smile. 'She's only for breeding, Father. That one wouldn't do Rathduff.'

Connie said:

'Father O'Flynn, I was up in Trimbat's Lane sympathising with the lads, and 'tis like a wake up there. They're all mourning, too, over the birds they lost.' Connie worked in the railway, and it was he who had consigned the six baskets of pigeons on their fatal journey to Ballycastle. He felt himself deeply involved in the present calamity.

Father O'Flynn was pleased to note that between the bird-men in Trimbat's Lane and those of Quarry Lane the old rivalry and jealousy had been buried in a common grief and mutual sympathy.

'One touch of sorrow makes the whole world kin,' he

mused. 'Tell me, Connie—do you get much pleasure out of the birds?'

'Well, Father O'Flynn,' said Connie, opening up on his favourite topic, 'when you'd be waiting for your little bird to come home from a long flight, you'd be up there in Griffin's field on top of Grawn early in the morning looking up at the scuds—up on your toes full of excitement, watching out for the birds. You wouldn't take your eyes off the scuds and look down for a hundred pounds. Suddenly you'd get a terrible start when some fellow shouted: "Look at 'em! look at them over there!" and he pointing to the north.

'And there they are, all together up in the sky. Then you'd see the whole flock stopping up and wheeling round—that's when the birds spotted home. Then they'd be saying to one another: "Look! that's our own Shandon—there's the barracks over on the other hill—and there's the North Chapel!"

'Then, Father, you'd go down off the hill, full of excitement, to the cage in your yard and wait for your birds. You'd see them circling over the houses, and then down into the cage they'd drop. You'd welcome them home, full of joy, like a long-lost pal, and feed them. While the birds are feeding you'd have your pipe in your mouth and you'd stand there listening to them talking to one another as they ate their food— talking about the journey they'd be—and you'd believe them, Father O'Flynn—you'd believe every word they'd be saying.'

Turning to Stephen, the priest asked him: 'Who are the best people to breed and fly pigeons?'

'Oh the Powers—the Powers of Commons Road, Father O'Flynn. No one can beat the Powers.' Then, lighting up with enthusiasm, he continued: 'Imagine, going over to Perth with four birds in your basket. Tossing up your birds at Perth!' He was pointing to somewhere at the end of the world with the stem of his pipe, and his imagination boggled at the idea of tossing up one's birds at Perth, for he was dumb for a moment.

Resuming in a calmer tone, he said: 'They'd fly up into the sky and take their bearings. They're true homers, Father O'Flynn— oh boy, they're true homers! None of your bankers, Father, that go down there to the quays and the distillery looking for grain.'

Seeing again in his mind's eye those four true homers spiralling into the sky over Perth, he exclaimed: 'Oh, they're what you might call *grand* birds—*bred* birds—Father O'Flynn! The Powers keep only bred birds. 'Tis in the blood of the bred bird to desire to come home, don't you know?'

But that glorious moment haunted him, for he referred to it once again with wide-eyed wonder.

'Imagine—tossing up your birds at Perth! And the little birds facing for home, facing the ocean and the winds of heaven, and next morning there they are, outside in the loft in the back-yard, as if they'd only done Rathduff.

'Them Powers, Father O'Flynn, they have a gift—they're bred themselves. They have it in 'em to train good birds. They're the best flyers in all Cork!'

Father O'Flynn said goodbye and started back for the presbytery.

'The nicest fellows I ever spent an hour with,' was how he later described Connie and Stephen and those other bird and dog fanciers.

'I was always impressed how nature conferred on those fellows who spent their days close to her in studying her ways a simple dignity and a nobility of mind that was not so evident among other people in the parish.'

Up by the Cathedral, the children who had been playing on the side of the street were attracted by the horse and the bread-van. They abandoned their game of 'pickie' and crossed the street to look on. Each had a satchel of books, for they were coming home from school. They sat in a row on the kerb-stone and laughed as they watched the pigeons waddling round the nose-bag and shouldering the sparrows out of the way.

Father O'Flynn came along the path. He heard the organ playing in the church. It was Herr Fleischmann, the fair, round-faced, squat and utterly dedicated organist and choir-master at the North Cathedral. He was practising a piece by Bach on the new organ which had been recently installed and was due to be blessed by the Bishop on Sunday. After the blessing, Herr Fleischmann would give a recital. Father O'Flynn liked Bach; he respected Herr Fleischmann. Though both loved music passionately they did not always agree on interpretation, and just then there was a coolness between them.

During Holy Week at *Tenebrae*, Father O'Flynn had sung the lamentations of Jeremiah. He sang them in the traditional style *Sean Nós*—from the heart. The poor people loved it—and many of them were moved to tears. 'It was awful sad,' they said. But Herr Fleischmann reacted differently. The choir saw him look to heaven, mutter something in German and plug his ears with his fingers.

On Easter Sunday, after High Mass, by way of pulling the professor's leg, the Canon had said: 'Didn't Father O'Flynn sing those lamentations superbly on Good Friday?'

'Oh mein Gott!' exclaimed the professor, 'please, do not call that singing—it was—murder! Father O'Flynn—he is a great artist, he has the drama, he has Shakespeare—and he has it all here'—he struck his heart—'but when it comes to music—O mein Gott! he thinks he has it—but I tell you he has it not and he vill not listen to me. He is stubborn. Do you know vhat I think, Canon? I think if der gut Gott in Himmel came down here on Good Friday and sang the lamentation, Father O'Flynn would shake his fist and say: "You're wrong Herr Gott! you're wrong. You're only singing notes—you haven't got the emotions correct"!'

The Canon repeated this to Father O'Flynn—and hence the coolness.

Maggie McCarthy came out of the church and spoke to Father O'Flynn.

'Father O'Flynn, for the love of God, will you tell Herr Fleischmann to stop that racket. I can't say me prayers—and the poor Sacred Heart have a pain in the head from it.' Then she began to weep, and through her sobs she continued: 'Father O'Flynn, I'm in the height o' trouble.'

'What is it, Maggie?' he asked.

'I'm up in Court tomorrow.' She cried again.

'And what would a decent woman like you be up in Court for?'

'For doing good, Father—for doing good.'

The priest was all sympathy with the old woman and they sat on the edge of the railings. When she recovered she explained her position.

'You remember poor Dotie Madden?'

'Sure—I saw her down to her grave last summer.'

'Well, that's me trouble, Father—the grave. Poor Dotie had no one belong to her. She was, as you know, blind and deaf at the end. When she wanted a bite or a sup she used to knock on the wall with the poker and I came in from next door and looked after her. When it came near the end she used to say: "Where will they bury me, Mag?"

'"Have you no grave, Dot?" says I.

' "No, Mag—I've no one belonging to me—they're all in America now and I never hear tell of 'em."

' "Where would you like to be buried, Dot?" I asked her.

' "I'd like to be buried with you, Mag,"' says she—"you were always a good neighbour."

' "You'll be buried with me, Dot," I gave her my word. So when she died, Father O'Flynn, I buried her with me own father and mother—up in White Church—for 'tis there I'll be going myself, when God calls me.'

'That was most charitable of you, Mag—the Lord will reward you for your kindness', commented the priest.

'But me cousins from the south side were mad when they heard about it. They come up to the house—and the language they used isn't fit for your ears. They're after dragging me into Court—for trespassing—and the solicitor says I haven't a leg to stand on.'

'When are you to appear in Court?' asked the priest.

'Tomorrow, Father,' she said.

'I'll be there to defend you, Mag.'

Father O'Flynn appealed for Mag, but justice had to take its course. She lost the case and had to spend a fortnight in the women's jail. Father O'Flynn told the Court that the law was an ass, and to prove it he'd visit Mag every day in jail. He did—and when she was released he called for her in his car and drove her home.

'The poor people like Mag,' he said later, 'knew little about liturgy, but they had, I think, the right end of the stick—they had the grace of contemplation: the love of God and their neighbour; I used to see them there praying with their gaze fastened on the tabernacle.'

The children sitting on the kerb opposite were too absorbed in their game to notice Father O'Flynn. When one of them clapped her hands, the mare jerked up her head, the sparrows flew to the eaves and the pigeons flapped noisily up to the bell-tower.

That source of amusement ended, the children now turned their attention to the large Dodge car. Sitting on the kerbstone, they could see themselves mirrored in the shining convex surface of the chromium hub-caps. There was much nudging of one another, and peals of childish laughter, as they noted the reflected distortion of their faces. They peered close, then drew back, for each had to get a turn at being in the centre. They pointed at the reflection; they mocked one another. It was wonderful fun, watching themselves thus distorted and exaggerated in the hub-caps of Father O'Flynn's car.

The priest stole over, and before they noticed him he too was sitting on the kerbstone and sharing in their fun. To add to their amusement he began to make funny faces himself, and this enthralled them no end.

'Will somebody show me their satchel?' he asked.

All rushed to be the first to give the satchel to the priest. He took the bag from a little girl of ten.

'What class are you in, Sheila?' He opened the satchel and took out the books.

'I'm in fourth class, Father,' she told him. He looked through the Irish Reader and Poetry Book; the English Reader and Poetry Book; the geography; the history; the tables book and catechism. He examined the box of pencils, the rubber and the ruler, and flicked over the pages of the exercise books with their lettering in English and in Irish, and the sums.

'That bag of books is a disgrace to the Minister for Education,' he murmured to himself. 'Nothing but letters, words, signs and symbols. . . .'

He opened the catechism. 'What questions did you have today?' he asked.

'Those two there, Father.' The child put her finger on the place on the page.

'Well, now, we'll see who knows their catechism.'

The four children instinctively stood up on the kerb and grouped themselves round the priest, feet together, standing bolt upright and with hands joined. It was what Father O'Flynn called 'the catechism stance'. He disliked it heartily.

'Now, Mary, what is grace?' asked the priest in a serious tone.

Mary added the final touch to her 'catechism stance' by closing her eyes. She paused for a moment, and then the answer shot out from the pigeon-hole in her memory like a bullet from a gun.

'Grace is a supernatural gift bestowed on us by God to enable us to do good and avoid evil.'

'Good girl you are,' praised the priest. 'What did the teacher say to you?'

'She gave me a sweet, Father.'

He was going to stop there, but the other children insisted that he ask them a question too. He noted how each in turn stiffened up, closed her eyes and shot out the answer pat.

'God help them!' he thought to himself. 'They're making catechism-machines out of the children—a mechanical and materialistic teaching of religion. They'll get "excellent" from the inspector for this sort of thing.'

He opened the English Reader. There was a poem in it by Padraic Colum: *The Old Woman of the Roads*. 'Did you ever learn that lovely poem?' he asked the children.

'Oh yes, Father—we all know that since last week.'

'Who'll say it for me?' he coaxed.

There was a silence, a little shy laughing, and then a hazel-eyed imp pointed at the child with the long fair hair and said:

'She's the best at it, Father,' thus getting herself out of a difficulty because she had forgotten it herself.

'Good,' said the priest. 'Then we'll hear Sheila.' Sheila now stood up on the pavement and adopted her 'catechism stance', except that instead of joining her hands she held them stiffly by her sides, her fists clenched. She, too, closed her eyes, shutting herself in from all human contact; and out shot the words of the poem in a jogging, staccato, class-room sing-song:

> *Oh-to-have-a-little-house*
> *To-own-the-hearth-and-stool-and-all*
> *The-heaped-up-sods-beside-the-fire*
> *The-stack-of-turf-beside-the-wall!*

The child put a strong emphasis on 'all' and 'wall'; otherwise the poem was spoken without thought or feeling; it was, the priest thought, like tapping out words on a typewriter.

'That will do,' he interrupted.

'But there's lots more—and I know down to the end.'

'I know there's lots more and I'm sure you know it all,' agreed the priest, 'but before you go I want to ask you a question.'

'What is it, Father?' she asked.

'Tell me, now,' he began, addressing the group: 'What would you like most in the world?'

'I'd like a sleeping doll, Father,' chirped up a little girl of nine.

'And I'd just love a currant bun from the shop down there,' said her sister of ten. This child's inflection impressed the priest.

'Say that again, Mary,' he asked.

'I'd love a currant bun. . . .'

'That's grand,' he said. 'Now listen to me, Mary, and say it again after me.' The priest now enlarged the inflection and evoked in himself the emotion of longing.

'I'd love a currant bun. Wouldn't it be grand?'

Mary imitated the priest. 'I'd love a currant bun. Wouldn't it be grand?'

The priest, noting the progress in her expression, now continued: 'Oh, to have a bun. The child repeated the phrase. The priest then got the other three to say the sentences: Wouldn't it be grand . . . oh, for a currant bun . . . I'd love a sleeping doll . . . oh, for a sleeping doll . . . wouldn't it be grand?'

Then gathering the children round him on the kerbstone, he explained: 'I'm a poor old woman, sitting here by the side of the road; I have no house, no home; and I'm weary and tired of walking round the roads and begging from people. Of all the things in the world, I'd love a little house of my own. Oh, wouldn't it be grand?' Then he spoke the first stanza of the poem, repeating after each verse the phrase: 'Wouldn't it be grand?'

Everything was forgotten. The children were intent, listening to the priest. They were moved by his rendering of the poem; and the priest was absorbed in teaching the children. They went on to the second stanza:

> *To have a clock with weights and chains*
> *And pendulum swinging up and down. . . .*

Their childish imagination was enkindled as the priest, with a gesture of his hand, showed them the pendulum swinging up and down. They wanted to imitate his gestures.

He opened wide his eyes with wonder to describe the treasures of the dresser:

> *A dresser filled with shining delph*
> *Speckled and white and blue and brown . . .*
> *Wouldn't it be grand . . . ah, wouldn't it be grand?*

The children were caught up completely in the imagery of the poem, and especially by the feeling that the priest had conveyed to them. He now enticed each child to express the different emotions of the poem: longing, wonder and contentment, and in the last stanza the beautiful transition to weariness, sadness and urgent prayer:

> *Ach, but I'm weary of mist and dark,*
> *And roads where there's never a house or bush;*
> *And tired I am of the crying wind and the lonesome hush.*
> *And I'm praying to God on high,*
> *And I'm praying to him night and day*
> *For a little house, a house of my own. . . .*

On the last line, the priest acted as if the wind and the rain were blowing in his face; he turned up the collar of his coat as if to protect himself:

> *Out of the wind and the rain's way.*

The children were charmed, delighted. They wanted to do the same.

Nobody noticed the Bishop. He was now a very old man, dressed in his soutane with a long black coat over it, a high-crowned hat on his head, an umbrella in his ungloved hand. On the opposite side of the street he was padding his way slowly towards the cathedral door. He was paying his daily visit to the Blessed Sacrament, where he would remain for an hour in prayer.

But the Bishop was observant. He noticed the large Dodge car parked outside the presbytery. He could not see the priest or the children sitting on the kerbstone, but he could hear them; and, recognising Father O'Flynn's voice, he crossed the deserted street.

The Bishop's shadow fell across the chattering group. They all looked up. They all stood up.

'Good day, my lord,' said Father O'Flynn, not one whit embarrassed. 'We were just reciting a lovely little poem here, and I'm sure Sheila would love to say it for the Bishop.'

The Bishop was not consulted as to whether he wished to hear it or not; but he couldn't very well say no, so he listened to *The Old Woman of the Roads* recited by the fair-haired child, and agreed with Father O'Flynn when he said that the child had grasped 'the fontal emotion of the poem'; all it needed now was developing.

The children then said good-bye to the Bishop and to Father O'Flynn, who gave them sixpence to buy sweets in the shop down the street.

'That's a very big car, Chris,' remarked the Bishop, in a casual way that concealed his disapproval of his clergy owning or using motor cars. He touched the tyre of the Dodge with his umbrella. 'How many horse power would that be now?'

''Tis eighteen horse power, my lord.'

'I suppose a car as big as that would need a lot of petrol,' the Bishop continued.

'Well, it does about twenty-five miles to the gallon.'

'Is that on the long runs or around the city?' asked the Bishop.

'On the long runs, my lord. I only get about eighteen to the gallon around the city.'

''Tis your car, then?' The Bishop rubbed the smooth, polished surface of the wing with his hand.

'Oh, no, my lord,' answered Father O'Flynn blandly. 'It belongs to O'Connor Bros., but by an arrangement with my brother—'

'They have come on very well in recent years—hiring out cars no doubt.' The Bishop was silent for a moment. Then he asked:

'How long have you been in the North Parish, Chris?'

'All my life, my lord.'

'I mean as a priest?'

'Well, I spent ten years as chaplain in the Asylum and I have been twenty-six years here as curate.'

'I suppose 'tis time you got a change . . . you know Passage West is vacant?'

'I do, my lord.'

'And now that you have a car it would not be too far away from you know where.'

'From the Loft, my lord?'

'From the Loft, as you call it . . . come up tomorrow and we'll see about it.'

'*Mon General!*' said Father O'Flynn, saluting the Bishop and then accompanying him across the street to the church.

A stream of water from one of the mains had been flowing along the gutter past the church. Two small boys were collecting mud from the gutter and piling it on the kerb.

'Look at those two little boys, my lord—they're engaged in art work.'

'Art work?—they're playing with mud.'

'But art is play—a joyful moulding of matter to a form; they're moulding something now—as God in the beginning moulded clay and made Adam!'

'We'll see what they're moulding,' said the Bishop and stooped down to speak to the children.

'What are you making there, little boys?'

'Priests!' one of them answered.

'Didn't I tell you, my lord,' Father O'Flynn smiled at the Bishop.

'And which of the priests is that?' continued the Bishop, pointing his umbrella at a shapeless lump of mud.

'That's him,' replied the child, pointing to Father O'Flynn. The Bishop chuckled.

'There's a sobering thought for you, Chris,' remarked the Bishop, and turned again to the children.

'Now that you're making priests, why don't you make a Bishop, too?'

'I can't,' said the child.

'Why not?' asked the Bishop.

'Because there's not enough mud!'

Father O'Flynn chuckled. 'I won't detain you any longer, my lord,' he said. 'You're going in to do your holy hour— no doubt we both have plenty of matter for meditation today!'

17

Pilgrim in Passage

I BOARDED the bus for Passage West, a drab straggly town some six miles below the city on the right bank of the Lee. Formerly, it had been a busy half-way house between the lower harbour and Cork city. On its wharfs the sailing ships from America unloaded their cargoes of grain and bales of merchandise. Ships of their draught were unable to navigate the upper reaches of the river. Huge stores built of stone were erected along the water's edge to house the grain and merchandise. Later, when better dredging deepened the channel, the ships sailed up to the quays at Cork. The heyday of the stores was over. After 1922, they crumbled and decayed.

In 1832 a modern dockyard had been laid down at Passage West. The hoisting windlass and swivelling crane, the scraping and tarring of hulls, the painting of decks, and the din of hammers on iron plates, meant work and money for the local people. Queen Victoria graciously named it 'The Royal Victoria Dockyard'.

There grew up among the young men a tradition of service in the British Navy and merchant fleet. Sailors' garments hanging out to dry were a familiar sight in Passage West.

Some who made their fortunes abroad returned home to Passage West and retired to the village up on the hills that an earlier generation of wealthy Hanoverian merchants had built. There, in faded elegance, they passed their declining years, enjoying a magnificent view of the harbour and the nostalgic tang of the salt in the breeze.

At the middle of the 19th century the railway came; the

Cork, Blackrock and Passage Line. In summer, especially on Sundays and Wednesday afternoons, crowds travelled from the city to enjoy the pleasant scenery and to take the air as they strolled along the banks of the river or crossed in the ferry to Carrigaloe. But when the line was extended to Crosshaven in 1904, Passage was forsaken for the more popular resort at the mouth of Cork Harbour.

By the middle of the present century all had changed. The railway line had been closed down. The old station was in ruins. The slates had fallen off the roofs of the great stores; their gaping windows let in wind and rain. They were empty save for the rats. The dockyard, idle for years, had been dismantled. Nothing remained of its former industry but a few rusting boilers; scraps of old engines; the bare ribs of a coaster's carcase lying in the stagnant water of the half-empty basin.

In the lean thirties many of the young men had emigrated to England in search of work. When World War II was over, their families began to follow them. The number of children on the school rolls fell. All around in Passage West, things rusted, crumbled and decayed.

To this parish of over two thousand people, Father O'Flynn was appointed pastor in 1946. He was then sixty-five.

When I got off the bus at Passage West, Father O'Flynn was waiting for me.

'We'll go up to the school right away,' he said, 'as I promised you last day you were here that I'd show you how we teach religion in Passage West.'

The Boys' National School was on the side of Church Hill, leading up from the town. Father O'Flynn trudged up the steep hill beside me as he talked of education.

We entered a class-room. The boys stood up; the teacher, whose name was Mr. O'Mahony, shook hands and welcomed us.

After a few words the priest left us at the window, waded in among the desks, and sat on top of one of them. The boys clustered round him. It seemed they were discussing my presence.

I looked round the room while chatting with the teacher. It was drab and stuffy. The furniture looked the worse for wear. The desks were scarred and furrowed. The blackboard was grey, and in time promised to be near-white. Two faded maps hung on the colourless walls; one of Ireland, the other a map of the world showing the hemispheres side by side. The dial of the clock had acquired a mellow tan, and a statue of St. Patrick looked cheerless and forlorn.

'We have a visitor today, and he'd like to see how we teach religion in Passage West.' Father O'Flynn backed out of the desks and nodded towards me.

He addressed a boy in the front desk.

'What is religion, Johnny?'

' "Come follow me," Jesus said,' the boy replied.

'That's right. Religion means the following of Christ. We must know him first. How can we know Jesus?'

'From the gospels.'

'Right! Out on the floor now, and we'll make the gospels live.'

'That,' whispered the teacher to me, 'is the catechism according to Father O'Flynn.'

'We'll do "Christ stilling the Tempest" today,' the priest went on.

The boys tumbled out of the desks and began to prepare the stage. They cleared a space in the centre of the room by shifting back the desks.

'Bring over those forms and make the boat,' directed Father O'Flynn. Willing hands placed two forms across the middle of the floor. 'Now get the chair and the cushion for the master.' The teacher's chair was placed at one end of the bench.

'Into the boat with the ten apostles! Peter and John stay ashore.' The boys straddled the form like oarsmen in a boat.

'There's the master over there talking with the sick.' Father O'Flynn pointed to a corner of the room where four boys stood. 'Where are the mad fellows—the demoniacs?'

'We're over here in Gargasa, Father,' two boys looked out from behind the blackboard.

'The winds—are ye ready up there?'

'Ready to blow the boat out of the water, Father,' replied a group of boys standing up on the desks.

'And the waves?'

'Ready to swamp 'em, Father!' Another group knelt down all round the barque of Peter.

'Ready, Peter?'

'Ready, Father!'

'Off ye go!'

The gospel sprang to life. . . .

Peter:	Are ye all ready, lads?
Apostles:	All ready, Peter.
Peter:	Where's the master?
John:	He's over there curing the sick.
Peter:	They never give him a minute's rest. Go over and call him, John.
John:	Righto, Peter.
John:	Master, Peter is ready to sail. All the lads are waiting for you.
Master:	I'll be with you just now. (To the sick) I must go to Peter. We're crossing over to Gargasa—I'll be back to see you soon again. I give you my blessing.
James:	Let the master go to sleep. He must be jaded.
Philip:	Why are we going to Gargasa, Peter?
Peter:	For a young fellow you ask too many questions. We're going because the master said so.

Peter: All aboard!
Apostles: All aboard!
Peter: Throw off the rope—slip the starboard stem firm!
            Port hard! Up with the sails!
All: We're off! That's a fair breeze.
Philip: Give us a song, John.
John: What would the master like?
Master: A song of David, John.

John stood up, and in a sweet soprano voice sang some verses
of Psalm 17 which Father O'Flynn had set to an Irish traditional
air:

> I love you, Lord, my strength,
> My rock, my fortress, my saviour.
> My God is the rock where I take refuge . . .
> From on high he reached down and seized me;
> He drew me forth from the mighty waters. . . .

Peter: Hush! Hush! The master is asleep.

I looked at 'the master' in the teacher's chair. His head had
drooped forward on his chest, and his eyes were closed.

'Hush—the master is asleep!' Father O'Flynn entered the
drama as a kind of chorus, and continued with a quotation
from Shakespeare:

> . . . the innocent sleep,
> Sleep that knits up the ravelled sleave of care,
> The death of each day's life, sore labour's bath,
> Balm of hurt minds, great nature's second course,
> Chief nourisher in life's feast.

'Continue on,' the priest said to the boys.

James: 'Tis dead calm.
Peter: 'Tis too calm. I don't like the look of it.
James: 'Tis the calm before the storm.

That was the cue for the winds and the waves, for they now

swung into action. The boys on the desks began to blow softly and rhythmically, but quickly louder and louder. Father O'Flynn conducted the wind like a choir. The boys who were the waves began to bob up and down and clutch at the boat, saying: 'Come on and we'll give 'em a ducking.'

Peter: Pull down the sails and put out the oars—here's the storm rushing down from the mountains!

In the twinkling of an eye, the room was in uproar; the blowing of the winds, the noise of the waves, and the cries of the apostles in the boat as they rowed frantically for the shore. The children revelled in it. Father O'Flynn, like Prospero, urged them to even greater fury.

Philip's voice was heard above the rest.

Philip: O Peter, turn back and head for Capharnaum!

James: Turn back, Peter, or we'll all be lost!

Peter: No! No! The master's orders were—on to Gargasa. We must keep on course, whatever happens.

Philip: Where's the master now?

John: Call the master!

Peter: He's here behind me, asleep.

Apostles: Wake him—wake him! Call him, Peter! We're lost —we're drowned! Lord save us, we perish!

The 'master' raised his head, rubbed his eyes, stretched his arms and yawned. I recognised the cavernous yawn that Father O'Flynn had taught us in the elocution class at Farranferris years ago.

The boy stood up and, with the gesture of a policeman stopping traffic, he rebuked the winds and the waves.

'Peace! Be still!'

Immediately the winds and the waves calmed down, and began to whisper to each other.

'He is the master. He is our creator. He is our Lord. We never knew he was in the boat. Of course we must obey him at once. Sorry, master! Sorry, Lord!' And they all bowed down in adoration.

The apostles, now recovered from their fright, began to question one another.

Apostles: What kind of man is he at all? Who is he? See how he calms the tempest! How did he do it?

James: We saw sickness obey him!

Philip: We saw devils obey him!

John: We saw death obey him!

All: What kind of man is he at all, when the winds and the waves obey him?

John: Master, we were terrified; we all lost our nerve and wanted to turn back home. But Peter said: 'On to Gargasa!'

Master: And Peter was right, John. Listen to me carefully all of you. Obey Peter—no matter how bad the storm—and ye won't go astray.

Peter: Lord, Philip asked me why we were going to Gargasa at all—there's nothing there but wild goats!

Master: There are two demoniacs over there—two poor fellows *as mad as the sea and wind when both contend which is the mightier*. And I want to bring them peace of mind.

('Excuse me, Father,' Mr. O'Mahony whispered to me, 'you'll notice how Father O'Flynn puts the master quoting Shakespeare!')

Apostles: (to each other): He's always thinking of others— how to bring them peace of soul.

Peter: Ship oars! We're running up on the beach. We've landed safely at last.

The master, Peter and the apostles climbed out of the boat. A sudden howling and screeching came from behind the black-board. The apostles, struck with fear, huddled round the master.

Philip: Lord, these must be the mad fellows who live among the tombs.

James: Iron chains couldn't hold them, they say.

John: The whole countryside is terrified of them.

The demoniacs came out from behind the blackboard, hair tousled, coats off, and shirts open.

Demoniacs: What have we to do with thee, Jesus, son of the most high God?

Peter: Listen to that, lads! The mad fellows have the truth that we all forgot in the storm. Son of the living God!

Demoniacs: Leave us alone! Go away! Do not torment us!

Master: Peace! What is your name?

Demoniacs: My name is Legion, for we are many. Do not drive us away out of this country—or if you do, then send us into that herd of swine over there on the hill.

Master: Depart, unclean spirit, and leave these poor men in peace!

Apostles: Look! Look at all the pigs running down the hill! There they go, all over the cliff into the sea!

Peter: Will ye look at that for power over the devils! Ah lads, we made an awful mess of it out in the boat. We should have trusted in the master and not lost our heads like a lot of kids. Sure he is the maker of the heavens and the earth. He controls the winds and the waves, and the storm thrown in. Ah—we should never have wakened him. No wonder he said we have little faith. We must admit it—we have little faith.

The two mad fellows were now kneeling at the feet of the master and clinging to him affectionately.

Demoniacs: We adore thee and thank thee, Jesus, son of the living God!

Master: My poor creatures, ye had a terrible time with those devils. But cheer up! Be of good heart! I have overcome the kingdom of Satan. My peace be with you always!

Peter and the Apostles: Lord, give us faith, like these poor fellows! Lord, increase our faith!

'That's the end of that section now,' Father O'Flynn said, joining us at the window.

'I'm amazed at what you have done with these boys,' I said.

'No need for amazement at all—for that was the Middle Ages way and the way our Lord himself taught his apostles: personal vital contact with reality; a real storm; real winds howling through the rigging; real waves splashing into the boat and drenching them to the skin; real fear and terror in their hearts that evoked a real cry for help: "Lord, save us, we perish!" The real encounter with the devils in the demoniacs; the terror, the power seen in the stampede of swine, and the reality of the peace in the hearts of those poor fellows as they clung to the legs of Christ.'

'Have the boys done any other incidents from the gospels in this way?' I asked.

'We begin with the babies down in the convent, and each year in each class we do two or three parables, which are the little art-dramas given to us by Christ our Lord, or miracles, in the way you've seen. By the time the children come to leave school at fourteen they have covered all the important events in the life of our Lord—and they love it! 'Tis thus we teach religion in Passage West.'

'What about the catechism?' I said.

'I wouldn't have anything to do with it.'

'Why?'

''Tis not in our tradition—it is of the same tradition as this murder-machine system of education—words, words,

words. I was talking to a doctor in Cork who is a social psychologist, no less, and she told me that she had visited a young man of twenty in Mountjoy Prison. He knew his catechism backwards—word perfect. But he knew nothing of the person or of the life of our Lord in the gospels. No wonder he ended up in Mountjoy, poor fellow.'

We said good-bye to the boys and to Mr. O'Mahony, and left for the girls' school down in the convent.

The idea of dramatising incidents from the gospels in order to put across the Christian message was very old, going back to the miracle and morality plays of the Middle Ages. Usually, with children, one gets a sing-song and rather wooden performance.

Father O'Flynn's class-room presentations of the parables and miracles of Christ were as live as the best of his Shakespearean productions in the Loft. The same principles were used. The priest accepted the children as he found them. He did not begin by correcting their mispronunciations or, Pygmalion-like, changing their inflections or accents. He concentrated on getting the meaning and the feeling of the part into the child's heart.

He wrote the scripts himself. He had an amazing facility for this, and there are dozens of such scripts among his papers. But he never brought a script into class. The children learned by listening to him. It was the traditional method: truth carried alive on wings of emotion from the live heart of the teacher to the heart of the child. This had the uplift in it which he was always anxious to achieve.

I saw his theory justified in the class-room at Passage West. So did many others.

'This method of teaching religion has another advantage,' he told me on the way over to the girls' school. 'It also teaches the parents. For when the children can act a parable, they go home and insist on doing it for their parents. Actors need an audience!'

Sister Theresita had assembled the choir girls at the end of the long class-room. She arranged them in three rows, placing the smaller children in front and the taller girls in steps of stairs behind them. They varied in age from seven to fourteen years, and they were obviously very excited by this unexpected call to sing before a visitor. Only the presence of the vigilant Sister Theresita kept their chatter within the bounds of decorum. She was herself an enthusiastic and competent teacher of traditional Irish singing. With her loyal co-operation Father O'Flynn had trained the children of Passage West Convent to be the best traditional choir in the country.

One of the first to recognise the unique quality of their singing was the Minister for Education, General Richard Mulcahy. He wrote:

'When first I met an tAthair Seamus Ó Floinn in Ballingeary in 1913, he was busy with an old phonograph on whose hard wax cylinders he recorded our traditional songs and melodies from the old singers of the district. The fogs of more than thirty disturbed years were to come between me and any further intimate knowledge of the man or his activities.

'Then came one night in the City Hall in Cork in 1949, at *Cór Fhéile na Scoil,* when for sweetness and beauty of its singing one choir stood out from the rest as if it were from another world. It was the children's choir from the National School of the Mercy Convent at Passage West, trained by Father O'Flynn. He was still recording, but this time on the hearts of children, our native songs he had so lovingly collected nearly forty years ago.'

Not long afterwards, the Department of Education invited Father O'Flynn and his choir to conduct the Summer School of traditional Irish Singing in Dublin. Radio Éireann made many recordings of the choir, and it broadcasted in a series of six programmes later.

In 1953, the Minister for Education, General R. Mulcahy,

visited Father O'Flynn at Passage West and brought with him some of the foremost people in Irish musical education. They included Messrs. M. Breathnach, Secretary to the Department of Education, S. McKenna, Deputy Chief Inspector, the three Music Inspectors of the Department, Messrs. P. Ó Ceallaigh, T. Kindlin and R. O'Sullivan. They had been asked specially by the Minister to attend a recital of traditional Irish singing by the Girls' Choir at the Convent of Mercy Schools, Passage West, which Father O'Flynn had trained. The songs selected by Father O'Flynn covered a very wide range of traditional music. About fifteen of these songs were recorded by the Radio Éireann mobile broadcasting unit that day. Mr. Fachnan Ó h-Annracháin, musical director of Radio Éireann, was present.

The songs were interspersed by short talks by Father O'Flynn on his methods of teaching. His talks were followed with interest by his distinguished and highly-qualified visitors.

At the conclusion of the recital the Minister thanked Father O'Flynn and his choir and the Sisters of Mercy for the important work they were doing—'fostering and cultivating the tiny seed of tradition that had come down to them from that "Hidden Ireland" of which Professor Corkery had so well written. I have found here much of the spirit of old Gaelic Ireland. It was for this that so many fought and so many have died that we, as a nation, might live as this man, An tAthair Seamus, lives and teaches others to live.'

The Minister felt that a future generation would look back on Father Christy O'Flynn as one of the greatest workers in preserving our culture and music. It was a magnificent thing to see the work that was being done in Passage West for Irish culture. His Department of Education were very much aware of the importance of singing and they had many schemes in mind for improving their methods.

Father O'Flynn replied: 'One thousand years before Christ

came on earth, David composed his psalms and set them to music. Then he organised the singers of Israel to sing them. Why? To uplift the degraded Israel that Saul had left after him. David, through song, carried truth to every heart with joy. His work remains to this day to elevate the Church—spouse of Christ—to her Saviour. We have organised this choir in Passage West and taught them our traditional Irish songs, to lift up the nation from the degraded tastes in music to which it has fallen, and to put it in contact with a tradition that ennobles.'

'Would you have a love song or a song of good life?' Father O'Flynn now asked me, in the words of Feste the Jester in *Twelfth Night*.

The children laughed at his drollery.

'I'd like to hear two love songs,' I said.

'What are they?'

'Two I heard during your recent broadcast.'

'They must have been *Fáth mo Bhuadhurtha* and *Eibhlín a Rún*,' Sister Theresita told us. 'We'd be delighted. But I feel the children would like to begin with a song they have just learned: *Mo Phaistín Fionn*.'

The children showed their enthusiastic approval. The song was evidently one of their favourites.

'This song depicts the rapturous joy of a woman hugging and kissing a beautiful little child, and her heartbreak that she had none of her own.'

He faced the smiling children. The sister raked them with a glance. There was absolute silence, and rows of serious eyes gave the priest their full attention.

The sister gave them the note on the harmonium. The priest hummed the opening phrase of the song. He paused; the choir awaited the signal. He raised his right hand before his face and closed it slowly, as if squeezing a sponge. Attention heightened. Suddenly the hand flew open wide, and the song was on the lips of the children.

Their fresh unaccompanied voices, the sure intonation and beautiful phrasing, were a musical experience never to be forgotten. Song after song contrasting in mood, in emotion and in rhythm, poured from the choir with ease and delight: *Fáth mo Bhuadhurtha; Muintir Connaithre; An Cuicin; Eibhlín a Rún; Fil a Rún Ó.*

It was of this style of singing that Professor Reeves Davies of Trinity College of Music, London, wrote later:

'I have thought many times of the singing of Father O'Flynn's children's choir from Passage West in Cork. It was an entirely new experience for me to hear these unaccompanied Gaelic songs sung with such ease, artistry, rhythm and obvious enjoyment. Is there a recording to be had, please? If so, I would like to purchase one; if not, why not, I wonder?'

'I prefer the solo singer to the choir,' Father O'Flynn said.

'Why?' I asked.

'In the choir individuality and personality are submerged in the interest of a uniform tone and quality. I like to give a different song to each child—a song to match each one's voice and personality. There is more real development of the child in that way.'

To conclude the recital, the choir sang the beautiful Plain Chant setting of the *Salve Regina.*

I was fascinated as much, all through the performance, by the conducting of Father O'Flynn as I was delighted by the sweet singing of his choir. He was alive with each song. It suffused his face; it played about his lips; it danced in his eyes. His hands were especially remarkable. He would raise his right hand, his huge fist clenched; there was power and tenderness in the gesture. With a swift thrust from right to left across his body, he marked the great accents of the melody. His arm would swing back again, drawing a smooth line with wrist bent and fingers splayed like petals on a pendent flower; then they would flutter with exquisite delicacy as if weaving out of the air the intricate pattern of the song's inner harmonies. His index finger marked each climax, and with his open palm he lovingly shaped each phrase and cadence of the song.

Here, it seemed, was music welling up from some secret source within the man. Like a spirit it possessed him, entranced him, and directed all his actions; mysteriously it flowed from him, out through his eyes and through his finger-tips to inspire the children in the choir before him.

We left the class-room and walked out into the summer's day. The view across the water to French's Point was magnificent.

'*Ailneacht in Uactar*,' I said.

'There's no arguing about that,' he replied. Then he began to speak of Plain Chant and Irish melody.

'All the beauty there before us, in the lines and folds of those hills, in the wide strong sweep of the river with all its lesser dynamics in the whirls and eddies and cross-currents, in the forms of those drifting clouds, in the graceful gliding of that gull—all that is captured and expressed in our Irish songs and in the Gregorian Chant. Both were inspired by the free rhythm and movements of nature, and not by the mechanical beats of a machine. But because we are living in a machine age and have geared our system of education to the factory belt and the machine, there is no appreciation of these melodies among the people today. Sometimes I think I am only blowing on a dying ember.'

We reached his home in Tureen Terrace, and climbed up the steep steps from the road to the front door.

When we had finished lunch, Father O'Flynn said grace and we got up from the table.

'Make yourself comfortable there.' He pointed to a chair by the window that looked out over the broad expanse of Lough Mahon.

I sat down and found myself looking up at a picture on the

wall. It was not a picture—but an illuminated Address. It began: 'We, the servants of Maynooth College. . . .'

'I see you're reading the Address,' he remarked. 'I cherish that more than a wall covered with Rembrandts.'

''Tis *Lear* you want to do today?' he continued, taking a volume of Shakespeare from the bookcase.

'Yes. I've been looking forward to doing it with you—especially since I saw it in Stratford some time ago.'

'I'm getting slow and heavy on the legs, like old Lear himself,' he remarked, crossing the room and joining me near the window. He sat heavily into the great lugged armchair, put his feet up on a leather footstool, and rested his head against the back of the chair. 'You saw it at Stratford? What did you think of it?'

''Twas a wonderful production,' I said. 'They had everything—except what you call "the main thing".'

'You mean they hadn't the emotion correct?'

'They had no emotion at all. It left me cold. Mind you, some of those actors had beautiful voices, and they gave us some of the poetry—'

'I know. Verse speaking—words, words, words—as dead as a waxed corpse. I've seen *Lear* myself in London long before the war. Sir X and Dame Y were acting in it. To relieve the boredom I shut my eyes and tried to identify the characters by their voices. Do you know what it is—I couldn't! All the voices sounded alike to me. The exact same vowel sounds most carefully shaped; the consonants finely chiselled; words were projected at us by a highly technical use of pitch, pace, power and pause. All those actors sounded as if they came from the same heartless school of elocution. There was not an ounce of emotion among them. The audience clapped the scenery at the beginning; they clapped the costumes at the end; and at the interval they clapped the thunder and lightning. Shakespeare how are you!

'But to get back to *Lear*—you were saying something about the opening?'

'The critics say that the opening scene of *King Lear* is highly improbable,' I said.

'Carry on,' said he.

'They say that Shakespeare's greatest tragedy has its source in a trivial domestic incident. This is dramatically faulty, and puts an undue strain on the audience at the very beginning of the play.'

'Keep going.'

'They say that the scene in which Lear proposed to divide his kingdom between his three daughters in proportion to the expression of their love for him is far-fetched—not true to life. Shakespeare in this scene falls far below his achievements in *Hamlet* and *Macbeth*.'

'You will find nothing far-fetched or improbable in the opening scene of *Lear* once you approach it from the right angle,' he replied. 'Shakespeare in his tragedies respects the power of love as something sacred. In *Lear, Othello, Macbeth* and *Hamlet* he lets us see the nobility and grandeur of the mightiest of all powers on earth—love. In these plays Shakespeare shows us love attacked by hatred, ambition and jealousy, and draws all humanity to pity most tender about its crucifixion.

'*Lear* is the tragedy of a man who had everything but true love; asked for it, and after great suffering got it, only to lose it by death. The movement is towards love.

'*Macbeth* is the tragedy of a man who put his happiness in power and ambition—only to realise at the end how empty these things were—without love.

> *And that which should accompany old age*
> *As honour, love, obedience, troops of friends,*
> *I must not look to have. . . .*'

Life without love leads to "dusty death"

'*Othello* is the tragedy of a man who loved "not wisely but too well" and the love in his heart for Desdemona being poisoned by Iago, he killed her and then himself, for life without love was ashes to Othello.

'In *Hamlet* the central emotion is broken-heartedness, because his loves for his father and his country, Ophelia and his mother, are all shattered and unfulfilled. *But break my heart for I must hold my tongue.*

'In real life we could die to see another as afflicted as we see these men in tragedy. In the theatre we shed tears of sympathy, and we can thank our hearts that caused such tears. Tragedy softens the features of the real. The copy is less vivid than the original. This is to the merit of art. But the lesson is more powerful than the real, in being in great verse and thrust home by the powerful dramatic emotions of the actor, without the pain reality inflicts.'

'About the opening of *Lear*—'I reminded him gently.

'The first thing to keep in mind,' he went on, 'is Lear's request for love. To the daughter who loves most he would give the largest portion of his kingdom to rule. In St. John's gospel, Chapter 21, we read that before Christ ascended into heaven he disposed of his kingdom on earth, his Church, to his apostles. On whom did he confer supreme power and authority?'

'On St. Peter,' I said.

'Right. And why? Let St. John tell us. Jesus said to Peter: "*Simon, son of John, lovest thou me more than these?*" "*Yes, Lord,*" he said. "*Thou knowest that I love thee.*" He said to him: "*Feed my lambs.*" Three times Jesus knocked on the door of Peter's heart asking for an expression of his love. Three times Peter responded generously. Christ made Peter the visible head of his kingdom on earth. "*Feed my lambs, feed my sheep.*" In the mind of Christ he rules best who loves most. What a disappointment to Christ had Peter refused to express his love!

'Lear was not so unreal or far-fetched in allotting the portions of his kingdom according to the love of his daughters.

'Recall, also, that God, our Father in heaven, asks only one thing of us his creatures—our love, our total love. "*This is the first and greatest commandment: thou shalt love the Lord thy God with thy whole heart and thy whole soul. . . . This do and thou shalt live.*" If we refuse to love God or refuse to express that love in worship and in the service of the neighbour, we know from the words of Christ what our lot will be: "*Depart from me. . . .*" Banishment from the presence of God who is light and life and love.

'Keeping these things in mind, you will find nothing improbable or unreal in Lear's request for love, and for the external expression of love; in his anger when refused by Cordelia, or in his banishment of her.

'The human heart hungers for love. It was made to love. Lear enjoyed to the full life's joys and pleasures. What is more human than that this old man should ask for love and should turn hopefully to his favourite daughter, Cordelia, for the most generous expression of it?

> *Now, our joy,*
> *Although the last, not least, to whose young love*
> *The vines of France and milk of Burgundy*
> *Strive to be interess'd, what can you say to draw*
> *A third more opulent than your sister's? Speak.*

'Lear knocks on the door of Cordelia's heart, asking for love. She slams the door in his face, so to speak, with a curt—

> "*Nothing, my lord.*"
> "*Nothing!*"
> "*Nothing.*"
> "*Nothing will come of nothing.*"

'This conflict of wills between Lear and Cordelia is the source of the whole tragedy. Her curt reply is utterly unexpected. It hits Lear like the sudden lash of a whip across the cheek. He reels under the blow. His reaction is swift and terrifying. He banishes Cordelia; he falls into a towering anger with Kent when he warns him of his folly. Kent is banished.'

'The critics,' I said, 'say that Lear's anger at Cordelia's refusal is absurd, and his sentence of banishment on her and Kent fantastic.'

'There's nothing absurd or fantastic about it when you know Lear. He was a man of titanic passions. He erupted with the suddenness and violence of a volcano. He lacked the virtue of temperance. Thwarted in his request for love, and his pride sorely wounded, he went wild with a delirious rage. It is an extreme but very natural reaction, and his banishment of Cordelia is simply the outcome of it.'

'The critics say that the suddenness of the action is unreal and strained,' I went on.

'It is in fact perfectly in keeping with certain things in nature. That "nothing" of Cordelia is like the pistol shot in the Alps that sets the avalanche moving. In a few minutes it hurtles down the mountain and destroys all life in the valley below. One moment a peaceful snow-clad mountain; then a pistol shot, and next moment disaster for all in the valley. The First World War began with a pistol shot in Sarajevo. In a few weeks all Europe had escalated into war. Millions of lives were lost. The beginning was out of all proportion to the holocaust that followed. It was what your critics say: unreal—far-fetched. Shakespeare is Bible, folk and classic. These critics that take it on themselves to fault Shakespeare's opening of *Lear* show themselves ignorant of the Bible and of the ordinary workings of the passions in folk life.'

'That certainly puts the opening scene of *Lear* in a new perspective, and seems to take the wind out of the critics' sails,' I agreed. 'But they say that while the beginning of *Lear* is unreal, the end of the play is unendurable.'

'They do—God help them! And for a few hundred years they altered it—to make a happy ending! The aptness of the opening scene comes out all the more strikingly in contrast to the end of the play. Lear, at the beginning, is like Job in some respects. He is a very successful and wealthy man. He had lived a long and full life, and had drained life's cup of joys and pleasures. Then he is suddenly and unexpectedly stripped of everything—even of his reason.

'*King Lear* is the tragedy of a man who asked for true love, and got it, but at an appalling cost to himself in terms of suffering. In the end he gained the pearl of great price he had asked for—but it was snatched from him almost at once, by the death of Cordelia. He died in an ecstasy of love for her.

'In his request for love Lear is true to the noblest human instincts. He is also acting after the image and likeness of God—as I have shown. But Lear in the opening scene is incapable of experiencing true love. He accepts, in fact, the false coin of Goneril and Regan in place of the true. He was proud, self-centred and imperious. He needed to be purified before his request could be granted. This could be achieved only by suffering. That is the main burden of the drama. It is a fruitful suffering, a purgatory. He is purged of pride and selfishness. He learns to see and pray with a Christian heart. In Act III, Scene 4, we see his new-found consideration for the Fool, and his deepening sympathy with all who suffer. He says to the Fool:

> *In boy, go first. You houseless poverty—*
> *Nay, get thee in. I'll pray and then I'll sleep.*
> *Poor naked wretches, wheresoe'er you are,*
> *That bide the pelting of the pitiless storm,*
> *How shall your houseless heads and unfed sides,*

Your loop'd and window'd raggedness, defend you
From seasons such as these? O, I have ta'en
Too little care of this! Take physic, pomp.
Expose thyself to feel what wretches feel,
That thou may'st shake the superfluous to them
And show the heavens more just.

'Christ the King, the wisdom of God incarnate, came to us as an infant lying in straw in a hovel. Lear the king found a new wisdom amid the straw in a hovel. The parallel may be fanciful, but it struck me years ago when we were doing *Lear* in the Loft.

'At the end of the play, Lear is a changed man. The old proud, selfish tyrant has become humble, sympathetic and docile—"*this child-changed father*," comments Cordelia.

'In a scene of melting pathos and beauty Lear and Cordelia are reconciled. He experiences the love he hungered for—for the first time in his long life. The enormous price he paid seems little.

'The circumstances contrast sharply with those of the opening scene when he possessed everything—except love. Now in defeat, in poverty, in prison, he has nothing but love; he has found the pearl of great price. United with Cordelia, he can give and receive ecstatic love in forgiveness, prayer, song and laughter.

Come, let's away to prison
And we two alone will sing like birds, i' the cage;
When thou dost ask me blessing, I'll kneel down
And ask of thee forgiveness: so we'll live,
And pray and sing and tell old tales and laugh
At gilded butterflies . . .

'Lear and Cordelia are led away to prison. But there, in defeat, in poverty, and detached from all the power and riches and pomp that surrounded him in the opening scene, he has what he longed for—love.'

We heard a noise in the hall as if somebody had stumbled.

'That must be Duggan—he always trips over the mat,' said Father O'Flynn.

The door opened and in walked Canon Tom Duggan.

'Didn't I tell you to get rid of the infernal mat—I nearly broke my neck again,' he remonstrated.

'But whom have we here?' he asked, tossing his head and pursing his lips as he tried to identify me. We had not met since I was a pupil in his maths class in Farrenferris fifteen years before.

'Don't tell me!' he interrupted Father O'Flynn when he began to enlighten him.

'If you were standing beside a blackboard instead of—I've got you now—Dick, isn't it?'

'Yes,' I told him. We shook hands.

'What may I ask are you doing in Passage West?'

'I'm on my bi-annual pilgrimage to Father O'Flynn.'

'And what mumbo-jumbo are the two of you up to?'

'We do some Shakespeare, some Irish songs—and dip into the Bible . . .' I explained.

'Ye amaze me!' he said.

When Father O'Flynn offered him a chair he said:

'I'll not sit down, for being as you know tone deaf and allergic to poetry, I'd only be out of place here. I've merely dropped in, Chris, to find out when you're holding your jamboree?'

'You mean—confirmation?' queried Father O'Flynn.

'What else would I mean?'

'The Bishop is coming next Thursday—as far as I know.'

'That's fair enough for me. I'll be here to keep you all inside the altar-rails—good-bye now—I'm off.'

I requested the Canon to give me a lift back to the city, which he very kindly did. . . . And so ended yet another of my many pleasant pilgrimages to Father O'Flynn at Passage West.

18

'Fair thoughts and happy hours'

'I'll be on the farm next Tuesday—but that need not put you off. Come up and I'll show you round. We can talk there as well as in Passage,' Father O'Flynn wrote in reply to my letter telling him of my proposed visit.

A taxi brought me by the North Cathedral and up Fair Hill. Then we turned left along a narrow road, and arrived at the farm in Churchfield.

Situated on the highest of the five hills that screen Cork city from the north, it commanded a magnificent view. Down in the broad valley the city, cut by the two branches of the river Lee, shimmered in a warm haze. Below and to the left, the golden hands of the clock on Shandon and the great golden fish on the steeple flashed in the strong sunlight. Westwards the view extended as far as the mountains in Kerry, and north-wards to the Galtees.

Father O'Flynn came down the drive to welcome me. It was autumn, and he wished to show me his fields of wheat.

'I love farming,' he said as we walked up the drive—'the earth and the smell of the earth in spring; its natural heat in summer; its nearness to the Creator and the sense of co-operating with him—with life itself.'

'How long have you been farming?' I asked him.

'I've been coming up here once a week—usually on a Tuesday—for about twenty years now. I find it a most satisfying and relaxing occupation—good for body and mind.'

We reached a gate that opened into a great field of wheat now almost ripe for harvesting.

'I sowed that wheat myself last spring—and another field

beyond it too,' he told me, 'and the inspector from the Department of Agriculture admired it a few days ago and said it was in first-class condition.'

We walked along the edge of the field, watching the golden sea undulating at the touch of a light breeze. Father O'Flynn pulled a few heads of wheat, rubbed them in his hands, and blew away the chaff. Then he explained to me the virtues of the grain.

'That's all the work of the sun,' he said. 'The sun is a great teacher. I was out here in June, looking at the young green wheat a few inches above the ground. It was devouring the sun. Down through the chlorophyll green into the roots it poured its energies, and lifted up that field of wheat inch by inch to where you see it now. That same sun has raised up millions of tons of wheat on the American prairies, and all over the world this summer. The power of the sun!

'The sun is a great teacher', he repeated. 'I called in to a house last June to see a child that was sick; a scrawny child it was, too. The doctor was there when I called.

' "Give that child plenty of sunshine," he said to the mother. "'Tis the most important item in its diet."

'I began to think over what the doctor had said. The sun is the most important item in our diet. We must eat the sun if we want to live a healthy life. But how can we eat the sun? It is over ninety million miles away; it is inaccessible. Besides, to draw near it is to be destroyed. Now I began to see a dilemma. To live, we need to eat the sun—but to approach it is to die. What is the solution?'

He looked over the field of wheat.

'There it is,' he said. 'The head of wheat has the secret of trapping all the vitalities and energies of the sun for our nourishment. We'll cut that wheat in a few days' time, and send it to the mill. The miller will grind it into flour; the baker will bake it into bread; then a loaf will appear on our tables. We cut a slice of it and—we eat the sun! Thanks to the head of wheat.'

'And some of your wheat there,' I remarked, 'may be made into hosts for the Mass and become the means of God's presence among men in the Blessed Eucharist.'

'That's what I meant,' he explained, 'when I said that I loved the spirit of co-operation with the Creator—that is part and parcel of farming. Heaven and earth are so close to each other here.

'Now take the Eucharist,' he went on. 'Our divine Lord said: "*Unless you eat the flesh of the Son of Man and drink his blood, you shall not have life in you.*" The people were shocked, and unless we experience something of their shock we lose the wonder of the Eucharist. Christ told the people that they must eat God or die. But God, they knew from their Scriptures, dwelt in light inaccessible. For a sinful creature to draw near his all holy Creator is to be destroyed. Again—the dilemma. To live, we need to eat God; to draw near him is to die. What is the solution? The Blessed Eucharist.

'I like the way John, in Chapter 6 of his gospel, describes how Christ made the people bread-minded. First there is their fast for three days; their weakness and their hunger for food. Then follows the miracle of the multiplication of the loaves. All get their fill of bread—and there are baskets of bread left over. At this point Christ begins his discourse on the living bread that is come down from heaven—the promise of the Eucharist. The people—and many of the disciples—were shocked. "How can this man give us his flesh to eat?" But Christ insists on faith in his person and trust in his word.

'The solution is astounding in its simplicity. At the Last Supper, Jesus took bread and wine. You will remember that in the beginning of his public life he had refused Satan when asked to turn stones into bread, and refused Mary his mother when first she asked him to provide wine at the wedding in

Cana. Now, when his hour had come, he took both these things—bread of wheat and wine of the grape in which are stored all the vitalities of the sun—and said: "*This is my body, this is my blood. Do this in commemoration of me.*" In the Blessed Eucharist are trapped all the divine vitalities and energies needed to sustain and increase the life of grace within us. God comes to his creatures in so humble a form. The simplicity of God's wisdom!'

We left the wheat-field and returned to the farmyard. He stopped at a pigsty and explained to me all the points of a prize sow he had bred himself, from the lines of her snout to the curl in her tail.

'I admire very much,' he said, 'those judges of livestock at the Spring Show in Dublin. Those men will look at twenty sows and pick out the best one. Now, that implies a standard— an ideal sow in the mind of the judge—and this ideal is the link with the prototype in the mind of the Creator. The more closely the real sow resembles the ideal in the mind of the judge, and provided that ideal reflects the Creator's prototype, the more the victory of truth is assured.'

This led Father O'Flynn straight into one of his favourite themes: truth—our need of it. With very little prompting he began.

'Truth lies all about us in the works of God's hands. Each item of creation, no matter how humble—even a blade of grass—contains truth. I have great respect for those scientists who sit down reverently before some item of creation and patiently observe it, analyse it, test it, and then record faithfully all it has to say of itself. In this way physicists got at the marvellous truth that lay hidden in the atom. But if the human mind is to see in scientific truth something more than an end in itself, to see it as a stepping-stone to the source of all truth, it needs something more than physics. It needs philosophy.

'Philosophy is a spring-well into which truth bubbles

from the great rocks of master-minds. Truth was extracted by these master-minds—men like Socrates and Aristotle—from the universe of created things. Such master-minds were the gift of the Creator to the human race. They're not made in universities. Drawing from some of the deepest and purest of these wells, St. Thomas Aquinas created a great reservoir of truth in his *Summa*. But these wells are in constant danger of pollution by the errors of lesser minds. They need care. The Church has always been at pains to keep the wells of philosophy pure.

'Philosophy is the effort of the mind to get into vital contact with reality and extract its deepest and inmost truth. That truth says that there lies beyond each item of creation, beyond species and genus, reality itself, which is the source of all things and whose mind is the source of all truth.

'But nowadays, the wonderful truths discovered by the scientists and taken over by philosophers do not seem to stimulate, as of old; to get to the source. Why?

'Because the modern mind is diseased with subjectivism, a mental malady that makes metaphysics impossible. Messrs. Descartes, Kant & Co. have a lot to do with it. Systems of thought and systems of education are the modern substitute for vital personal contact with individual real items of creation. Result: mental myopia.

'Man has a duty from his creator to get at the objective truth about creation, and to conform his thinking and his living to that truth. To do otherwise is to court disaster. Even the ordinary stone-mason must be directed in his operations by the objective truth—the pull in the lead of the plumb-line. If not, he'll build a crooked wall. The captain on a ship and the pilot in the airliner depend on the pull of the magnetic north on the needle of the compass to direct them. The objective truth is in the compass. Unless the navigators take their bearings from it, all head for disaster. Truth, the objective truth, must direct our lives. Only a sot like Shakespeare's Stephano would say: "Thought is free."

'As the human eye cannot make light, neither can the created mind make truth. Given light the eye can see and the whole body is enlighttened. Informed by truth, the mind can function correctly; a healthy intellectual life ensues, and the spirit grows in the image and likeness of its Creator.

'There is no progress except along the road of truth. It is with the objective truth that we put ourselves right, our house right, our town right, our nation right, the world right. The Catholic man knows that he must conform his mind to the uncreated mind of God if he is to stand in the truth. The Catholic man understands that his finite created intelligence is to the infinite uncreated mind of God as the sensitized needle of the compass is to the North Pole. What value is the compass, even though it be made of gold and studded with diamonds, if its needle is unresponsive to the pull of the Pole? Scrap!

'What may we expect from leaders of the people whose minds, tainted with subjectivism, are unresponsive to the pull of the eternal truth that is God's mind? Nothing but "systems" vitiated with falsehoods and injurious to men. The Catholic man is humble enough to realise that, if he is to reach his goal safely, he must make sure that the needle of his intellect remains delicately responsive to the pull of the divine intelligence. It is by faith, nourished by humble prayer, and by obedience to God's law as made known to him by the Church, that the Catholic man keeps responsive the needle of his created intelligence.

' "*In lumine tuo videbimus lumen*".'

We had arrived at the house, and as we passed through the kitchen on our way to the parlour the housekeeper called me aside and warned me.

'There's to be no more King Lear! Father didn't get a

proper sleep for three nights after your last visit due to all the allegations ye had over King Lear. He's getting too old for that now.'

I took the hint, and as we settled down at opposite sides of the fireplace I reminded him:

'You mentioned in your letter, Father, that you would have a few points for me on the Bible and Shakespeare.'

'And so I have. You'll find a Bible on the shelf behind you. Take it down and have it handy. I'll look after Shakespeare.

'The man—the nation that lives close to nature, respects her ways and grows up with roots firmly planted in the soil of a good natural tradition, will quickly feel at home when reading the Bible or Shakespeare, for both are great nature books, outdoor books; the two books that most educated people presumably would wish to have with them on a desert island. Why? Because between them they cover the human scene. Both treat of man in this fallen world. The Bible views him from above, from the creator's point of view, and gives us divine truth; Shakespeare views him from below, from the creature's point of view, and gives us the truth as grasped by a great artist. Frequently, both points of view coincide. Open the Bible at psalm eight and you'll see what I mean.'

I opened the book of psalms and read:

> *What is man that you should be mindful of him,*
> *or the son of man that you should care for him?*
> *You have made him a little less than the angels*
> *And crowned him with glory and honour. . . .*

'There you hear David singing of the nobility and dignity of man and that's God's point of view,' Father O'Flynn commented. 'Now listen to Shakespeare,' he continued:

' *"What a piece of work is a man! How noble in reason! How infinite in faculties! in form and moving how express and admirable! in action how like an angel! in apprehension how like a god!"*

There is the statement of a great artist, truth from below! The Bible and Shakespeare are at one. Truth triumphs!

'Take another point,' he continued. 'The heart of the Bible's message is: "Thou shalt love God and thy neighbour." Love is a biblical imperative and there are no half-measures; it must be with the whole heart and the whole soul. Neither are there any exceptions: it must embrace all mankind. Shakespeare shows us in his dramas that love is life's most urgent need. In plays like *Twelfth Night* and *As You Like It*, where love is enthroned in the human heart, life becomes a heaven on earth. In his tragedies, particularly in *Macbeth* and *Othello*, where love's place is usurped by ambition or jealousy or some other vice, disaster follows and life becomes a hell upon earth. Again—the same truth from heaven and from earth, from the Bible and Shakespeare: if life is to be fulfilled, love must be central.'

'Could you give me specific examples to illustrate your point?' I asked him.

'Nothing easier,' he replied. 'Take the love scene in Shakespeare's *Tempest*. Ferdinand, the prince of Naples, is shipwrecked on a magic island. Prospero, the magician, holds him under his spell and constrains him to do slave-service. Because of his love for Miranda, Ferdinand's labours are turned into joy.

> *This my mean task*
> *Would be as heavy to me as odious but*
> *The mistress which I serve quickens what's dead,*
> *And makes my labours pleasures.*

Miranda, who has fallen in love at first sight with Ferdinand, comes on the scene. Moved with compassion, she offers to help Ferdinand in his lowly task. But his love for her will not hear of it.

> *No precious creature;*
> *I had rather crack my sinews, break my back,*
> *Than you should such dishonour undergo,*
> *While I sit lazy by.*

They reveal their love for each other and then Ferdinand says:

> *I am, in my condition*
> *A prince, Miranda; I do think, a king;*
> *I would not so!—and would no more endure*
> *This wooden slavery than to suffer*
> *The flesh-fly blow my mouth. Hear my soul speak:*
> *The very instant that I saw you, did*
> *My heart fly to your service; there resides*
> *To make me slave to it; and for your sake*
> *Am I this patient log-man.*

'Shakespeare is saying here that the most exalted person may render the lowliest service and lose nothing of his personal dignity when the task is done out of love for the neighbour.

'Now open St. John's gospel at chapter thirteen and read the first sixteen verses.'

I read aloud the account of the washing of the disciples' feet by Christ at the Last Supper.

Father O'Flynn commented: 'There we see our divine Lord—fully conscious of his dignity, his divine origin, his power and his sublime destiny—putting aside his outer garments, girding himself with a towel, taking water in a basin and kneeling before his disciples to render a service that was usually done by the lowest slave in the Roman household. The creator washing the feet of his creature! But notice, no loss of personal dignity, no shedding of his nobility—because the service was dictated by divine love, and that ennobles all tasks. Again, the Bible and Shakespeare utter the same truth: one on the divine level, the other on the human.'

The housekeeper entered and announced that there was a man out in the yard who had come to arrange about the combine-harvester to cut the wheat. That ended our discussion; and as we parted at the gate, Father O'Flynn said to me:

'Fair thoughts and happy hours attend thee.'

19

Golden Jubilee

ON June 20 1959, Father O'Flynn had completed fifty years of active priestly ministry. It was his Golden Jubilee. He had no plans to celebrate the anniversary except with the immediate members of his own family, his brothers and sisters and their children. But his pupils of the Loft made their own plans. They formed a committee and decided to mark the occasion by giving a luncheon in honour of the priest. Invitations were sent out to all members, past and present. The replies poured in, and included subscriptions to present the priest with a chalice. He was told a week before the event. Would he come to luncheon at the Imperial Hotel? His old pupils of the Loft wished to congratulate him on his Golden Jubilee. He rarely dined out, and hardly ever in hotels. Yes, he would be delighted to come—'but let it be a simple meal', he requested.

When Father O'Flynn arrived at the Imperial Hotel that Sunday afternoon in June 1959, all his pupils—past and present—were lined up in the foyer to greet him. Some had not seen him for twenty, twenty-five or thirty years. They had been abroad. Tears brimmed in their eyes when they saw the change the years had effected.

He walked in among them, white-haired, heavy on the feet and slow—but still very erect—'and that which should accompany old age as honour, love, obedience, troops of friends'. It was all there for him—their priest—the priest of the Loft—that day at the Imperial Hotel. Father John Forde, on behalf of the pupils, presented Father O'Flynn with a gold chalice. It was Canon Tom Duggan who composed the Latin inscription. It said:

> '*I was made in the jubilee year, 1959, at the request of the pupils of Father J. C. O'Flynn, P.P., to perpetuate his memory, who was a great priest, a true lover of his country and a cultivator of the arts.*'

Artist by nature, priest by vocation and patriot by choice, James Christopher O'Flynn had lived life to the full on these three levels, and by his living had enriched the lives of many people. Patently he had succeeded in integrating these three powerful drives into one harmonious personality: Father Christy O'Flynn, the priest.

Among the tributes paid to him at that jubilee celebration in the Imperial Hotel, Edward Golden, of the Abbey Theatre, Dublin, said:

'You who were my contemporaries in the Loft cannot doubt my idolatry of Shakespeare—but there had been too much emphasis on him. It was the priest who made the Loft and it was the priest who opened many windows on life for me. He taught me now to find places of refuge, culturally speaking, or, if I may steal a phrase from the poet Auden: "*Sudden mansions of joy*"; and by that I do not mean in art alone, but especially in the appreciation of the simple happiness of everyday life— again, refuges. Had we not got these things from the priest we could have ended up spending our spare time playing pitch and toss at a corner.

'People may say that the vistas he opened to us were there for all. They were, but it was the priest who grasped me by the shoulder, turned me towards the window, flung it open wide and said: "Look, Eddie!" For that he will always have my gratitude and my love.'

James Stack, producer and now a director of the Cork Opera House said: 'How many of us, I wonder, could be doing the

things we are doing today, were it not for the priest? Take
Father Jack Curran there: he would agree that only for Father
O'Flynn he would hardly be a priest today. Is it not the same
with many more of us?

'I wish to speak of Father O'Flynn as an actor. In all the
more difficult Shakespearean roles and in their most difficult
speeches—in Lear, Hamlet, Macbeth, Falstaff and Shylock—I
have never seen anything like him anywhere, and I've seen
most of the greatest Shakespearean actors of our time. It has
been said by a well-known critic that a certain great English
actor interpreted Shakespeare in flashes of lightning. I can
assure you that in my time in the Loft we certainly saw those
flashes very often. You remember how we would be chatting
and talking, and suddenly there was silence while the priest
acted some part to demonstrate to a pupil how it should be
done, and we were spellbound. The chatting and laughter
gave place to tears, so deeply did he move us boys and girls
by his acting. Tears of sympathy were, as you all know, the
baptism of the Loft. If Father O'Flynn had not been called to
the very much higher walk of the priesthood, he would have
been ranked among the greatest actors of our time.

'He is a great actor and he has taught us all we know about
acting.

'Men like Father O'Flynn don't happen often. We were
most fortunate in having been so closely associated with you,
Father. We look on you as a father, and we love you as our
father always.'

There were many other speakers, all expressing the gratitude
and the indebtedness of his pupils to the priest.

Canon Tom Duggan, in a brief speech, said that he offered
congratulations and good wishes of the priests of the diocese, to
Father O'Flynn on the occasion of his Golden Jubilee. For fifty
years he had taught elocution at the seminary in Farranferris,
and if the priests of Cork did not all speak with the perfection

of their teacher, Father O'Flynn, it was not his fault, for he had done his part.

'When it comes to art and acting, I'm afraid, I'm out,' said the Canon. 'My own acting career was both brief and undistinguished. The man who was to play the part of the second grave-digger in *Hamlet* got ill. The producer was at his wits' end. I was called in.

' "Can you hold a shovel in your hand and speak a few lines in a rough and ready fashion?" he asked me.

' "No bother at all," I replied.

' "Then you are elected," he said.

'I was thrilled. I remember the fuss in the green-room and the putting on of the grease-paint. I liked the smell of it—and did not wash it all off for about four days. I considered that I had acquitted myself very well—and half expected an offer from the Old Vic. But to my dismay, I was not invited to take part in any further theatricals! We've celebrated Father O'Flynn's Golden Jubilee—here's looking forward to his Diamond Jubilee in ten years' time.'

Father O'Flynn stood up to reply. He spoke the old message—the same message he had preached for forty years: education of the heart—'Be loyal to truth, to goodness; pursue the beautiful and the noble.' Then he continued:

'Hearts ever taught hearts; lesser hearts plugged in to the greater hearts. It is thus we become human, and unless we are human we are nothing. The human heart is the bond between God and man since God became man. Christ, our Lord, was the educator par excellence. All uplift, all ennobling of human life comes from vital contact with God through the Sacred Heart of Christ, the heart that was opened by a lance for us in his passion of divine love—the noblest of all the emotions. This is the only power in the world today to preserve us from Cains with atom bombs.'

He concluded by reciting Mangan's *My Dark Rosaleen*.

Father O'Flynn returned to Passage West. That evening, when devotions had ended in the parish church, the people gathered in Chapel Square to congratulate him on his Golden Jubilee. He was presented with a cheque by Mr. Jack O'Callaghan on behalf of the parishioners. He took it with one hand, and gave it away with the other to Mr. Paddy O'Mahony and Miss Nora Coughlan to be used for the study and promotion of the Church's Plain Chant under the patronage of St. Pius X.

'The more the people came to appreciate the beauties of Plain Chant,' he said, 'the less they could escape the beauties in the traditional music of Ireland. That tradition was now a dying ember—all but extinguished. Those in authority, who professed to know all about it, in fact did not understand. They were treating it as modern music and killing the free flow of the melodies. The key to our musical tradition is the poetry—but who cares about that poetry today?

'The people of France up to A.D. 1300 sang with the Church, in the church and in the fields. . . . But the later musicians who tried to put in notation the troubadour songs failed to do justice to them. They could not strait-jacket the free ancient rhythms—and this is exactly what has happened in Ireland in 1959.

'We have the loveliest melodies that exist. Schubert, Mozart, Gregorian Chant and our own traditional melodies are a quartet unchallenged in the whole range of the art.

'We walk in fields of gold and we are persuaded by ignorance in authority that our tradition in music is rubbish.'

'Where in art have you come across the most moving expression of human sympathy?' I asked Father O'Flynn that evening in Passage West.

He paused, as he always did before replying, as if drawing from some deep source within him.

'What would you say yourself?' he asked.

'I would say at the end of *Lear*, in the scene where the old King and Cordelia are re-united.'

He quoted Cordelia:

> *Was this a face*
> *To be opposed against the warring winds?*

He went on. 'The sympathy of Cordelia for her poor old father—'twould make stones melt. For sympathy, that's unsurpassed in literature. But my own experience is that the *Pieta* of Michelangelo in Rome is the perfect expression in stone of human sympathy—Mary's compassion for her divine son. Since I saw that sculpture in Rome, I always link it with the prayer in the Mass immediately after the Consecration, where the priest says: "*hostiam puram, hostiam sanctam, hostiam immaculatam*", and makes the sign of the cross each time over the Host and chalice.

'For a long time those crosses struck me as odd. Surely the priest was not blessing what was infinitely holy? What then did these gestures mean? This is how I worked it out: After the Consecration at Mass, we're all gathered at the foot of the Cross. Christ, our victim, is present on the altar. Mary held that body in her arms when it was taken down from the Cross, and she embraced it and stroked it with gestures of sympathy for her son and for her God. She did this because it is our nature to act thus when moved by sorrow and sympathy—tenderly to stroke the victim. Now, at the Mass the priest, on behalf of the Church, takes the place of Mary, and with these gestures immediately after the Consecration he does what she did on Calvary: he expresses the grief and sympathy of the whole Church for its saviour whom it has crucified by its sins, but for which it now repents. "*Hostiam puram, hostiam sanctam, hostiam immaculatam*"—that, to me, is the finest expression of sympathy in art, in literature or in liturgy.'

Next Sunday, as was his custom before beginning Mass, Father O'Flynn turned to the congregation and said: 'We, the people of God in Passage West, are about to ascend before the throne of God our Father in heaven; through and with and in his divine son, Jesus, we offer him in this Mass all honour and glory and thanksgiving.'

And so he began the fifty-first year of his priesthood.

20

'It happened to me'

'I HAVE met many great humanitarians in the course of doing documentary programmes for television, but Father O'Flynn was the greatest of them all.

'What impressed us all about him was his tremendous love of his fellow-man as well as for God. To us he epitomised the Christian.'

These might well have been the words of an Irish Catholic gentleman justly praising the excellence of his fellow-country-man—Father Christy O'Flynn—but not so.

'The Irish are a very just people, they never speak well of one another,' Doctor Johnson had observed. They leave that to the foreigner. It was thus with Father O'Flynn.

'Christy, of course,' Canon Duggan had remarked, 'is an extraordinary genius. What it is he's got I'm not quite sure, and being one of our own we don't bother to find out. But this I would say: If they had his likes in England today, he'd be on the BBC every other week.'

The Canon was prophetic. The words quoted above were written by an English Protestant, James Buchan, Production Controller of Grampian Television, Ltd. He and the son of a Welsh Nonconformist Minister, Hywel Davis of the BBC, share the honour of having attracted the attention of the world and focussed it for one half-hour on Father O'Flynn and his work by the excellent documentary television film, *It Happened To Me*.

While Father O'Flynn had ever aspired to the noble and the sublime in art—and inspired many young people to pursue that ideal—he had always identified himself with the poor and the lowly in life. That he enjoyed a vision that was wide, noble and sympathetic, no one could deny; that he had achieved a unique nobility of mind and heart was apparent. But he had not achieved fame—except in a local sense.

That he deserved more seemed to his friends but bare justice. That BBC Television was the means of winning that wider fame merits their lasting gratitude.

Father O'Flynn was slow—even reluctant—to accept the BBC invitation to appear on television. It was heartening and disappointing at once. He was pleased that certain aspects of his work, the Shakespearean drama in the Loft, Irish music, and his speech therapy, would at last be given some recognition. He was disappointed that that recognition should come from foreigners rather than from his own.

'I was as surprised at the invitation as poor St. Peter was when he found the net breaking with the miraculous catch of fishes. Whoever would have thought that recognition for my work would come from the BBC? My first reaction was that of St. Peter: Depart from me, for while my work is valuable, I am nothing.'

When they wrote again, Father O'Flynn replied:

'Pictures of the children—certainly, but please arrange so that I can be left out. I am nothing.'

Luckily, other counsels prevailed—largely those of his friends, Canon Duggan and Father John Forde.

The team from the BBC television arrived in Cork in September 1960. James Buchan was the producer and Hywel Davis the commentator and interviewer. The other members of that team were—Margaret Barr, Charles Clifford, Gordon Mackey, Norman Shepherd and Alan Woods.

Father O'Flynn welcomed them, but he was very slow to do anything. For four days they interviewed him. All that time he was interviewing them and getting the feel of those strangers.

It was only when he was convinced of their sincerity and understood clearly the purpose of their visit that he responded. Then he gave all they asked and in addition took them to his heart.

Hywel Davis wrote of those days with Father O'Flynn:

'For a number of years, James Buchan and I had worked together as producer and interviewer in a series of programmes called *It Happened To Me*. Together we had presented on the television screen remarkable accounts of hardship and courage and goodness: stories about homeless tinkers on the Mull of Kintyre, about hopeless alcoholics in a Manchester claypit, about the loneliness of deaf children in Oxford. Buchan is himself an unusual producer, a man who is both subjective and objective towards his material; in the sense that a surgeon can weep for the man and dissect the body. Two years ago he asked me to enter in my diary some dates for a programme in Cork. "What's the story?" I asked him. "I don't really know," he said, "but it's about an old priest who cures stammering. Sounds a bit thin to me, but I'll let you know if it is and we'll switch the Oxford story earlier."

'And that's how I met Seamus O'Flynn. I first saw him in the Loft, above a tiny toffee factory in a Shandon back street. When I climbed the stairs and opened the door, I saw a cluster of children around a broad back and head of white hair; and I heard a voice in the rapt silence speaking softly and compellingly to a row of bright eyes which ignored completely the passage of a stranger across the room.

'I spent four days in his company. In this business of broadcasting you have to get as close to a person as you can in a short spell of time; as close as you can, as close as you are allowed, in order to portray his character and personality as truly as possible in thirty tight little minutes. I think I got close to him very quickly for the simple, shining reason that he liked to get as close as he could to any human being. I have never met, nor think I ever shall, such a mixture of strength and tenderness, of purposefulness and compassion and generosity, and of downright devilment and fun. He reminded me from our first meeting, disturbingly and warmly, of my own father who had died at the age of eighty, three years earlier; the heavy shoulders, the strong jaw, the soft hands, the humorous eyes, the overwhelming love of poetry and people of God.

'So many things happened in those strange four days that I find it difficult to shape a narrative in retrospect. I think the only narrative was the man himself, and that the rest will remain a remembered and cherished confusion of remarkable moments. There was a moment in the Loft when he recited the Seven Ages of Man and a little girl burst into sobbing tears at the prospect of *sans* everything; a moment in Passage when his table bore a baron of beef and a shoulder of lamb and plate of cold ham and potatoes and swedes and cabbage and pudding and stout and a hallelujah of laughter; a moment when a tiny boy was aloft in his arms with a big black biretta on the small head and a little hand on the white hair; and a moment when the firm stubby forefinger prodded the stammering stomach of an uncertain youth and the voice said: "That's where the trouble lies, my boy, and we're going to get rid of it, together."

'Six weeks after he died, we heard that our television programme about him had won the highest award at the International Catholic Festival in Monte Carlo. He would have been the last to understand that it was not James Buchan and I and the others who won the trophy. It is a bronze dove which graciously the BBC gave me as a personal possession. I have it in my home and it will always be there. It will remind me that a craft is made in the image of man; and that men are made in the image of God; and some more truly than others.'

Desmond Forristal reported in *The Furrow*, March 1962, on the films shown at the International Conference of Catholic Television at Monte Carlo:

'The second category was *reportage*. The first entry was obviously a predestined winner. It was an Italian film on the life of Pope John XXIII. . . . It closed with an informal address given by the Holy Father to a group of journalists in which his warm and lovable personality came across more freshly and immediately than in any other film I have seen. It was obviously, as I said, a winner in its category (one disgruntled producer was heard to mutter that there should be a special category for popes), but it was run a close second by a film made in Cork. It was the excellent BBC programme, *It Happened To Me*, about the life and work of the late Father O'Flynn, which told the story of the School of Drama in the Loft where so many young people learned to love Shakespeare and beauty and God. The sincerity and simplicity of the old man spoke across the language barrier to the polyglot audience on Radio Monte Carlo and its close was greeted by a burst of spontaneous applause. Those who saw the programme either in its first showing or when re-transmitted recently by Telefís Éireann will understand the reasons for its impact. It had many memorable moments—the boy cured of his stammer, the wide-eyed choir of little girls, the circle of children moved to laughter and tears at the touch of the priest's voice. But the most memorable belonged to Father O'Flynn himself, exhorting, encouraging, scolding, praising, or—in the lovely closing shot—just sitting quietly and looking into eternity. . . .'

The impact of that 30-minute film on viewers all over England, Scotland and the Channel Islands, when it was first transmitted in January 1961, was sensational. Father O'Flynn received hundreds of letters of congratulation, of appreciation, of encouragement in his good work—and seeking his advice and help for those who suffered from speech impediments. He had won fame overnight, but with fame came more and more work for others; and he had only one more year to live.

Letters asking for his advice poured in each day. They came from people of all religious beliefs and of none. A housewife from Aberdeen wrote: 'It is good to know such men as you live in this troubled world of ours.' Some people wrote asking for a personal interview. No one was turned away.

Raymond Smith, the journalist, called on Father O'Flynn at Passage West and describes the situation:

'When I called at his house I found him sitting in his famous old armchair in front of the fire, replying to a letter from a Scottish housewife whose brother had a defect of speech.

'My eye was immediately caught by the big bundle of letters, divided into two piles—those already answered and those yet to be answered.

' "It's so easy to show how stammers can be cured, but so hard to put it across in writing," he said with a sigh.

' "But surely you cannot possibly answer all those letters?" I said, aghast at the magnitude of the task facing a man of his years.

' "People are in need of help and we must give it to them," was his simple reply.

'And it was given freely. Any money enclosed was immediately sent back; also money sent for special prayers by people with worries and problems, many of them non-Catholics, who had been deeply moved by the television programme. They unburdened themselves to a priest whom they had never met personally, but who had suddenly exerted a compelling influence on their lives.

'There was one pound note which Father O'Flynn could not return, for all that was enclosed with it was a covering note that read: "From a black Ulster Protestant." '

The reaction of his pupils who knew him intimately over the years is accurately expressed in this letter from Harry Weldon:

The Éire Society of Boston,
47 Avalon Road, Milton 87,
Mass., U.S.A.

A Athair Dhil,

Congratulations on the fabulous success of your television appearance in *It Happened To Me*. I have been speculating what such recognition would have meant had it come thirty years earlier. . . . We who worked under you night after night for years on end knew infinitely more than one-night viewers of your TV appearance how great you really are and how much more of you there is.

Very few realised, in those early days in the Loft, that you were giving us something more than Shakespeare—you gave us a way of life which those of us who had to emigrate thanked God for and will continue to do till the end of our days.

I often reflect on how empty our lives would have been, we children of working-class parents, were it not for the priest, the class and the Loft.

This latter affectionate name for you, when I first heard it from my seniors—Tom Vesey and Eddie Golden—shocked me a little, I must confess, but in a short time I was to realise that it was a term of reverence. And therein lay your influence and your power for good. You not only preached but superbly practised true Christianity.

21

Last lesson

A 'PHONE call from Cork, Saturday, 6 January 1962. It was Eileen Curran.

'Father O'Flynn is sinking fast,' she said. 'He asked me to contact you: "Tell Dick of my condition—I would like to see him," he said.'

'I'll be down on Tuesday,' I told her. 'That's the earliest I can make it.'

Tuesday, the 9th of January, was a dry, sunny day, almost spring-like. As I had to be back in Dublin that night I left for Cork soon after breakfast. The roads were clear of traffic and I made good time. Now and then I glanced at the landscape flashing past. It looked cold and lifeless. Winter's dead hand lay upon the earth and nothing stirred. I sped by a line of beech trees which in summer made a long green tunnel, but now, stripped bare of their leaves, they stood stark against the white sunlight.

From a chalky classroom in Farranferris came a memory, an echo of Flynnie. 'In winter nature shows us the outlines of things, and there is a beauty in that too.' Yes, there was a kind of beauty in those 'bare ruined choirs where late the sweet birds sang'.

Farranferris . . . my mind wandered to Canon Duggan. He had resigned his parish in Cork at the age of 72, and left for Lima, Peru, the preceding October to serve on the missions. After a month he was dead. A few days before, he wrote his last letter to Father O'Flynn:

Padres de Santiago Apostol,
Miraflores, Lima, Peru.
29th November, 1961.

Dear Christy,

Excuse this horrible pen. I have about seven of them and they are all gone sour on me.

Things are not going at all badly with me. A succession of fine summer days and good full breeze off the Pacific to keep things cool.

The flora of the place are not very interesting but the fauna are various. You remember poor Jerry Coughlan (R.I.P.) and his sensitivity to fleas. . . . Thanks be to God, I don't share it.

I am trying to cram in Spanish. It is not hard, but to come on it suddenly. . . . However, I think I am making a little progress.

So far I have been living at the Headquarters in company with the nicest collection of young priests you ever met. God help them (and me!), I am slated to give them a four-day retreat in early January.

I hope men and things are going well with you. I say a prayer for you every morning.

Looking at things through the perspective of seven thousand miles I see you as one who has brought and continues to bring light and glory to us all. I'd venture to say that in fifty years' time you will be the only one of us to be remembered.

Tell Josie that the Peruvian cows lead too hard a life to be worth eating. As against that, if fruit made any appeal, this is Paradise.

Now to wish you *ex imo corde*, again and again all the blessings of Christmas.

Ever your friend,
Tom Duggan.

I had heard that on the day this letter arrived, Father O'Flynn got the news that his friend had died. He did not see anyone for three days. . . .

It was a lonely journey.

Arrived in Cork, I went straight to the North Infirmary. It was opposite the Loft and under the shadow of Shandon steeple. Directed to the first floor, I went up the stairs and walked along the corridor looking for his room. I saw a door open. It was his. They said he liked the door open to feel near the people, to see them passing by. I went in.

I was shocked by what I saw. Lying back on the pillows of that white hospital bed lay the ruins of his magnificent physique. The glorious manhood of him, shrunk to this little measure! The terrible disease had eaten him up. I tried to hide my feelings. I sat by the bed at once. He clasped my hands, and I wondered at the great strength in his.

'You're very good to come,' he said, in a thin, high-pitched voice. 'Don't mind what you see at all,' he went on, evidently conscious of the great change since our last meeting in early November. 'Things are not as bad as they look. I collapsed on Christmas Eve and they carried me in here for dead. But the nuns did a wonderful job on me. Everything is going grand now.'

He was trying hard to cheer me up after my journey from Dublin. My eyes strayed to a vase full of daffodils near the window. The sun was shining full upon them.

'They're very early,' I thought, 'out of season.' Then I turned to Father O'Flynn, and in a flash I recalled that laughing April day in the library at Farranferris many years ago, when Flynnie walked into class with a golden daffodil in his hand. . . . '*Fair daffodils, we weep. . . .*' The wonderful world of truth and goodness and beauty and love the man had opened up for us.

Now he was dying. He knew it, and he knew that I knew it. No point in pretence; he abhorred it all his life. He spoke:

'We're doing *Macbeth* in the Loft, and mind you they're quite good. They have the feeling of it. They are working hard for the drama festival in February.'

I was a little taken aback that his mind should be on such things now. Then he continued softly: 'Poor Macbeth—how those juggling friends deceived him!' My mind went back to an evening in Passage West when I opened a conversation with him: 'I can't sympathise with Macbeth at the end of the play.'

'Can't you now?' he had said with a whimsical smile, and began at once to act some passage from the last scenes of the play. He pointed strongly to the contrast between the outward brash bravado of:

> *Bring me no more reports, let them fly all*
> *Till Birnam wood remove to Dunsinane*
> *I cannot taint with fear. . . .*

And the inner heart-break and bitter disillusion of:

> *my way of life*
> *Is fallen in the sear, the yellow leaf.*

I could hear again his tones of lamentation and despair:

> *Tomorrow and tomorrow and tomorrow*
> *Creeps in this petty pace from day to day. . . .*

'Here you have the very cadence of an Irish *caoine*,' he told me. I changed my views on Macbeth.

Now he spoke again. 'Sympathy is the feeling of the Good Samaritan. It is like a ring. In many that ring is narrow— our hearts are small and cold and hard. Our life should be spent in widening that ring out and out in ever larger circles, until like Christ on the cross we embrace all mankind.' He had always something fresh to say, even now at the end. He lay back on the pillow.

'You used to say, Father,' I reminded him, 'that Shakespeare got *Macbeth* from David's first psalm: the story of the two men who went different ways—Banquo to the right, Macbeth to the left.'

'Yes,' he answered, 'David had it long before Shakespeare— and they say Shakespeare was not a Catholic!' This with a flash of the old fire and sarcasm in his weak voice.

I read for him:

> *Happy the man who follows not the counsel of the wicked*
> *Nor sits in the company of the insolent*
> *But delights in the house of the Lord.*

His eyes closed, he took up from here:

> *He is like a tree*
> *Planted by running water.*

Raising himself a little, he opened his large blue eyes and looked at me.

'How beautifully David expresses that!' He sank back again and closed his eyes. He muttered very softly: '*Out, out brief candle* . . . poor Macbeth—the smoking flax,' his mind swinging back to the last scene of the play. 'God help us all to take the right turn,' he prayed.

He asked me to read Psalm 8, one of his favourites:

O Lord, our Lord, how glorious is your name all over the earth . . . so often on his lips when we were doing *Hamlet* in the Loft, always comparing it favourably with Shakespeare's: *What a piece of work is man.* 'Shakespeare viewed man from below,' he used to say, 'the psalmist viewed him from above—"*You have made him a little less than the angels and crowned him with glory and honour!*"'

We said the *Miserere* together in Latin; we both knew it by heart since our days in Maynooth, where as students we recited it daily en route from the chapel to the refectory.

At the end he was silent for a little while. I did not interrupt his peace. Then 'great things can come of great mistakes—David's psalm from David's sin,' and he repeated one or two favourite verses: '*Amplius lava me ab iniquitate mea . . . cor mundum crea in me, Deus.*'

I read a few verses of Psalm 83, with its ardent desire for God:

> *How lovely is your dwelling place, O Lord of hosts,*
> *My soul yearns and pines for the courts of the Lord. . . .*

He lay back and spoke a little further of the Loft and the choir children. 'They're being ruined by the system of education —words, words, words—no education of the heart.

'In the schools of today, Shakespeare is a bore and Irish is a grind—and an arid legalism is paralysing the mind of the nation . . . I'm afraid the mould is broken.'

He paused to get his breath and then continued: 'The only hope now is the little children and the Holy Ghost—I should have put the Holy Ghost first'—he smiled at me—'and these will be always there.'

Then he appeared to slip back to his North Cathedral years. 'I loved all those poor people up the lanes, and the children . . . and the young fellows and the hurlers and bowl players . . . the harrier and the bird boys. I tried to get the children off the streets with the spirit of song and dance and . . . Shakespeare. They know I love them all . . . even the poor fellows who take too much to drink in the pub. . . .'

Then, opening wide his eyes again and looking intently at me, he grasped my hand and said: 'It was a great grace . . . a very great grace to have lived among those poor people.'

He paused, he looked at me intently; tears were brimming in my eyes. As I fumbled for a handkerchief he smiled faintly and continued in a calm, steady voice: 'You have come all the way from Dublin to give me the gift of your tears . . . the nicest present I got since I came to hospital.'

I was astounded at the endless freshness of his mind. Here he was, interpreting my tears to me in a way that removed any embarrassment that I might have felt.

'And I'll tell you this,' he continued, 'if you went back to Dublin without shedding those tears your whole journey would have been in vain. . . . Give me your blessing now before you go,' he asked quite firmly.

For the moment it struck me as odd that I should bless this old and saintly man. Up to this he was always giving to me. It was the first time he asked anything of me.

I stood over him at the head of the bed to give my last blessing. I began '*Benedictio Dei Omnipotentis . . .*' and then my eye caught sight of the great hollows in his shoulders and around his neck, revealed now by the open nightshirt; his head, the white hair thinning on top, bowed beneath me, and his large bony hands clasped tight. My voice broke; I barely finished the formula.

He took both my hands in his and kissed them on the palms and, looking up at me, a little smile about his lips, said quite simply:

'*Vita mutator non tollitur*' (Life is changed, not taken away).

I left the room and walked down the corridor, not seeing where I was going.

It was my last lesson.